LIVING TIME

AND THE INTEGRATION OF THE LIFE

LIVING TIME

AND THE INTEGRATION
OF THE LIFE

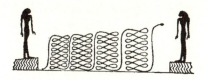

Maurice Nicoll

*Eternity enters into time, and it is in time
that all movement takes place.... Eternity is
not limited by the conditions of time, and time
is eternal in virtue of its cyclic recurrence.*
HERMETICA, ASCLEPIUS III

*Contracting our Infinite sense we behold
Multitude, or expanding we behold as One.*
WILLIAM BLAKE

EUREKA EDITIONS
UTRECHT – THE NETHERLANDS

FIRST PUBLISHED IN 1952
VINCENT STUART PUBLISHERS LTD
REPUBLISHED IN 1998
by EUREKA EDITIONS
by the same author
The New Man
The Mark
Psychological Commentaries on the Teaching of Gurdjieff and Ouspensky
Selections from Meetings in 1953
Simple Explanation of Work Ideas

CONTENTS

*The drawing of Apophis in the mystic celestial ocean bet-
ween the goddesses Isis and Nephthys, on the title page,
is reproduced from* The Journal of The Transactions of
THE VICTORIA INSTITUTE, *vol. vi, 1873.*

Give me Nepenthe
            With the lulling eyes
To shut away the world!
            To sleep, to dream,
And in this clover-scented air
            Slip through imprisoning Time
And find my Spirit free!
            Alas, not thus
Shalt thou escape from Time.
            Thou wilt return again
And yet again
            Till thou hast paid
The uttermost farthing.
            Didst thou not know
Time is a debtor's prison?
            Whom dost thou owe?
Owe not Nepenthe.

INTRODUCTORY NOTE

PLATO SAYS THAT to become a spectator of Time is a cure for meanness of soul. We live in a narrow reality, partly conditioned by our form of perception and partly made by opinions that we have borrowed, to which our self-esteem is fastened. We fight for our opinions, not because we believe them but because they involve the ordinary feeling of oneself. Though we are continually being hurt owing to the narrowness of the reality in which we dwell, we blame life, and do not see the necessity of finding absolutely new standpoints.

All ideas that have a transforming power change our sense of reality. They act like ferments. But they necessarily lead us in the direction of affirmation. To see more wholly, more comprehensively, requires affirmation, an assent to the existence of new truth. If there is buried in us the sense of truth, we must admit that there is a great deal superficial to it that fights against it. It is always much easier to deny than to affirm.

One reason for this is that the soul is turned towards the senses, while ideas are internally perceived as distinct from the inrush of outer things, and if there is no feeling of the separateness of one's existence, no sense of essential invisibility, and no effort made in this direction, it is unlikely that we will ever be aware of them. Plato described two gods or ruling powers, one outer and one inner. Under the power of the outer, the soul is tossed about in every direction and is like a drunkard. Turned towards the world of ideas, she begins to become sane and to remember.

In the following pages a number of quotations, notes, and observations have been brought together that refer in the main to the *invisible* side of things. How can we begin to understand the 'invisible'? The invisible nature of man and the corresponding invisible side of the world are here dealt with from the standpoint of *dimensions* (not taken mathematically) and also from the related

5

standpoint of *higher levels of consciousness*. The question of a new understanding of Time, and of what the life means in the light of this understanding, is discussed. The possibility of a change in the time-sense, with a changed feeling of *oneself*, enters into this question.

The meaning of *eternity*, about which we have really erroneous notions, comes under consideration, and finally the idea of the *recurrence* of the life is reviewed.

It is necessary to begin with a general approach which takes into review some of our ordinary 'notions of things', as derived from the world that is shown to us by our senses. In this connection some reflections about the visible and invisible side of people must be first made.

CHAPTER ONE

INVISIBILITY OF ONESELF

WE CAN ALL SEE another person's body directly. We see the lips moving, the eyes opening and shutting, the lines of the mouth and face changing, and the body expressing itself as a whole in action. The person *himself* is invisible.

We see the outside of a person much more comprehensively than the person can himself. He does not see himself in action, and if he looks in a mirror he changes psychologically and begins to invent himself. He appears very distinct and visible, very definite and clear to eye and touch, although he is not so to himself. We are distinct and clear to him, appearing to have a very real and solid existence, but to ourselves it does not seem that we have this real and solid existence.

Because we see the visible side of people plainly and they see ours plainly, we all appear much more definite *to one another* than we do to ourselves. If the invisible side of people were discerned as easily as the visible side, we would live in a *new humanity*. As we are, we live in visible humanity, a humanity of *appearances*. In consequence, an extra-ordinary number of misunderstandings inevitably exist.

Let us consider our means of communication with one another. They are limited to muscles, mainly to the smallest. We signal by means of muscles, either in speech or gesture. To reach another person, every thought, feeling, emotion, must be transmitted through muscular movements and rendered visible or audible or tangible in this way. We communicate badly, partly because we never notice how we are doing it, and partly because it is an extremely difficult matter to communicate anything save the simplest observations, without the danger of our signals being misinterpreted. Also, as often as not, we do not exactly know

7

what it is we are trying to communicate. Finally, nearly everything of importance cannot be expressed.

But in a general sense it is because we communicate so
badly and because other people understand our signals in their way,
adding their own thoughts and feelings to them, that an inex-
haustible supply of misunderstandings and unhappinesses arise.
This is seeing the matter from one point of view, for if our invisible side were more easily demonstrated to others, new difficulties
would arise.

Now all our thoughts, emotions, feelings, imaginations, reveries, dreams, fantasies, are *invisible*. All that belongs to our sche-
ming, planning, secrets, ambitions, all our hopes, fears, doubts,
perplexities, all our affections, speculations, ponderings, vacui-
ties, uncertainties, all our desires, longings, appetites, sensations,
our likes, dislikes, aversions, attractions, loves and hates – all are
themselves invisible. They constitute *oneself*.

They may or may not betray their existence. They usually
do so much more than we believe for we are both much more and
much less obvious to others than we suppose. But all these inner states, moods, thoughts, etc., are in themselves invisible and
all that we see of them in another is through their expression in
muscular movement.

No one ever *sees* thought. No one knows what *we* are
thinking. We imagine we know other people, and all these
imaginations we have of each other form a world of fictitious
people, that love and hate.

It is impossible for me to say that I know anybody, and it is
equally impossible to say that anybody knows me. For while I see
all *your* bodily movements and outward appearances so easily and
have a hundred thousand visual impressions of you that do not
exist in your mind, and have seen you as part of the landscape,
part of the house, part of the street, and have a knowledge of
you that you always wish to know about – what impression you

make, how you look – yet I cannot see into you and do not know what you are, and can never know. And while I have this direct access to your visible side, to all your life as seen, you have direct access to your invisibility – and to your invisibility only *you* have this direct access, if you learn to use it. I and everyone else can see and hear you. The whole world might see and hear you. *But only you can know yourself.*

We are thus like two systems of levers, one working with all the advantage in one direction, the other with all the advantage in the other direction.

Now to the reader all this may appear obvious, but I must assure him that it is not at all obvious. It is an extremely difficult thing to grasp and I will endeavour to explain why this is so. We do not grasp that we are invisible. We do not realise that we live in a world of invisible people. We do not understand *that life, before all other definitions of it, is a drama of the visible and invisible.*

The reason why we do not grasp it is because it is an idea. In this book, which is about one or two *ideas*, I mean by the term something which has the power of altering our standpoint and changing our sense of things. An idea is, of course, invisible and we may never have any ideas in the sense that I mean, throughout our entire existence. We think that only the visible world has reality and structure and do not conceive the possibility that the psychological world, or inner world that we know as our thought, feeling, and imagination, may have also a real structure and exist in its own 'space', although not that space that we are in touch with through our sense-organs.

·   ·   ·

Into this inner space may come *ideas*. They may visit the mind. What we see through the power of an idea cannot be seen when we are no longer in contact with it. We know the experience of suddenly seeing the truth of something for the first time.

9

At such moments we are altered and if they persisted we would be permanently altered. But they come as flashes with traces of direct knowledge, direct cognition.

The description of an *idea* is quite different from the direct cognition of it. The one takes time, the other is instantaneous. The description of the idea that we are invisible is quite different from the realisation of it: only in thinking in different ways about this invisibility of everybody and ourselves we may attract the idea so that it illuminates us directly.

Such ideas act directly on the substance of our lives as by a chemical combination, and the shock of contact may be sometimes so great as actually to change a man's life and not merely alter his understanding for the moment. The preparation of ourselves for the possibilities of new meaning, which is more desirable than anything else, since meaninglessness is a disease, cannot be separated from contact with *ideas* that have transforming power.

We can think of an idea, in this sense, as something that puts us in contact with another degree of understanding and takes us out of inner routine and the habitual state of indolence of our consciousness – our usual 'reality'. *We cannot understand differently without ideas.*

It is easy enough to say in words that we are invisible, but just as we sometimes catch the meaning, for the first time, of a common phrase that we have often used, we may catch the meaning of our invisibility, suddenly, if we repeat often enough the sentence: *I am invisible.* The realisation of one's own separate existence begins at this point.

It is not a 'natural' idea, because it is not derived from sensory experience or perceptible fact. While we know it in one sense already, it is not *distinct*. We know a great deal, only not distinctly, not authoritatively, through the inner perception of its truth. This half-discerned knowledge at the back of us cannot, I believe, be brought into focus save through the power of ideas. For, ordina-

10

rily, what influences us above everything is the outer, sense-given, visible world of appearances.

This great sensory world with its noise, colour and movement, rushing in through the open channels of sight and hearing, overwhelms the faint understanding. If I realise my own invisibility, and reach for a moment a new sense of my own existence, I am the next moment lost in the effects of outer things. I am aware only of the noises in the street, and I cannot reach the experience again. I return again to my 'natural' mind to which everything perceptible appeals, and for which the evidence of the senses is mainly the criterion of truth. Having experienced something 'inner', I find myself back in the 'outer', and the truth that was demonstrated to me directly, as internal truth, I can no longer demonstrate to myself with my natural reason, save as a theory or conception.

Now I would say that all *ideas* that have the power of altering us and letting new meaning into our lives are about the *invisible* side of things and cannot be demonstrated directly or reached by reasoning alone. Because they relate to the invisible side of things they are not approached by reasoning according to the evidence of the senses. Before coming to the *idea* of Time with which this book is chiefly concerned and which can only be understood by getting away from appearances and by thinking about the 'invisible world' from the standpoint of dimensions, we must make some effort to grasp the invisibility of ourselves. For I believe that we never understand anything about the 'invisible' world if we do not grasp *our own invisibility* first.

This demands a certain kind of effort, the nature of which is similar to the effort required to get some realisation of the essential invisibility and unknowableness of another person. In this connection I believe that we can never realise the existence of another person in any real way unless we realise our own existence. The realisation of one's own existence, as a real experience, is the realisation of one's essential invisibility.

11

Our usual sense of existence is derived from external things. We try to press into the visible world, to feel ourselves in something outside us, in money, possessions, clothes, position; to get out of ourselves. We feel that what we lack lies outside us, in the world that our organs of sense delineate to us. This is natural because the world of sense is obvious. We think, as it were, in terms of it, and towards it. The solution of our difficulties seems to lie in it – in getting something, in being honoured. Moreover, we do not support even a hint of our invisibility easily and do not reflect that while we are related to one obvious world, on one side, through the senses, we may be related to another world, on another side, not at all obvious, through 'understanding' – to a world which is just as complex and diverse as the world given by sense, and which has just as many desirable and undesirable places in it.

.   .   .

Our bodies stand in the visible world. They stand in the *space of three dimensions*, accessible to the sense of sight and of touch. Our bodies are themselves three-dimensional. They have length, height, and breadth. They are 'solids' in space. *But we ourselves are not in this world of three dimensions.*

Our thoughts, for instance, are not three-dimensional solids. One thought is not to the *right* or *left* of another thought. Yet are they not quite *real* to us? If we say that reality is confined to that which exists in the three-dimensional world *outside*, we must regard all our thoughts and feelings *inside*, as unreal.

Our inner life – oneself – has no position in that space which is perceptible to the senses. But while thought, feeling, and imagination have no position in space, it is possible to think of them having position in some other kind of space. One thought follows another in passing-time. A feeling lasts a certain time and then disappears. If we think of time as a fourth dimension, or a higher dimension of space, our inner life seems to be related to this

12

'higher' space, or world in more dimensions than those accessible to our senses. If we conceive of a higher dimensional world we might consider that we do not live, properly speaking, in the world of three dimensions that we touch and see, and in which we meet people, but have more intimate contact with a more-dimensioned form of existence, beginning with *time*.

But before coming to the subject of dimensions let us first consider the world of *appearances*, i.e., the world which our senses reveal to us, and make some reflections on two ways of thinking, one of which starts from the visible side of things and the other from the 'invisible'.

    .   .   .   .

All that we *see* falls on the retina of the eye, upside down, as in a camera. A picture of the world refracted through the lens of the eye falls on the surface of the retina where it is received by a great number of nerve endings or sensitive points. The picture is two-dimensional, like that on a screen, upside down, and distributed over separate recording points. Yet this picture is in some way transformed for us into the smooth solid world we behold. 'Out of pictures I have imagined solid things. Out of space of two dimensions, as we call it, I have made space of three dimensions' (W. K. Clifford, *Lectures and Essays*, Vol. I, P. 260, 1879, from lecture: 'Philosophy of the Pure Sciences').

Now the outer world seems close to us, not as if we were in contact with it but as if we were in it. We are not aware of being in contact with it only through our sense organs situated all over the curtain of flesh. We do not have the impression of *looking into* the world through the little living nerve-machines of the eye. The world merely seems there, and we right in the middle of it. Nor does it seem to be a quantity of separate impressions (coming through our various senses) that combine by the action of the mind into a composite whole. Yet we know that if we had no eyes or ears, we could not see or hear anything. Simultaneous sensations coming through the different senses, and combined in the mind, give us the appearance and qualities of a rose. The rose is actually created *for us* out of all these separate impressions; yet it is practically impossible to realise the matter in this way. For us, the rose is simply there.

When we consider that the picture of the world on the retina is two-dimensional and that this is the source of contact with the outer scene, it is not difficult to understand that Kant came to the conclusion that the mind *creates* the physical world, and lays down the laws of nature, owing to innate dispositions in it that arrange the stream of incoming sensations into an organised system. The senses merely give us messages, and out of these we create the visible, tangible, audible world by some inner action of the mind, by something which is more than the messages. But it is extremely difficult to persuade ourselves that this is so, because in order to do so we must detach ourselves from the overwhelmingly *immediate* impression of an external reality in which we are invariably immersed. Now this effort is of the same peculiar nature as that required to bring to us a realisation of the invisibility of ourselves or other people.

We are immersed in appearances. This is one of the meanings in the idea of *Maya*, in Indian philosophical thought. We are not separate from the outside because we take it for granted. We are mingled with it through sense, and our thinking is moulded on it – that is, on our senses. Two ideas appear here: one, that we follow what the senses show us of the world in our forms of thought: two, that we take the external as real in itself and not as a matter connected with the nature of our senses. What do we mean by appearances? Let us include in this term all that the senses show us. They show us a person's body, the outward appearance of him. They do not show his consciousness, spirit or soul, or his history, his life, all that he has thought, done, loved and hated. They show us *practically nothing* about him, yet we fasten on the apparent side

14

of him as the chief thing. They show neither the invisible side of a person nor the invisible side of the world, yet what we think of as real and existing we always confound with what the senses reveal.

Let us consider the composite picture of the world that is built up for us internally (according to some older thinkers by the action of the imagination). What we see comes to us through the medium of light, transmitted through the 'ether'; and what we hear, through the medium of sound transmitted through the air. Touch is by direct contact. Each of the senses works in a remarkably separate manner, fashioned for its own medium and responding only to its particular set of stimulations. Yet all these messages from such different sources are united together into unitary meaning. We see a person, hear him, touch him, and do not get the impression of three persons, but one person; and this is really extraordinary.

Now there are many reasons for saying that our senses respond to only a very limited part of the external world. Take the eyes: they respond to vibrations of light which travel at 186,000 miles a second in the 'ether', but what *we* call light is merely one octave of vibrations out of at least fifty other known octaves of vibration that travel in the ether at the same speed, and reach us from sun and stars and perhaps galaxies.

So that it is only this *one* single octave, out of all these, that our eyes are open to. Seen as a unity, or whole, light appears white, but split up into separate notes, it appears as colours. The violet side of a rainbow is the seat of vibrations of about twice the frequency of those on the red side, so roughly speaking there is an octave in between. But beyond the violet there are three (ascending) octaves of ultra-violet light, i.e. of increasing frequency. Beyond that, seven octaves of what are known as X-rays; beyond that still higher octaves of higher frequencies, and shorter and shorter wave-lengths, so much so that they can pass through a great thickness of lead with ease.

15

Below the red end of the rainbow are descending octaves of lower frequency – infra-red rays, wireless waves, etc. But the eye sees only *one* octave out of all these.

Our picture of the external world, which we take as our criterion of the real, is relative to the forms of our external senses. It does not necessarily exist, indeed it cannot, for itself as we see it. Whatever it really is, we see it merely *in a certain way*. Its appearance is conditioned by our organs of perception. There is a vast *invisible* side that we can never enter into as direct sensory experience, as we enter into the experience of light. Light enters into our consciousness directly, but X-rays or wireless vibrations do not. There may be insects or plants which are conscious in one or other form of radiant energy apart from light, and so live in a world different from our world. It is even possible that our brains may be receptive organs, apart from that side open to the sensory influx from skin, eyes, nose, ears, etc. The extensive arborisations of nerve-cells at the surface of the cortex might suggest vast receptive arrangements, like the branching of trees towards the sun; but we have no evidence for this.

But, considering the great ladder of vibrations which is the *Universe* in terms of energies, we cannot say that our senses reveal the totality of things. Our eyes clearly answer to only a limited range of vibrations in the ether. 'The universe may be conceived as a polygon of a thousand or a hundred thousand sides or facets – and each of these sides or facets may be conceived as representing one special mode of existence. Now, of these thousand sides or modes, all may be equally essential, but three or four only may be turned towards us, or be analogous to our organs. One side or facet of the universe, as holding a relation to the organ of sight, is the mode of luminous or visible existence; another, as proportional to the organ of hearing, is the mode of sonorous, or audible existence' (Sir Wm. Hamilton: *Lectures in Metaphysics*, Vol. I, page 142).

This passage was written before the opening up of the world of radiant energies by scientific investigation. Whether consciousness be response to energy or energy itself, it is evident that we live in a world filled with different energies and are conscious of only a few. Since physics has resolved matter into forms of energy we can no longer think, in a crude way, of a material universe – of mere lumps of matter. It would seem obvious, rather, that we are in a universe of *energies* in different scales, and are given naturally a response to a fraction of them.

I have mentioned that it is an extraordinary thing that stimulations coming into us through our senses from such widely separated sources in the natural scale should fall together so easily into composition. But this composition is relatively valid.

If a gun is fired close at hand we see the flash and hear the report *simultaneously* and so connect one with the other. But if the gun is fired far away at sea at night, we see the vivid flash and many seconds later hear the air shaken by the report, because sound travels very slowly in comparison with light. Comparatively it crawls in the medium of the air at about one mile in four seconds, while light flashes through the ether at one hundred and eighty thousand miles a second. If we had had no previous experience we might not even connect the flash and the report. At a distance the composite picture of the world presented to us by our senses shows signs of falling apart – or rather, assuming another aspect in regard to *time*. And even though light messages travel so fast, when we look up at the heavens we see stars shining where, ordinarily speaking, for themselves they are not. We see them in their past – where they were thousands of years ago. Their past is present for us. Even the sun, which is close, is not where we see it in space, because its light takes eight minutes to reach us. So we see it where it *was* eight minutes ago.

We cannot, then, be certain that what we see is the unchallengeable reality of things. If our senses worked in a different way, if we had more senses, or fewer, what we customarily call *reality* would be different. The matter has been expressed by Kant in many passages, in one of which he says that if 'the subjective constitution of the senses in general were removed, the whole constitution and all the relation of objects in space and time, nay, space and time themselves, would vanish'. And if our senses were changed the appearance of objects would change, for 'as appearances they cannot exist in themselves but only in us. What objects are in themselves, apart from all the receptivity of our sensibility, remains completely unknown to us. We know nothing but our mode of perceiving them – a mode which is peculiar to us, and not necessarilyshared in by every being.'

What is it in us that begins to raise objections to this view of the *relative* reality of the visible world? We are firmly anchored to what the senses show us. Perceptible reality is the starting point of our thought. *Sense-thinking* characterises the natural action of the mind, and we refer to sense as final proof.

It is not necessary to think that appearances themselves are illusions, or that the senses show us an illusory world. They show us part of reality. Is not the starting point of illusion rather the taking of appearances for all ultimate reality and the belief that sense perception is the sole standard of the real? The seen world is real but does not embrace reality. It is built out of invisible realities which surround it on every side. The visible world is contained in a much greater invisible world (invisible to us) and we do not lose one by studying the other but enlarge one *into* the other. But as our natural everyday logic is so closely connected with sense-thinking it fights against this enlarging of the world, and its actual *form* of understanding becomes a psychological barrier to further understanding.

If we could in some unknown way apprehend the totality of things apart from the senses we would, according to many early authorities, perceive the universe as the *unity* that its name originally implies. 'If the senses were eliminated the world would appear as a unity' (Sufi literature). An example of the experiencing of the universe as a *vast coherence* will be given later.

Now the senses split up the totality of things, and in following their evidence we collect an enormous quantity of little separated facts. We forget that they are all merely little bits of one gigantic system. These little facts intoxicate us easily. We do not merely think that we have discovered something, but created it. We forget we start out from an *already prepared and connected world* which lies behind any little facts that we can discover about it. We too easily forget that we start *from a given world.* The little facts seem to explain things, to do away with mystery, so that in our conceit we begin to think in a certain way, seeing life as a question of innumerable little facts and human existence as something that can be regulated by facts. An immense quantity of labour is expended in collecting further facts, till it seems as if this gathering of facts were going to replace all real life and living experience.

.   .   .   .

The search for facts began with the study of the outer phenomenal world, i.e. with science. *It made truth seem to be only outside ourselves* – in facts about matter. It sought to find the basic principle of the universe, to solve its riddle, to find it out, in something outside – in the atom – believing that the 'explanation' of everything would thus be found and the ultimate cause of the universe and all that it contains would be laid bare. Everything was submitted to weighing and measuring, and the mathematical treatment of phenomena began. *One kind of thinking* became predominant, which, starting from the visible, concerns itself only with what can be termed external truth and particularly with quantities.

The older, prescientific thought concerned itself mainly with *qualities.*

19

Now regarded only as a physical body man is an infinitesimal quantity of *matter* in the universe of matter. Taken as a measurable quantity in a universe of measurable quantities he is ruled out of the picture. Conceive his material bulk in comparison with the earth! He vanishes; so that thinking only *quantitatively* about ourselves and the universe, and starting from the visible, demonstrable, weighable side of things, we think in the direction of our own annihilation as individuals.

Man is composed of qualities and these do not lend themselves to measurement or to mathematical treatment, save fictiously. It is impossible to say of a man: let his courage = x and his capacity for affection = y and in this way represent him in mathematical symbols.

With the increasing predominance of 'external' over 'internal' truth, all that truly belonged to man came to be looked upon as *secondary* and unreal, and the primary and real field for investigation was held to lie in that which existed independently of man's mind in the external world. The transition between the quantitative and qualitative standpoints is well expressed in the following passage:

'Till the time of Galileo (seventeenth century) it had always been taken for granted that man and nature were both integral parts of a larger whole, in which man's place was the more fundamental. Whatever distinctions might be made between being and non-being, between primary and secondary, man was regarded as fundamentally allied with the positive and the primary. In the philosophies of Plato and Aristotle this is obvious enough; the remarks hold true none the less for the ancient materialists. Man's soul for Democritus was composed of the very finest and most mobile fire-atoms, which statement at once allied it to the most active and causal element in the outside world. Indeed, to all important ancient and mediaeval thinkers, man was a genuine microcosm; in him was exemplified such a union of things primary and secondary as truly typified their relations in the vast macrocosm, whether the real and primary be regarded as ideas or as some material substance. Now, in the course of translating this distinction of primary and secondary into terms suited to the new mathematical interpretation of nature, we have the first stage in the reading of man quite out of the real and primary realm. Obviously man was not a subject suited to mathematical study. His performances could not be treated by the quantitative method, except in the most meagre fashion. His life was a life of colours and sounds, of pleasures, of griefs, of passionate loves, of ambitions, and strivings. Hence the real world must be (it was thought) the world outside of man; the world of astronomy and the world of resting and moving terrestrial objects' (E. A. Burtt: *The Metaphysical Foundations of Modern Physical Science*. Kegan Paul, Trench, Trubner and Co., Ltd., London, 1925).

Since ultimate truth and reality were sought in something outside man, investigation naturally passed into the world of atoms. But the atom turned out to constitute no simple, easy, & non-ethical basis for the 'explaining away' of the universe. The atom proved to be a system of extraordinary complexity, a small universe in itself. Searching more and more into small parts and seeking always to explain the whole by its parts, science reached further mysteries. On its philosophical side it now begins to turn towards ideas that are similar to those with which prescientific thought was concerned. But what we have especially to notice is that the form of thought which starts from the visible, from fact, tends to rule man out of the picture. People have the delusion that it puts him more strongly into the picture, partly because they do not understand that man is himself essentially invisible. All that is most real for him lies in his invisible life and, relatively, the visible is not nearly so real to him, although the power of appearances makes it seem so.

If we start with the visible, then in order to explain it we must pass into its parts. If we seek to explain man by his organs, his organs by the cells composing them, the atoms by electrons, we lose sight of the *man* as a whole. Under the microscope the *man himself* completely disappears.

.   .   .   .

It is obvious that we can explain a chair by its parts, but this is only one way of thinking about it, one form of truth. The chair is also to be explained by the idea in the mind that conceived it. No quantitative investigation, no chemical analysis or microscopic examination can detect this idea or give us the full meaning of the chair's existence. If we ask ourselves what is the *cause* of the chair, how can we answer this question?

The chair exists before us as a visible object. Its cause has two sides. On the visible side, it is caused by the wooden parts of which it is made. On the invisible, it is caused by an idea in somebody's mind. There are thus three terms – *idea, chair, wood.*

Naturalism or scientific materialism lays stress on the third term. It lays stress on the separate material parts which enter into the composition of any object, seeking in them for 'cause'. The idea behind organised matter is overlooked. That which is manifest in time and space engages its attention, and so it cannot help looking for causal origin in the smaller constituent parts of any organism – and also in *preceding* time, i.e. in the past.

Now the moment of the origin of the chair in time and space can be taken as the moment when the first piece of wood is shaped for its construction. A chair is begun, visibly, with the first piece of wood, a house with the first brick. But prior to the beginning of the chair or house in time or space, the idea of either of them exists in someone's mind. The architect has already the whole conception of the house in his mind before the first brick is laid down.

But in translating this idea into visible expression the *smallest* part of the house must appear first in passing-time. The architect thinks first of the whole idea, of the house as a *whole*, and from that proceeds to smaller and smaller details. *But in manifestation in time this process is reversed.* The force of the idea, in order to become manifest in expression, must first pass into the smallest detail, e.g. a single brick is the first point of the manifestation of the *idea* of the house. The first expression in time and space of an idea is one single elementary material constituent. Yet the idea is already complete in the architect's mind, but invisibly so. When the house is finished it expresses the idea in visible form. The house has grown up, so to speak, as something intermediate between the first term, *idea*, and the third term, *elementary material part.*

When the house is completed (as the second term), the first and third terms, through which the construction of the house was effected, drop out. The idea has found expression in time and space and the separate bricks are no longer thought of as such, but become an aggregate which is the house itself. It is possible to analyse the house into the bricks and mortar which compose it; and it is always possible to say that the bricks are the cause of the house. But it is inadequate, because the whole structure of the house, its form, and the integration of its separate parts, have their ultimate origin in the *idea* in the architect's mind – and this idea is not in time or space. I mean that it is not in the phenomenal or visible world.

It is obvious that the first and third term – that is, idea and elementary brick – are both *causal*, and that we must think of causality in two categories. All that scientific materialism finds as *causal* is correct on the phenomenal side, but ultimately insufficient. And *idea* by itself cannot be cause. Both the first and third terms are necessary, acting in conjunction.

In a broad sense, two types of mind exist, one that argues from the first term and the other from the third term. It is a union of both standpoints that is necessary.

The difficulty is that, owing to the laws of time, even the fullest formed and most complete idea must necessarily express itself sequentially, in visible manifestation, in the most elementary form first of all. A long period of trial and error may be necessary before it can be properly realised in manifestation. And it will always appear (to the senses) that the first elementary material starting-point of the idea, in passing into visible manifestation, is itself the *cause* of all that follows. It looks that way, and because it looks that way the modern doctrine of evolution has arisen.

Consider the plastic material elements of organised living matter – the world of atoms, of carbon, hydrogen, nitrogen, oxygen, sulphur, and phosphorus – this marvellous paint-box, where valency is the mingling power, and from which arise an infinite diversity of combinations and groupings and an endless variety of products! This constitutes the third term, the material elements, out of which the world and its life are built. Man has a far more limited range – a far grosser range – of plastic material that he can use directly. If his ideas could play directly and easily into the atomic world, what material transformations could he not effect? If my mind could play directly into the atomic world of this wooden table upon which I am writing, I could change it into innumerable substances without difficulty, by merely rearranging the atoms which compose it. And if I had this power over the atomic world and I knew the *idea* of life, I could create life. But it would be mind and idea, not the material elements themselves, that would be true *cause* in such magic.

.   .   .   .

I mentioned that naturalism lays stress on the third term as cause. Through its eyes we tend to see everything as quantity and material arrangement rather than quality, meaning, or idea. The emphasis is on one side – on the external, extended, sense-given side of the universe. It corresponds to an attitude that everyone must know and recognise in himself. The world is as we see it, and somehow or other it is self-derived. Somehow or other the atoms comprising it fell into certain arrangements, and visible masses of matter as well as living creatures somehow or other appeared.

What does naturalism take away from us? It leads, of course, to a somewhat dead view of things. In its extreme forms it takes the view that we live in a gigantic and mechanical universe, a meaningless machinery of planets and suns, in which man has accidentally appeared as a minute speck of life, negligible and ephemeral. Stressing the third term alone, this view is true enough. It means that if man is to improve his life, he must only deal with the external, visible world. There is nothing 'real' save what man can reach through his senses. So man should invent and build new machinery and amass as many facts as possible about the visible world and set about to 'conquer nature'.

This standpoint turns man outwards. It makes him see his field of activities as only outside himself. It makes him think that by discovering some fresh facts about the material universe he will be able to assuage his own sorrow and pain. There is today a very remarkable turning outwards of mankind, connected with scientific developments, and an increasingly diffused expectancy that new discoveries and inventions will solve man's problems. The attitude of scientific materialism, which especially characterised the later part of the nineteenth century, has reached the masses. it has also reached the East.

Mankind now sees the solution of its difficulties lying in something outside itself. And with this attitude there inevitably goes the belief in mass organisations of peoples, and a corresponding loss of the inner sense of existence, the effacement of individual differences, and a gradual obliteration of all the rich diversity of custom and local distinction which belongs to normal life. The world becomes smaller and smaller as it becomes more and more uniform. People lose the power of any separate wisdom. In place of it, they imitate each other increasingly. And it is just this that makes possible mass organisation. Hand-in-hand with this goes the linking up of the world by rapid transit and wireless communication, so that the entire world abnormally responds to a single local stimulus.

And above all this hovers the strange chimera, that seems to shimmer in the imagination of all humanity today, the phantasy that science will discover some secret, some solution, that will rid the earth of its brutality and injustice and restore the Golden Age. This idea, that we can discover *final solutions* to the difficulties of life, and that mankind as a whole can reach 'truth' at some future date, ignores the fact that every person born into the world is a new starting-point. Every person must discover for himself all that has been discovered before. Every person must find truth for himself. Apart from this, what can we see today as the result of man's belief that he can organise life merely by scientific knowledge?

From the practical side, we only see that man's inventions increasingly take charge of him. We see machines becoming disproportionate to human life. It is surely obvious that the development of machinery is not the development of man and it is equally obvious that machinery is enslaving man and gradually removing from him his possibilities of normal life and normal effort, and the normal use of his functions. If machinery were used on a scale proportionate to man's needs it would be a blessing. If people could only understand that the latest discovery is not necessarily the best thing for humanity, and become sceptical of the word *progress*, they might insist on bringing about a better balance. What we fail to grasp is that the pressure of outer life is not necessarily lessened by new discoveries. They only complicate our lives still further. We do not only live by *bread* but by *word*. It is not only new facts and facilities that we need but ideas and the stimulation of new meanings. Man is his understanding – not his possession of facts or his heap of inventions and facilities. Only

26

through his own hard-won understanding does he find his centre in himself, whereby he can withstand the pressure of outer things. Yet it is obvious that nothing can check the general momentum of events today. There is no discernible force in western civilisation strong enough to withstand it and the modern world has yet to learn that the standpoint of naturalism is inimical to man in the long run. To lay stress only on the third term – on the visible and tangible – seems logical enough. But man is more than a logical machine. No one can understand either himself or another person merely through the exercise of logic. We can indeed understand very little through logic. But the tyranny of this faculty can become so great that it can destroy much of the emotional and instinctive life of man.

.   .   .   .

Contrasted with naturalism is the older standpoint which puts man in a *created* universe, part visible and part invisible, part *in* time and part *outside* time. The universe as we see it is only one aspect of total reality. Man, as a creature of sense, knows only appearances and only studies appearances. The universe is not only sensory experience, but inner experience as well, i.e. there is inner truth as well as outer truth. The universe is both visible and invisible. On the visible side (the third term) stands the world of facts. On the invisible side (the first term) stands the world of ideas.

Man himself stands between the visible and invisible sides of the universe, related to one through his senses, and to the other through his inner nature. At a certain point, the external, visible side of the universe leaves off, as it were, and passes into man as internal experience. In other words, man is a certain ratio between visible and invisible.

Because of this, the outer scene does not complete him and no outer improvement of the conditions of life will ever really satisfy him. Man has inner necessities. His emotional life is not satisfied by outer things. His organisation is not only to be explained in terms of *adaptation* to outer life. He needs ideas to give meaning to his existence. There is that in him that can grow and develop – some further state of himself – not lying in 'tomorrow' but above him. There is a kind of knowledge that can change him, a knowledge of quite a different quality from that which concerns itself with facts relating to the phenomenal world, a knowledge that changes his attitudes and understanding, that can work on him internally and bring the discordant elements of his nature into harmony.

.　　　.　　　.　　　.

In many of the ancient philosophies this is taken as man's chief task – his *real* task. Through inner growth man finds the real solution of his difficulties. It is necessary to understand that the direction of this growth is not outwards, in business, in science or in external activities, but inwards, in the direction of knowledge of himself, through which there comes *a change of consciousness*. As long as man is turned only outwards, as long as his beliefs turn him towards sense as the sole criterion of the 'real', as long as he believes only in appearances, he cannot change in himself.

He cannot grow in this internal sense. Through the standpoint of naturalism, he cuts himself off from all possibilities of inner change. He must relate himself to the 'world of ideas' before he can begin to grow. That is, he must feel that there is *more* in the universe than is apparent to the senses. He must feel that other meanings are possible, other interpretations, for only in this way can his mind become 'open'. There must have come to him the feeling of *something else*. He must have wondered what he is, what life can possibly mean, what his existence means. Certain kinds of questioning must have occurred in his soul. Is the meaning of existence more than it appears to be? Do I live in something greater than what my senses reveal? Are all my problems merely outer problems? Is knowledge about the external world the only possible knowledge?

CHAPTER TWO

QUALITY OF CONSCIOUSNESS

THERE IS LITTLE doubt that we take our consciousness for granted in much the same way as we take the world as we see it for granted. Our consciousness seems final. It seems the *only* kind of consciousness that we can possibly know. While we may doubt our memory, or even our powers of thought, and sometimes our feelings, we would scarcely think of doubting our consciousness. We would never regard it as something that makes our life what it is. The fact, for example, that our experience seems divided into opposites, into black and white, into yes or no, into contradictions, would not seem to us to be due to the nature of our consciousness (or to the kind of mind we have, which is a direct result of our degree of consciousness) but to something inherent in external things themselves.

Through some experiences, and through experiments made on himself, William James concluded that 'our normal waking consciousness, rational consciousness, is but one special type of consciousness, while all about it, parted from it by the flimsiest of screens, there are potential forms of consciousness entirely different'.

Convinced of the existence of other states of consciousness, through which we experience things in quite a new way, and through which we meet life in a new way, he realised that no account of the universe can ever be regarded as final which leaves out these other forms of consciousness. Nor can any view of *ourselves* be final if we accept that our present consciousness is final.

Consciousness is usually defined as *awareness*, but this definition is actually inferior in meaning to the implication of the word itself. Consciousness means, literally, 'knowing-together'. A development of conscious-ness would therefore mean knowing 'more together', and so it would bring about a new relationship to everything previously known. For to know more always means to see things differently.

But even if we take 'consciousness' merely as meaning 'awareness' we cannot imagine that it is all possible awareness. It must be a *degree* of awareness and one through which we are *related* in a particular way to whatever we know.

Our ordinary consciousness relates us to ourselves and to things. During sleep the quality of our consciousness is changed. It gives one sort of awareness and relation. When we awake, the degree of awareness and the form of relation is changed. But though we may admit the truth of this, we do not think that still further kinds of consciousness may be possible, giving new degrees of awareness and relation. Nor do we think that many of our insoluble difficulties, perplexities, and unanswered questions necessarily exist *because of the kind of consciousness we naturally possess*, and that a new degree of consciousness would either cause our awareness of them to disappear or bring about an entirely new relation to them.

Consciousness is sometimes compared with *light*. An increase of consciousness is likened to an increase of light. But we shall see eventually that an increase of consciousness does not mean only that we see with greater clearness what was formerly obscure. The *quality* is changed. For the moment, the man who experiences it himself is changed. It is not merely the *quantity* of consciousness that is altered, but its very nature.

.   .   .   .

What evidence is there, from the *physiological* side, about levels of consciousness in man? What does neurological teaching say?

In his teaching about the nervous system, Hughlings Jackson, the forerunner of English neurology, conceived it as an integrated system of nervous levels, in which the higher holds the lower in check.

We must understand that the nervous system is not one thing, of one composition, a uniformity. It is a *structure* of different groupings of nerve-cells, fitted together and linked up on the principle of *scale*, and apparently presided over by the cortex of the brain, which itself shows different strata or levels of nerve-cells.

Jackson taught that if the action of a higher level in the nervous system is weakened the activity of a lower level is released. A lower function takes the place of a higher function. The main point he emphasised was that we could never understand the action of the nervous system, physiologically considered, unless we took into review this factor of release, because many symptoms of disordered nervous function consist in *phenomena of release*.

It is necessary to understand clearly what he meant. Imagine a schoolmaster in charge of a class of boys, and suppose that the schoolmaster represents a higher level, the boys a lower, and that the whole class constitutes an 'integrated system' which works in a certain way. If the schoolmaster goes to sleep, the lower level is 'released' – that is, the boys begin to behave as they like, and the system now works in quite a different way.

This is due not merely to the fact that the schoolmaster is asleep (which Jackson would have called a negative factor – that is, it does not *itself* give rise to any manifestations or symptoms) but rather to the release of the boys from control, with resulting disorder. In other words, if a higher level of the nervous system is not working, *its absence of function cannot be discerned in itself.* It will only be the released activity of the lower level that will be manifested and this only can be studied. The function of the higher level will merely be absent and *it will be impossible to deduce its nature* because we will only be able to perceive and study the released activities of a lower level.

31

Suppose that the schoolmaster becomes invisible when he falls asleep and that we know nothing about the proper working of a class. We see only a number of boys in a state of disorder. We can deduce nothing about the proper working of the class from this disorder. It will remain unknown to us.

In the absence of higher function lower function necessarily appears, and this latter is of a *different order*. The higher function cannot be deduced from the lower. If we think of the question from the standpoint of *levels of consciousness*, then beneath our ordinary level exists a lower level, of another order. When the level of ordinary consciousness is disturbed, Jackson observed that there is often a marked rise of *dream-like states*, which he ascribed to the release of the activities of a lower level.

Another quality of consciousness manifests itself, for at this level things can be connected together in a way that is impossible at the usual level and we are exposed to fantastic influences, nightmares, etc., which do not exist at the higher level. When there are very remarkable contradictions in the personality, this dream-state has a tendency to arise at any time and interfere with the life.

We have no right to believe that our ordinary level of consciousness is the *highest* form of consciousness, or the sole mode of experience possible to man. We cannot say that the range of the internal experience of oneself is necessarily limited either to dream-states or to ordinary consciousness. We have to consider the possibility, not only that there is a level above our ordinary level of consciousness, to which we are only occasionally awakened, but that *our ordinary consciousness becomes integrated into a larger system when this happens.*

From this point of view our ordinary consciousness would have to be regarded as a *release phenomenon*. We would have to study ourselves from the angle of being *disintegrated and not integrated* individuals. From the physiological standpoint what can be said,

32

in respect to evidence, is that the nervous system seems certainly far from being fully used under ordinary conditions. But this kind of evidence, clinically speaking, is not easy to marshal. It is necessary to approach the subject from the psychological side.

There is a very old idea that man cannot find any integration or harmony of being as long as he is on the level of a *sensual* outlook. As a creature of sense, thinking only from sense and turned 'outwards' towards visible life, he remains *dead* in regard to that which is *himself.* Nor is he quickened by any demonstration coming from the sensible side of the universe.

In the older views of man, which were much richer and more complete than are the modern views, man was placed in the framework of a vast *living* universe as a created being – that is, created in and out of the living universe. So not only was man in the world, *but the world was in him.*

The idea of *scale* or 'degree of excellence' permeated most of the older notions about man and the universe. The universe is on different scales. And man was taken as a very complex creation having *within* him a scale consisting of different levels of mind, consciousness and understanding. Of these levels the *sensual* was taken as the lowest.

I will connect the sensual with the 'materialistic' outlook of today. The point to be noticed is that if there be potential degrees of development hidden as a scale within man, no one can rise in this scale of his own potential being unless he transcends the purely sensual or material outlook.

The psychological implications behind this view are really of very great interest and importance. A sensualistic or materialistic outlook limits us *psychologically*, in the fullest sense of this word, so that if there be higher degrees of consciousness we will be incapable of reaching them if we believe only in the 'evidence of things seen', or seek only for proof from the visible, tangible and matter-of-fact side of things, or regard the world simply as we *see* it.

.   .   .   .

What is the standpoint of materialism? It is not by any means so easy to define as we may think. We are 'materialists' without knowing it, and 'materialism' is a much deeper problem to each of us than we imagine. But, in the first place, from its standpoint we look *outwards* (via the senses) for the explanation and *cause* of everything. We start from phenomena as absolute truth.

Speaking first of ultimate issues, we seek proof of the existence of 'God' from phenomenal life itself. If life takes on an evil aspect we think there can be no 'God'. Scientifically, we seek for *causes* in the phenomenal world. in both cases we are doing much the same thing. In the first case we are looking for 'spirit' in visible material life. In the second case we are looking for the principles behind phenomena in the minutest forms of matter. As materialists we look for *cause* in the elementary material particle. We look for the final explanation of the mystery of life in minute physiological processes, in bio-chemistry, etc. We might compare this with looking for the causes of a house only in its minute structure, as if we could find its real 'cause' in the elementary bricks of which it is composed, and not in the *idea* behind it. For, to materialists, the world must necessarily be idea-less. It can be no masterpiece of art – for where is the artist? Neither telescope nor microscope reveal his actual existence.

If the originating principle behind all manifestation is not in the phenomenal world itself, if it lies in *idea* working via chemistry

34

(that is, through minute elementary particles) into visible form, we must, as materialists, ignore this factor and assume that the chemical processes belonging to the world of atoms themselves establish life. The development of the germcell into an embryo is, from this side, merely a progressive series of chemical changes, starting from the initial shock of conception, each chemical change determined by and following upon the previous one, and thus leading to the budding up of the embryo. Looking only at the chemical changes we will ignore the controlling principle or *law* acting behind them. Whatever we do not find in the three dimensions of space we will ignore, not seeing life as unfolding events but rather as aggregations of physical mass.

Strictly speaking, materialism gives sense and physical matter *priority* over mind or idea. In the tenth book of the *Laws* Plato put the standpoint of materialism, as it existed then, clearly enough. The materialist was a person who regarded *nature as self-derived*. Elementary particles of *dead* matter somehow or other combined together to form the entire universe and all the living beings contained in it. Matter accidentally raised itself up into the most complex living forms. Matter created its laws. And *Mind* itself resulted from these accidental combinations of inanimate matter. 'They say that fire and water and earth and air all exist by nature and chance.... The elements are severally moved by chance and some inherent force, according to certain affinities among them, of hot with cold, or of dry with moist, etc. After this fashion and in this manner the whole heaven has been created, as well as animals and plants ... not by the action of mind, as they say, or of any god, but as I was saying, by nature and chance only' (*Laws*, 889 B).

From this standpoint physical nature is necessarily the *first* cause of the generation and destruction of all things. Mind is secondary – an accidental product of physical matter.

Can we really believe that mind and intelligence accidentally came out of dead matter? If so, then in order to face the problem sincerely, we must grant to original matter – which, chemically speaking, is hydrogen – extraordinary properties, and assume that all organised beings were potentially present in the first matter of the nebular system, that is, if we believe that the universe 'started' at some distant point in passing- time.

But the customary standpoint of scientific materialism is that primary matter is dead – and the universe is dead and nature is dead – and a dead nature can, of course, aim at nothing. It cannot be teleological.

Since Plato's time science has passed far beyond the region of the unaided senses. It has turned matter into electricity, and the world of three dimensions into a theoretical world of at least four dimensions. It has passed beyond *natural*, i.e., sensual concepts, beyond the visualisable and matter-of-fact. Physicists today are trying to understand what we are in. What is this 'world-field' in which events happen? Does one event really cause another? What is this four-dimensional continuum called space-time? And what, for that matter, is electricity? We are in a mysterious and incomprehensible universe. Nevertheless, psychologically speaking, the standpoint of materialism prevails and spreads its effects over the entire world. How can we better grasp what materialism consists in, as regards its psychological effect? Why can it limit us psychologically?

.   .   .   .

Let us glance at an entirely different standpoint. The Platonic view of visible or phenomenal reality was that there is behind it an invisible and greater order of reality. There is invisible *form* or figure (only mentally perceptible) over and above all form or figure that we can apprehend through our senses. These invisible forms or figures, with which our term *idea* came to be connected,

36

are prior in scale to, and therefore much more 'real' than, any perceptible form or figure. Thus the world of sense, all that we see, is a very limited expression of *real form* and, properly speaking, science studies that which is *indicated* in the visible object. '... the object of anything that can be called science in the strict sense of the word is something that may be indicated by the world of sense, but it is not really of that world, but of a higher degree of reality' (Burnet, *Platonism,* p. 43,1928).

The geometer, for example, studies triangles and finds that the three interior angles of any sort of triangle are always equal in sum to two right angles. But this is not true of any triangle that we can perceive with the external senses because it is not possible to draw an absolutely exact triangle. So that *'triangle'* itself belongs to a higher degree of reality than any visible representation of it. The triangle as *idea* – the 'ideal' triangle – does not exist in passing time and space. It is not visible, but is only apprehended by the mind. In a similar way, anything that has the semblance of beauty, relation and proportion in the visible world, as seen by us with our organs of sight, has behind it beauty, relation and proportion belonging to a higher degree of reality, which art strives towards, and of which we may catch glimpses in flashes of consciousness above the ordinary.

But for materialism a higher degree of reality is not countenanced. I think it would be absolutely inexplicable on the basis upon which materialism rests. There may be a *below* but there cannot be an *above*. There can be no existing higher degree of reality. There can be no superior order behind the phenomenal world, nothing *prior* to it in scale. For the universe must be a mindless product and body must be prior to mind. There can be 'no thought without phosphorus'. Matter must be prior to function and use, and sensation prior to meaning.

To admit a higher order of reality behind known reality is, in fact, to reverse the direction of materialism. For it is to affirm by an act of the mind what the senses by themselves do not directly show, but what, at the same time, the senses really indicate. And it is exactly in this that Plato puts *the turning point of a man's soul* – in this recognition of an existing higher order of reality that explains this obviously imperfect, suggestive world in which we live.

.   .   .   .

If the universe be in man (as a scale of reality) as well as man in the universe, then if a man gives an inferior explanation of the universe it will react on himself; he will limit himself and remain inferior to his own potential being. He is then left nothing else to do but to study a dead material world outside him, out of which his own life and his mind accidentally come.

If there be energies in us capable of seeking another direction, they will then necessarily find no goal. For if there be 'things of the spirit', if there be higher degrees of consciousness and re-alness within, then all those impulses which in their right development should separate man from the tyranny of outer life, and create inner independence of soul through the realisation of these higher degrees within, will become fused with the things of outer life into one common outer influence; for, having no inner goal, their goal will seem to lie outside him. The hypnotic power of outer life will then be increased. The 'outer' will then tend to be felt *fanatically*, i.e. religiously. And that is perhaps why in this age of materialism men seem doomed to sacrifice themselves more and more to mass organisations, to war, to machines, to speed, to gigantism and ugliness of every kind, in order to get emotional satisfaction. Seen from this angle, the attitude of scientific materialism really increases man's inner weakness, which is always too great. In all that belongs to himself, in all that is necessary for the dawn of individuality, it renders him more and more impotent, giving him the illusion that he can gain absolute power over a dead material world. And with this increasing inner weakness he seeks more and more to put himself under some dominating personality, to surrender his thinking, to cease to be a man at all. What paradox could be stranger?

.   .   .   .

The emotional attitude belonging to materialism is necessarily quite different from that belonging to 'idealism'. As materialists we think we can lay bare the secrets of nature, and as often as not we assume the credit of being the actual creators of whatever processes we have discovered. It is extraordinary how a very superficial descriptive explanation satisfies us that we *know*. For example, by chemical analysis we can find out the quan-ti-tative composition of a substance. Vegetation is obviously green-blooded. Chlorophyll is its most important constituent. Man has red blood and haemoglobin is its chief element. We can find by chemical analysis that their structure is rather similar and that each contains so many atoms of carbon, oxygen, hydrogen, etc. We tend then to assume that we have discovered *what they are* – by discovering the quantity and kind of elementary constituent bricks in these substances. But their use, and the idea behind these substances, belong to quite a different order of thinking – and this is what, as materialists, we tend to ignore. We ignore what they represent, what place they have and what part they play in *a connected universe*. We ignore quality; for, as materialists, we do not admit a connected or intelligent universe in which everything has its definite role or function. Comte actually said that quality was no positive entity, the most positive entity being quantity. But is not the meaning of a thing *as a whole*, its function and use, the part it plays in the life of man and in the life of the universe, its most positive aspect? And is not the fact that, quantitatively speaking, different chemical structure transmits such an infinite variety of qualities, the greatest mystery of all?

The most positive aspect of a thing is the thing as a whole. We never really explain or understand a thing by the mere reduction of it to its elementary parts, while ignoring its patent qualities and uses and purposes when taken as a whole. Such a way of 'explaining' a thing gives us a wrong sense of power, a conceit, a superficiality of standpoint, which seem to me to lie at the very root of 'materialism'.

I remember my first contact with chemistry at school. Everything seemed to become amazingly simple. Everything was merely *chemistry*, merely different quantities and combinations of elementary particles. A living being was merely a combination of different quantities of atoms, of infinitely small bricks, of carbon, oxygen, hydrogen, sulphur, nitrogen and phosphorus – certainly in vast and inconceivable quantities, but still 'nothing but' atoms. Even a person whom one loved was 'nothing but' a prodigious quantity of atoms. Explanations seemed to be fascinatingly easy on this basis of quantities. Is not this the obsessing fascination of explaining the greater by the less – the root of all obsession? It seemed as if the secret of the universe had been handed over to me, particularly because at that time people in general seemed to be quite ignorant of chemistry.

It was only when I began to ponder over the meaning of the periodic law of the elements – the law of the octave as the English chemist, Newlands, called it – whereby the same sort of elements repeat themselves at regular intervals, that I realised that something stood behind all these atoms and behind all chemistry. There is law, there is 'order', which determine their action, their properties, their position, their affinities and relations. Behind these elementary particles stood another 'world' – the world of law, order, form and principle, that connected all these particles together and made all chemical changes and relationships possible. But it is understandable how anyone, who has not yet begun to think, can become intoxicated by the powers that science seems to put into his hands. It seems possible to explain every-thing, to know everything, to understand exactly why everything is what it is; and this first contact with science produces in some people an extraordinary contempt for and intolerance of anything like 'idealism' – that is, of a world behind this visible world that explains this visible world. They cannot see that we cannot really know or understand or even explain anything, simply through the method of science – and that all our explanations are nothing but descriptions of processes that remain a mystery.

.   .   .   .

The 'natural' man of the eighteenth century writers and the carnal-minded or sensual man of the ancient writers, is the outward-turned, sense-bound and sense-minded man. But we all have this 'natural' man as a particular part of our being. Today, this side of human psychology is intensified by the marvels of science, whose general standpoint has reached the masses. Intel-lectually, we appear to have only what Paul called 'the mind of the flesh'. And even if we vaguely believe in realities higher than those we can contact with our senses, the 'natural man' in us haunts us with the idea that such higher realities, if they exist at all, will eventually be *proved* by some grand scientific demonstra-tion – or finally dismissed.

But can we suppose that any *demonstration* of higher realities – I mean one that could somehow appeal to the senses – could ever take us off the sensual level of understanding? Nothing that can be demonstrated to the senses, no scientific discovery of any sort, no demonstration that can be *proved* to us, will ever lift us from that level of understanding. Why is this so? Perhaps we have never really considered the question.

If there be potential degrees of higher 'reality' within us no-thing coming from the side of the senses will alone open them.

41

We do not understand this easily. Yet is it not obvious that *man himself is not changed by discoveries in phenomena*? No matter how far we investigate the minute side of the phenomenal world we will never escape from *materialism*, however subtly it may be presented. We can never prove, discover or realise *mind* through sense. An extraordinary discovery, such as that of wireless telegraphy, does not change us in ourselves in the slightest degree. We merely get used to it and expect more. The quality of our consciousness undergoes not the slightest change. A sense of the miraculous does not leaven it – in fact, the contrary happens. We become more blind, more bored, more sure. If a change in consciousness is possible it does not seem possible that it can come from the phenomenal side.

Suppose, even, it were possible to prove to the senses the existence of a 'deity' – what would be the result? Suppose a deity could be demonstrated. It would mean that all that side of things which the inner spirit of man must search after and seek to apprehend individually, as self-revealed and self-realised truth, would become a matter of sensory and general evidence. Were a divinity to appear in the sky the whole inner construction of man would be violated and rendered sterile. Man would be *coerced* through his senses in just what belongs to his highest and most individual issues. The deepest theme in the drama of invisible and visible would be anticipated in the most wretched way, and our situation would be far more intolerable than it is.

From this angle we can perhaps see why all arguments in favour of higher intelligence that reach out ultimately to external sensory proofs – as Paley's argument from design, the alleged existence of spirits, proof by external miracles and magic – when brought too close to us, as evidence, profoundly repel us.

Outer cannot coerce inner. Indeed, in all such matters, outer 'proof' of the marvellous does not help us. The miracles of the modern world in physical science have not helped us to reach deeper values. An increase in the range of known or expected phenomena obviously does not awaken man's spirit.

Life is sufficiently miraculous already – *only we do not notice it.* If we catch a glimpse of its mystery, we border momentarily on new emotions and thoughts, but this comes from within, as a momentary, individual awakening of the spirit.

.   .   .   .

Eckhart says that we are at fault as long as we see *God* in what is outside us. It is not a matter of sense or of sensory evidence or of collective demonstration. He is not the prodigious and terrifying whirlwind, nor earthquake, nor fire. As long as we have this external view a hindrance lies in ourselves, and we fail to understand something of tremendous importance. Why is this so? Apparently we cannot begin from outer proof, from the phenomenal side; through our senses we cannot reach a necessary 'place' of understanding, though, whether we know it or not, our sense-mindedness is always trying to do so. 'Where creature stops, there God begins.' All the liberating inner truth and vision that we need, apart from outer truth and facts about things is, Eckhart says, 'native within us'. It is an internal matter, to be realised *first* as being in us. Yet it is far more difficult to understand what this means than we imagine, for we are born and nurtured in sensation, and so cannot help thinking sensually. Sensation – the sensory – is our *mother*; and she is very difficult to overcome. Our incest with matter is universal. The most important and convincing evidence for us remains the outward evidence of the senses. We see our salvation lying in that kind of truth, and therefore, now-a-days, in some great discovery, in some fresh facts. We cannot comprehend the psychological significance of such a statement as: 'We are saved by hope; but hope that is seen is not hope; for who hopeth for that which he seeth?' (*Romans* 8.24).

.   .   .   .

43

One point, then, about materialism, as regards its limiting effect upon man, would seem to lie in the attitude it takes towards the existence of higher degrees of reality. Man's reason is taken to be capable of attaining to a complete knowledge of the laws and the nature of all things. His consciousness, while it is capable of including more and more facts, is not regarded as capable of attaining a new quality. Higher degrees of consciousness and higher degrees of truth and entirely new forms of experience are excluded.

We see, then, that such a view certainly does not include scale. Scale must necessarily imply an above and a below, a higher and a lower, and also a special way of connecting things on different levels of reality. Materialism, having no sense of scale, cannot therefore admit either that which is greater than man or that which is greater *in* man.

But is the sole mode of experiencing or understanding life by way of the method of science? Is not science merely one mode of experience? And are we to believe that the quality of our ordinary consciousness is so fine that further states of consciousness are inconceivable? Are not further states of consciousness most likely to be the key to the understanding of the complexities and contradictions that have arisen in the realm of physics? The synthetic power belonging to our ordinary consciousness may well be of such a kind that it is unable to assimilate into a *whole* the various separate findings of scientific research.

If we argue in this way, it would mean that scientific materialism is limiting to the psychological development of man simply because it takes the consciousness of man for granted and therefore does not concern itself with problems as to how man can reach a higher state of development in himself – by what methods, by what kind of knowledge, work, ideas, efforts and attitudes. With all this latter we see at once that what is usually called 'religion' has always, on its inner side, concerned itself. The

44

so-called gap between science and religion seems to lie exactly at this point. *Man cannot understand more because he is in a state of inner disorganisation.* The quality of his consciousness is too separative and coarse. Yet he starts out in his investigations of the universe without any idea that he will be unable to penetrate beyond a certain point because he himself is an unsuitable instrument for this purpose. He thinks only that he is limited by a lack of scientific instruments of sufficient precision, or by a lack of data. He thinks therefore 'outwards' and strives only to overcome the 'outward' difficulties.

All that ancient religion and philosophy concerned itself with, and all that great art has reached after, will seem to him to have no possible connection with the difficulties he experiences in attaining final knowledge and ultimate truth. The finer qualities of consciousness and the new meaning and interpretations that art and religion have sought to reach will not seem to be of any importance to him; nor will he suspect that the inevitable contradictions that he is bound to find awaiting him at the end of his investigations result from the *quality of his own consciousness* and his own inner disorganisation.

.   .   .   .

For Plato the world is not only our sensation of it, as it must be if man is merely in the world. The world is also in man, so man can know from 'within' as well as from 'without'. The ideas behind all discernible reality are touched by man through the existence in him of *innate notions*. These 'innate notions' in the soul of man have as their true object the *Ideas* which are the archetypes behind all temporal manifestation. So, while our knowledge is developed by worldly experience, it contains elements which are not derived from experience. In its contact with the sensible world, which contains imperfect representations of the 'eternal' Ideas, the soul is awakened in greater or less degree to an awareness of the Ideas themselves. This awareness comes, not from the side of the senses, but internally, from the side of the mind. The soul *recollects* the *Ideas* through perceiving the manifold objects of nature into which the Ideas are reflected. The soul stands between the sensible world and the world of Ideas — between two orders of 'reality'; and becoming aware of this she takes from the world of sensible objects all those impressions which remind her of a higher order of reality, not giving to sensible nature that which does not belong to it, *but extracting from it that which belongs to an order above it.* So her whole mode of experiencing temporal life and gaining impressions becomes quite different from the mode of experience belonging to the soul that is 'glued to the senses' and sees all as outside her, attributing the first *causal* principle to physical nature itself. For the awakened soul all is really *within*. The real world is within, and is only apprehensible within. And a man whose soul has reached this position is no longer 'natural' or sensual man, although all that sense reveals to him is immeasurably intensified. He sees clearly — with increasing clearness — because he has become a meeting-point of two worlds, one reached within and through himself, and the other reached without, and through his senses.

.   .   .   .

How are visible objects representations of *ideas*? How do the eternal Ideas enter the three-dimensional world in passing-time? Plato suggests that they enter through the most minute — through the *dimensionless*. 'It is evident that generation takes place whenever a principle (*arche*, originating principle) attains to the second dimension and coming as far as the third, arrives at such a state as to become an object of sensation' (*Laws*, 894A). This seems to mean that he thought that the higher world enters the known world through its finest divisions. But it must be clearly understood that Plato's suggestion concerning the source

46

of generation is not a refined materialism aided by a theory of
dimensions. Originating cause is for him quite distinct from any
matter that we can reach externally through scientific research.
Idea enters into manifestation through what *for our sense-perception
is dimensionless*. Let us conceive an illustration.

Idea enters as seed. The seed is the elementary material constituent or third term. Between the first term, *idea*, and the third
term, seed, there grows up flower, animal or child as second term.
Only in one sense is the seed *cause*. The seed is fertile because of
the first term, idea, which is nihil, nothing, dimensionless, invisible in the phenomenal world. If the material organisation of the
seed be faulty, the *idea* to which it is conjoined will be unable to
manifest itself in space and passing-time rightly. The spermatic
power is really in the *idea* rather than in the seed, and flows as a
current through the seed when the right conditions for nurture
exist. Yet, thinking naturally, we see the full cause of a flower, or
an animal or child in the seed alone – in the minute speck of organised matter. And in the case of sterile hybrids we think rather
of a state of the seed than of the confounding of two distinct *ideas*,
each of which can only manifest itself in an appropriate seed.

.   .   .   .

In consequence of the quality of our consciousness, which
gives us an outward direction, we cannot see *ourselves* distinctly.
We take the effects of outer life upon us as 'ourselves'. We can
scarcely discern our states and moods apart from what appear to
be their outside causes. Governed by our senses reality appears
to be outside us. Sensually we do not realise the invisibility of
ourselves and others, for this is not a matter of 'perceptual consciousness'. Our *outwardness* prevents our reaching of inner harmony.
There is nothing in ourselves so much more real that it is capable
of isolating us from the continual effects of the world that is entering via sense. We are controlled by the sense-given scene – and

so we are outside ourselves. But we imagine that we are controlled by our reason and set firmly in ourselves.

Speaking of the conditions of higher consciousness, Ouspensky remarks that 'it is necessary that the centre of gravity of
everything shall lie for man in his inner world, in self-consciousness
and not in the outer world at all' (*Tertium Organum*, p. 331). He
is speaking here of self-consciousness as the full consciousness of I
– of a state of consciousness in which the centre of gravity of our
being – that is, I – is in ourselves. With our present consciousness
we are, as it were, fused with the world and continually distracted by its changes. And the form of our thought, which is based
upon what the senses show us, is 'natural' – that is, it follows the
world of sense and passing-time and is grounded in the evidence
of things seen. To get the centre of gravity of our being into ourselves, to become possessed of an internal sense of I in place of
the continual reactions of the moment to which we say I, another
'reality' of all things in general is necessary. Our natural concepts
are not sufficient to change the quality of consciousness or to get
the centre of gravity of our being into ourselves. Man must not
only overcome the sensual view of life by theoretical thinking but
he must look within – away from the senses – and become an object of study to himself. And he must get beyond merely sensible
knowledge and even rational knowledge.

Eckhart observes that there are three kinds of knowledge:
'The first is sensible, the second is rational and a great deal higher.
The third corresponds to a higher power of the soul which knows
no yesterday or today or tomorrow.'

Eckhart is referring to a phrase used by Paul: 'Pray that
ye may be able to comprehend with all the saints what is the
height, breadth, length and depth.' He is pointing to a state of
consciousness where time, as we know it, vanishes and there is no
'yesterday' or 'tomorrow'. Not only does a change in the sense
of I belong to a higher quality of consciousness, but the natural

concept of time derived from our sensory contact with the world disappears and a new knowledge or sense of time takes its place. What higher mathematics touches theoretically (in relation to dimensions) is perceived by direct cognition.

From this point of view higher mathematics lies in between the understanding belonging to our ordinary consciousness and the understanding belonging to a higher level of consciousness. This is how I understand Plato's view that *numbers* differ from *ideas*, and occupy the interval between ideas and sensible objects. The Ideas belong to a higher degree of reality than do sensible objects, and in between come numbers. But we must understand that to arrive theoretically at the conclusion that the world is four-dimensional is quite different from the realisation of it through an actual change in the time-sense.

.   .   .   .

We have considered three of the factors limiting to the development of consciousness: first, the question of our sensualism and the necessity for overcoming the sensory and literal point-of-view with which the attitude of materialism is connected; second, the need for change in the sense of *I*; third, the need for a new understanding of time. The fourth factor relates to the quality of our love. Let us touch on that briefly before continuing the subject of levels of consciousness.

.   .   .   .

Our love is little else than *self-love*. The more we study what self-love is the more does it become apparent that it puts, paradoxically, the centre of gravity of our being outside ourselves. Or, putting the matter in the reverse way, because the centre of gravity is outside ourselves, we only know, broadly speaking, self-love. Self-love always requires *audience*, either imagined or actual.

49

Perhaps the simplest way to begin to understand the nature of self-love is to study it from the side of falsity of action. Whatever we do from self-love we do in a false way, from a conceit, from the standpoint of producing some impression. We are not really doing what we are doing. We are not doing it from ourselves but from a curious relationship of ourselves to others, or to the idea of others and ourselves.

The great writers on self-love often take the subject back to the central point of attack in Christian psychology – to the *Pharisee* in us, who does all things *'to be seen of men'*. The criticism, I suggest, is directed against the lack of any real psychological starting point within ourselves. We probably take this *Pharisee* too concretely, imagining we know the kind of people to whom the term can very well be referred. I will take it as referring to a difficulty that exists in everyone, and one that is a feature of our form of consciousness. *We have no real I.* We have no real *self-consciousness.* Our love of self is not love of anything real. So we cannot act from anything real in ourselves but only from a continual mirror-like process within us which is not self-initiated but automatic. So that, in considering what puts the centre of gravity outside ourselves we have not only the factor due to the senses turning us outwards, making us see all as lying outside us, but also the emotional factor of the 'self-love'.

.　　　　.　　　　.　　　　.

In Indian thought bondage to *Maya* is, from one angle, bondage to the surrounding objects of sense. Not only our passion to possess objects is meant, but that everything outside us affects us or has power over us. We are continually distracted, just as a dog is distracted by everything he sees, hears, or smells. The tumult of sense-impressions, the riot of thoughts, the surgings of emotions and imagination, the throngings of desires, have nothing central between them to steady them. Between that which is pouring in from outside through the senses, and that which is going on within, nothing permanent intervenes to subject all these random activities to order, to bring them into alignment and produce a point of consciousness between inner and outer. The self-love disports itself in this chaos, glancing at itself in the mirror of every activity.

Speaking of the chaotic inner state of man, Ouspensky remarks that the first aim that an individual can have, as regards his own development, is 'to create in himself a permanent *"I"*, to protect himself from continual strivings, moods and desires which sway him now in one direction and now in another' (*A New Model of the Universe*, p. 244, Kegan Paul). But we must clearly grasp that such a state would mean a new state of the individual. It would mean a new *quality* of consciousness. It would mean the attainment of a higher degree of reality within. Such a permanent I could not be a derivative of the self-love, which is changing its direction every moment, trying on every costume as it were, and admiring itself in every possible pose. For everything relating to the self-love, and the passion for approval and self-approval, can have no stability in itself. The creation of a permanent I must take place somewhere beyond the sphere of self-love. It must be brought into existence through a series of acts which cannot be initiated by self-love and so cannot start from the admiration of oneself. And for this reason many things are necessary before such acts can be *self*-initiated. The whole standpoint must change. The standpoint of mate-rialism or sensualism cannot provide the right basis from which to start. Only the recognition that there are higher degrees of reality, *and the emotions that such a recognition can rouse*, can begin to give the right starting point. For such emotions do not lie in the sphere of the self-love.

In the Christian psychological system many interesting things are said about 'love of neighbour', which are usually taken in a sentimental way — that is, from the side of the self-love. But *the conscious discrimination of one's neighbour implies an actual development of consciousness.*

The quality of our ordinary love is so coloured by self-love that we are unable to feel the real existence of others, to feel *them*, save momentarily. They are little more than associations with our self-love. In connection with this Swedenborg says that our self-love demands as its main object a favourable reflection of ourselves in others. That is its goal. If we believe this reflection exists we feel joy. This joy changes to dislike, self-pity or hate, once we imagine the reflection is unfavourable. This is our ordinary 'love'. *It cannot become different – save momentarily – because the quality of our consciousness makes this impossible.*

To see another person, apart from our subjective notions and images, to realise another person's actual objective existence, is exactly one of those momentary and genuine experiences which give us hints of further possible states of consciousness. For then, during one moment, we awaken to entirely new and wonderful forms of experience. But falling back we forget them, because an inferior level of consciousness cannot reproduce the experiences belonging to a higher level. It is not so much that we forget, but *cannot* remember.

I will connect the self-love with a definite psychological direction. The old conception of two paths that man can follow, as represented originally in the ancient Pythagorean Y, is usually interpreted as referring to virtue and vice, as conventionally understood according to period and local custom. 'Where the Samian Y directs thy steps to run, to Virtue's narrow Steep and Broadway Vice to shun' (Dryden). This is the superficial explanation. But it may have originally referred to two possible paths in life, one *real* and one *sham*: along the sham direction let us imagine there lies the great spectacle of life, with all its honours and rewards. Its motive power is the gratified and ungratified self-love, its governing fear the loss of reputation. Along this path we all seek, in some form or another, audience. Usually we seek open approval. Connected with it is a very remarkable *perpetual-motion machine.* The great are flattered by the homage of their inferiors, and the inferiors are flattered by the recognition of the great. Thus the machinery turns unceasingly in this mutual self-satisfaction.

Bernard de Mandeville saw in this machinery the driving force of *every* form of society. He distinguished this aspect of self-love as self-liking. It is the passion of self-liking, he says, which is generated in children in the nursery by the chorus of praise which surrounds them, that is not only the foundation of all society but is the source of *honour* and *shame*, through which the appetites of people are held in check, and men and women are made virtuous, though not in any real sense. Through the passion of self-liking people may *imitate* all the virtues of the Christian life. He said, indeed, that there are no Christians – which roused the greatest indignation.

Along this sham path life is chiefly a dressing-up, an emptiness, a make-believe, in which we seek to be *like* something rather than really to *be* something. In this sense, then, no one is really doing what he appears to be doing, and nothing is what it pretends to be. Everything is governed by the complicated reactions of the gratified, the wounded, or the expectant self-love. Thus no one is 'pure' in heart – that is, the emotions are not real.

The general cause is that no one has *created himself.* No one has real existence in himself. We only attain to a fictitious self-existence. And if we are frank with ourselves, we know that we feel empty or locked-in. We do not know what to do. Through the incessant mirror-action of the self-love, we are always turned outwards, towards audience, *away from the direction of self-existence.* So, we are turned outwards not only by our senses and sense-mindedness, which can be said to belong to our natural constitution, but also by the infinite psychological ramifications of our self-love.

When the self-love is wounded or when we feel our

reputation is damaged or lost, we feel depreciated, 'inferior' or annihilated. Actually, such a state of affairs might be regarded as a starting-point for something new. But in life this does not happen.

The starting-point for some entirely new state of oneself, above what life produces, can never lie along the direction of what is generally approved or applauded, for it will then only administer to the self-love, which is the point of danger. For nothing, says Swedenborg, can produce such a brilliant effect upon oneself as the fully gratified self-love. For its delight, he says, reaches to every fibre of the body, and is felt far more intensely than is the gratification of any of the physical appetites. So also are the effects of wounded self-love equally intense. Swedenborg defines the first step beyond self-love as the *love of uses*. Anyone who can be simple enough to take real pleasure in what he does, and be genuinely interested in what he works at, obviously moves a step beyond self-love.

.   .   .   .

We must imagine a range of conscious experience lying *above* that which we ordinarily know. Intervening between it and what we ordinarily know is a discontinuity, a gap. We cannot bridge this gap save through lending ourselves to ideas, views, and ways of taking things that *ultimately belong* to the higher range of conscious experience.

Remaining 'sensual', the gap is not bridged: taking things in the ordinary way, retaining our ordinary views and natural ideas, we never attain the potential in us. All systems of 'religion' have this attainment in view. But not understanding the *doctrine of potentiality*, which regards man as a seed, we take all that we class as 'religion' in a moral way, as something merely urging us to be good. And the more obscure side of religion – the hints that belong to its internal meaning and esoteric side – we usually entirely ignore or contemplate with idle curiosity. We certainly see no *science in that*. But if there be a higher reality of oneself there must be an actual science of that higher reality of oneself – a science higher than any we know and one which will comprehend in itself all the ordinary forms of knowing, such as belong to philosophy, art and the sciences.

And having this view in mind – that there is a higher science of man – we can perceive that observation of the following kind probably finds its place just in this higher science. Boehme said that we could come into a new reality of our being and perceive everything in a new relation 'if we can stand still from self-thinking and self-willing and stop the wheel of imagination and the senses'. These are plain psychological instructions. *But in what sense psychological?* Not as we understand 'psychology' today. For what possible meaning can they have for us if we deny the possibility of any qualitative change to man? If there be no 'higher reality' there is no sense in such instructions, no *psychological* meaning.

And if, to obtain a higher reality of oneself, *the centre of gravity of one's being must be in oneself*, then this qualitative change in being will clearly remain impossible as long as we are turned only *outwards*. The centre of gravity of oneself must not lie *outside* through the action of self-love and the senses. It must not lie outwards in this *foreign* world which we can never *directly* reach, but within, in this invisibility that is the beginning of *oneself* and can become something, and through which we can reach 'neighbour'. And for this to happen a *qualitative* change of standpoint is necessary, and a willingness which starts from a conviction that there is something else that is essential for us. For we can only begin from *our own* willingness and *our own* conviction.

I believe that as long as we think that the world, as displayed to our senses, contains all that we need, and holds the key to our happiness, then we must always go in the wrong direction. We must overcome *that* degree of materialism to begin with, that kind of sensual understanding, and with it also overcome the effect of all those evidences in which the sensual man within us finds so much complacent comfort – as, for example, in the outward solidarity of a religious or a political movement, or in the increase of its organised and outward form. We must understand that we can rest upon *no proof* – such as the sensual understanding will seek and accept. The extra-ordinary confusion that arises when we confound the truth of ideas with the truth of the senses must disappear. We can no longer say that we will believe 'provided we have the proof'; or that we cannot believe 'because there is no proof'. A man's understanding must not stop at that point where things can no longer be satisfactorily demonstrated and proved to everyone. We have comprehension far above the sensory field, and experiences quite apart from it. Faith and belief belong to *orders of understanding* quite distinct from sensual understanding and sensory proof. The greatest initial barrier of all lies in the inability to distinguish between the truth of ideas and the truth of sense. It is a confounding of two orders – of what belongs to the inner man and what belongs to the outer man – and until it is passed, the inner life is rendered sterile because it cannot receive food. Even when a man reads or hears about truth belonging to ideas he holds it off by arguing that 'no one really knows', or that 'it cannot be proved'. Yet the outward-turning side of us must first taste life in full seeing the solution of all things as lying *without*. As the prodigal son, it must go out into life and experience, tasting from every cup, avoiding, if it can, the 'cup of bitterness'. As prodigal sons, we must first go further and further from source, until there awakens in us, earlier or later, fleeting realisations *that the direct approach to outer life cannot give us what we are looking for.*

The sensual man thinks of the outer as the most familiar and easy, the most satisfying and real and the most easily reached.

Does it not come to be the most foreign and most incomprehensible, and in the long run the most unsatisfying? Can you ever directly understand, or possess, or reach, even the simplest object lying in it? Certainly you will know you cannot if you already know your invisibility. Karl Barth says: 'Men suffer, because, bearing within them an invisible world, they find this unobservable inner world met by the tangible, foreign, other outer world, desperately visible, dislocated, its fragments jostling one another, yet mightily powerful and strangely menacing and hostile' (*Commentary on Romans*, p. 306, Oxford University Press). We are, indeed, in such a desperately foreign world, in such a strange land, that we may well ask ourselves how it has ever been possible to believe that we have been mechanically evolved through countless millions of years solely in order to be directly in it and of it.

    .   .   .   .

If the doctrine of potentiality is true and man is incomplete but capable of reaching further states of himself, any psychological system that does not take these possibilities into consideration must be inadequate. Actually it must be *negative* in character. It will not be enough to take known life alone. A positive psychological system, as that inherent in Christianity, must teach that man can be different and be based upon the view – the actual knowledge – that man is capable of *a very definite kind of development* that mere response to known life does not give, and that *some definite transformation* can take place in him. The ideas belonging to such a system will not, of course, be understandable in any ordinary way. They will not be about the phenomenal world, about matters of sense, about the third term. Nor will such ideas be verifiable through historical considerations, which are of minor importance. One does not prove the truth of an *idea* by demonstrating that its founder lived. The evidence of its truth can only lie in a man's own experience of it when it enters into him. Such

57

ideas cannot be compared to ordinary scientific ideas. We shall not find them in books on the physical nature of the universe. And unless we can distinguish between ideas of this kind and ordinary or scientific ideas, we will never be able to give them any germinating place in our mind, or perhaps never even grasp what they refer to.

CHAPTER THREE

DIFFERENT LEVELS OF REALITY
IN MAN AND THE UNIVERSE

THERE IS A GREAT amount of literature dealing with records of new experiences in consciousness that point to the existence of higher forms or levels of consciousness than we ordinarily know.

On the psychological side, the idea of levels in man is a very old one. It is found in ancient teachings, and appears in most mediaeval philosophical systems.

The idea of scale, which is also an old one, is bound up with the idea of levels. But since the time when the external world became the main object of study it has been nearly lost sight of. The senses show us apparently everything on the same scale, though of different sizes and at different distances. The eye can pass from a star to a human cell under the microscope without any particular difficulty. Yet we are passing from one order of things to another, and they cannot be taken on the same scale. The quantitative approach to things does not give the sense of scale, which is qualitative, although the idea of scale exists in the numerical series, for the numbers, 1, 2, 3, 4, 5, 6, 7, 8, 9, are followed by the repetition of the same numbers on another scale, the strange symbol nought or 'nothing' being used to indicate this.

Not only was *scale in the mind* conceived of in older thought – that is, different levels of consciousness – but the universe itself was regarded from the standpoint of scale. 'Higher' and 'lower' are in man and the universe. Sometimes these levels were spoken of as being discontinuous, that is, separated by 'nothing'. Let us study briefly some of the earliest conceptions of the structure of the universe in conjunction with the conceptions about man.

At the dawn of our civilisation Pythagoras taught that the universe is a 'harmony'. The word had distinct meanings. The Pythagoreans connected it with the musical *scale*. Burnet points out that it had the meaning of octave. In the second place, harmony meant the 'tension of opposites' held in balance. 'The harmonious structure of the world depends on opposite tension, like that of the bow or the lyre' (Heraklitus). Some thought that the universe could be represented by a *scale* of numbers. This was a definitely Pythagorean idea. Burnet believed that these numbers signified dimensions, i.e. one meant a point, two – a line, three – a plane, etc.

The harmony of the world was called the *soul* of the world. Just as musical harmony depends on certain numerical proportions in the length of strings, the universe was thought to be constructed so that its various parts were in harmonic relationship. From this point of view the universe is not haphazard, but an established order. For this reason Pythagoras gave to it the name *Cosmos*, a word which came to mean *order*.

The soul of man was also regarded as a 'harmony'. Plato speaks of the different elements in man as lying in a state of disorder but being capable of reaching a harmony on the principle of scale, as in a musical chord, where the various notes on different levels are brought into accord.

The lowest and most irrational part of man touches the world of the senses. The highest approximates to the world of *Ideas* and is beyond the level of logical reason. Plato describes these degrees in man as being comparable to four levels of mental development. In his theory of knowledge they correspond to four forms of knowing. The lowest is little more than a simple consciousness of the images of objects. This lowest state (*eikasia*) gives the most superficial view of the world and conveys the least knowledge. The mental state is nothing but a series of images and dreams. 'Shadows, images and dreams are the most obvious types of unreality and the contrast between them and realities is very striking to early thinkers, as it is to a mind which is just beginning to think' (Nettleship).

In the well-known analogy, Plato compares the ordinary mental state of man to that of a prisoner chained in a cave with his face to the wall, on which are thrown the shadows of real things outside the cave, of which latter he can begin to have no true idea unless he realises his situation and turns himself round. (This allegory is given in full later, page 221.) This is the state of *eikasia*, and it is characterised by continual uncertainty and vagueness, a living, as it were, in a dream world of shadows and fears. In this state of illusion man is simply a dim reflex of the changing world in time, a procession of images caught by the senses.

We are mainly in this internal state of *eikasia*, for the major part of our lives. This is the state in which the soul lives at the bottom of the scale of reality within us. For while the 'harmony' or scale is sometimes called the soul itself, at other times the soul is spoken of as an energy that can be related to the higher or lower gradations in this scale.

The next stage defined by Plato is that of *pistis*. In this state we get to know by experience some of the tangible facts of life. We feel certain about some things and form definite opinions, or opinions are formed in us by imitation. These opinions may be quite contradictory if we come to examine them. But because each of them gives us a feeling of certainty we do not investigate them deeply, and do not wish to do so. It is sufficient that we have something to hold on to. This is the stage of *pistis*, or belief and opinion; and however naive it may be it gives some feeling of certainty. So we find people in different countries with certain similar beliefs in the tangible things of exis-tence and quite different beliefs about the nature of things in general, but having some feeling of certainty in common. While there may be truth in some of these beliefs, as mere *belief* the inner perception of their truth is hindered.

Both the above states of mind were classed by Plato as *opinion* (*doxa*). Belief, and the perception of shadows, are not the waking reality. They are not *understanding*. One may hold a correct opinion but as long as it is an opinion it is not the perception of truth but only a kind of dream about it, i.e. the mind is not awakened.

When people begin to examine their opinions and find contradictions in their various beliefs, they begin to search for principles, or some unity underlying variety. Plato calls this stage of mental development *dianoia*. When we reason from hypothesis as in geometry, we use this dianoetic thinking; or when we try to find a law connecting together various perceived phenomena. These two examples are, of course, not similar. Scientific thought is dianoetic in that it endeavours to abstract from the mass of sensible things in order to establish simple laws that explain phenomena descriptively.

Above this he puts the highest level in man, *nous* (mind). We may perhaps be able to see dimly something of what was meant by this term. If we could see all the relations and affinities that an object has, *simultaneously*, instead of as a confused collection of separately noticed properties, which often seem to be contradictory, we would be on the *noetic* level of conscious experience. 'Suppose that different men of science had set themselves to work to exhaust all the properties of an object, and that all these properties came to be understood, we should regard the object as the centre in which a number of laws of nature, or what Plato would call forms, (ideas) converged' (Nettleship). The separate sensible properties of the object would be merged into its *total significance*. It would be seen as an expression of the universe, so that while nothing that our senses told us of it would be lost sight of or wrong, it would be invested with a meaning that transcended all sensible perception and would become a manifestation of 'intelligible form' or *idea*. At this noetic level the world would be experienced in a new way, i.e. as regards the interconnection, relation, meaning and significance of everything that we perceive.

Noetic experience can only be individually known. The sharing of knowledge by a number of people, who know different sides of the same question, could not possibly give *noesis*, as Nettleship seems to imply.

Since the noetic level of conscious experience and Plato's world of forms or ideas are closely related, we must look for a moment at the cosmological theory in which the latter appears.

All visible creation is regarded as an imperfect copy of invisible ideas or forms which can only be apprehended by mind (*nous*) at its highest level. Our senses reveal to us only copies. These copies exist in passing-time, *for everything visible, every sensible object, exists in passing-time.* The ideas are apart from time, but they are reflected into objects in time.

Man thus stands between a sensible world of copies and an intelligible (mentally perceptible) world of true forms, of which these copies are representations. This cosmological theory contains *three* terms: (1) that which *becomes*, which is the copy in time; (2) that wherein it becomes; (3) the model on which that which becomes – the copy – is based. 'We may compare the recipient with the mother, the model with the father, and that which arises between them with their child' (*Timaeus* 50, D).

Visible creation in time, or nature, therefore, does not exist of itself. It is not the cause of itself, but is an ever-changing copy of something which lies behind appearances. *The recipient, or mother, is three-dimensional space, which must be empty of all properties in order to receive the impress of the model. The copy is in time. The model (idea) is outside our space and time.*

Since the copy is in time it is always changing, always manifesting itself only partially. The full expression of itself lies in this first pattern or original model, beyond our time. If, then, we ever reached the noetic level of experience, our inward perception of the model would invest the outward copy with intense significance. Our intuition of the model, as direct cognition, would be free from all properties of sense. It would be knowledge apart from sense, but inasmuch as it met the sensible copy in outer space, it would exalt it into its total significance, because its *whole* form would be internally perceived.

Plato observes that at this level of conscious experience the world presents itself as a scale or series of orders of existence, each connected with the one above it and the one below it.

One form of preparation for the reaching of this state is indicated – the exercising of the power of *seeing together* the relationships that exist between the various branches of available knowledge, i.e. progress in knowledge is progress in the perception of the unity of knowledge. If we imagine that a branch of knowledge can exist separately by itself, we are in error, for everything is connected, in order of scale or 'harmony'.

Let us pass from Plato to one psychological aspect of the Christian doctrine. It is a necessary idea of religion that *there is a higher state of man.* In Christian terminology man is *hylic, psychic and finally pneumatic. This is surely not so much a question of types of men but of levels in man.* At the hylic level we have a purely sensual conception of nature as cause of itself (hyle = matter). At the psychic level, which I am unable to define, we can have apparently all sorts of opinions and beliefs about life, right or wrong, that are *imagination*. It was the awakening of the *pneumatic* or spiritual nature that was the object of the Christian teaching just as the aim of the Platonic discipline was to awaken the level of *nous*. The 'natural' or sensual ideas that we derive from our ordinary experiences of life are not sufficient to awaken this third nature.

.   .   .   .

We find the attribute of *unchangingness* always associated with the highest level of conscious experience. *The experiences of truth are always similar.* There is the changing mind, following time and change; and the unchanging mind behind it. There is the

64

order of natural reasoning that goes with changing phenomena, and another above it. 'For examining what caused me to admire the beauties of bodies, celestial or terrestrial, and what I used in judging things changeable and in pronouncing "this ought to be thus, and this not" – examining, I say, what was the cause of my so judging, seeing I did so judge, I found the unchangeable and true eternity of truth above my changeable mind. And thus by degrees I passed from body to the soul, which perceives through the senses of the body, and thence to its inward faculty, to which the bodily senses communicate external things; and so far even beasts possess this....'

This is the imagination, in the original sense of the word. The senses lead into a receptive image-forming organ which we possess in common with the beasts. Beyond this is the reasoning faculty 'to which is referred for judgment whatsoever is received from the senses and when this found itself in me also to be a changeable thing, it raised itself up in its own understanding, and drew away my thoughts from the power of habit, withdrawing itself from those contradictory phantasms; that so it might discover what that light was, whereby it was bedewed, when without any doubtfulness it cried out "that the unchangeable is to be preferred to the changeable"; whence also it knew the unchangeable itself, which unless it had in some way known, it had had no sure ground to prefer it to the changeable. And thus with the flash of one trembling glance it arrived *at that which is*.' In these words Augustine describes the ladder of levels in man, as known by him through his own experience, and the similarity between his description and that given by Plato is evident.

In his philosophical system Augustine took the spirit of man as a substance, different from body and yet everywhere present in the body, manifesting itself through the organs of the body as different functions, e.g. through the cerebellum (according to him) as the power of voluntary movement. In itself he regarded it as divided into seven degrees, i.e. as a harmony, or scale. The highest degrees transcended the natural reason. Regarded spiritually, man is nothing but will, but the quality of his will is different in these different degrees. As a creature of self-will (self-love) he has no being, no real existence. He is only the lowest level of himself. He has no centre of gravity in himself – an idea which seems at first sight paradoxical.

His truest being lies in the topmost degrees in the scale of spirit and unless these degrees begin to open in him, we are told he is incapable 'even of doing good'. The source of all truth lies in 'unchangeable truth' which is above the level of reason, and it is the internal perception of this unchangeable truth that endows man with the highest grade of being. This unchangeable truth is the divine logos or ordered plan and in identifying *knowledge* with the logos, or 'word', Augustine is in agreement with the Platonists.

We must understand that the perception of this truth is an internal experience. It is not of the same nature as external truth which comes from the direction of the senses, or when we reason about the outer nature of things. Some writers have said that all true knowledge must be born in man, and that he cannot have any real knowledge (even of nature) apart from this, because the natural reason can only trade in the outside surface of things, take measurements, weigh, etc., but cannot in this way reach the understanding of any person or thing. In other words, the point of view is that there is an order of truth in us and once born into the light of consciousness it is its own proof. But when it is lost sight of and we begin to reason and dispute about it, we enter a circle of irreconcilable contradictions, for the logical reason does not belong to that level which we are to connect with the internal perception of this unchanging truth. For this reason, the real truths behind religion and philosophy inevitably become matters of dispute, which lead to wars and persecutions. For the natural logical reason (in mystical terminology) has no higher birth than the 'spirit of this world'. It can only view things in a certain light derived from sensible experience and is turned outwards towards the phenomena of space and time. And psychologically it is bound up with self-love — that is, with the feelings of I from which we derive the ordinary sense of our value.

Now the Platonists regarded *thought* in its purest form as actual vision, the object of the vision being unchanging truth or the 'intelligible world' — the realm of meaning itself. This pure 'thought', which is not really thought as we understand it, lies above all the processes of reasoning and argument. Flashes of it are said to transform momentarily the entire understanding. This is the *transforming power* latent in man, i.e. a higher level of conscious experience. The later Platonists took the view that every contact with the intelligible world, or world of ideas, transformed the soul, which ultimately could reach the degree of comprehending the whole perfection of the intelligible universe. In this breadth of insight, we are told, evil disappears, merely because the true and necessary relation of everything is seen aright.

I would call the reader's attention to the point that if we believe a higher level of consciousness is latent in man, any experience of its activity must act in a direction entirely different from what is usual. In following the evidence of the senses we accept the sum of reality more or less as lying on the side of the senses. That there is anything else, more real in its effect is not something that we can easily be convinced about. But if noetic experience is possible, it must come from another side, and so must involve a *reversal* in ordinary process. Here we are dealing with a question which does not belong to the order of time.

If we believe in the temporal progress of man, then we also believe that he will *eventually* discover all possible truth. From this point of view one sees truth as something lying *far ahead in time*, towards which mankind is pressing. Some day, we think, people will find out everything. But if we put a higher level above all the changeable processes in man, and connect with it a form of consciousness that gives us insight into truth beyond any given by the form of consciousness we ordinarily know, then truth is not something lying in time, in the future, but is something here, now, only above us, *above our present consciousness*.

For some people it is difficult to think except in terms of time. They cannot conceive orders of existence, or degrees of understanding, or levels of consciousness, as forming part of some inherent structure of things, always present. To think from this latter standpoint requires, I repeat, something of a *reversal* in our customary way of thinking. To this I will return in a later chapter.

.   .   .   .

I must ask the reader to consider some of the other older cosmological theories, particularly because they do not regard the visible world in time as the sum-total of reality. Let us take the system of Erigena and examine it briefly. This system belongs to the tenth century a.d., and its general standpoint, like that of the Pythagorean-Platonic one that we have glanced at, can be expressed by the phrase: *visibilia ex invisibilibus*. The visible is derived from the invisible.

It is a system based on scale. According to all systems of this kind, we live in a created universe, in which nothing lives of itself; for the entire universe, including that part of it on which our senses open, is *connected together*.

At the top of the scale of reality Erigena puts Mind itself, or Deity, defining it as that which creates but is not created. Where, then, is this Mind from which the order of the whole universe is derived? We are told that God is *neither in space nor time*; that Mind, in the supreme sense, the power that gives *order* to all, can-

68

not be understood by our *'passive'* reason, upon which are impressed natural ideas derived from our sensible experience, and that no natural thought can compass its measure. For it is outside the visible world set in space and running in time. We next learn that from this Mind is first derived the order of Ideas (of which we have already spoken) of which all created things are copies. This order cannot, of course, be apprehended through natural sense.

Thus the Ideas, the *second* order, are created, and in their turn they create. They create, ultimately, the order of life with which we are familiar, the visible world of people, animals and plants.

We can imagine an architect informing some pupils of his plans and leaving them to carry out his instructions. But we must also imagine that the conditions under which these instructions are to be carried out are definitely limited.

As working-examples or experiments of the Ideas we are subject to passing-time, in which nothing can be instantaneously realised. Everything must conform to a process of transition from moment to moment. The third order is, therefore, the order of created things – including ourselves – that we perceive in time, which are necessarily imperfect copies of the Ideas that proceed from Mind. We understand, therefore, that the phenomenal world is actually a world of effects whose causes lie *at a higher level in the scale of reality.* While these effects are themselves related to one another in a certain sequence in time-order, which we can study scientifically, we cannot reach causes in a proper sense.

We learn further that what is outside time is free from opposites and inner contradictions. In time, we experience everything in the form of opposites and our thinking is based to a large extent, if not entirely, upon opposites. It follows that *Mind* itself is beyond our natural level of thought. For this reason Erigena says that we cannot apply any name or known quality to *God*. He can be called Truth, Good, Justice, or any name we like, but all such predicates imply an opposite. Since we think by means of words to which we can find an opposite, it is impossible for us to conceive the nature of God.

The world-scale of Erigena thus appears as a scale of descent, from the whole and perfect into the divided and less perfect, from pattern to copy. I have given the scale as briefly as possible.

.   .   .   .

In one sense it is easy for us to admit that the visible is derived from the invisible, because all visible matter is built out of smaller and still smaller parts, and finally out of atoms and electrons, which in themselves are quite invisible. These older systems, however, regarded the universe from the standpoint of man's position in it, his significance with regard to it, his possibilities, etc. If we think of the world as merely composed of electrons and say that only they constitute the 'invisible' world, we cannot really connect this view with *ourselves*. It does not increase our understanding or show us any possibilities. We may establish the view that the atom is like a small solar system in which the electrons revolve in orbits. Further, the view may be established that these orbits represent discontinuous *levels* of energy and that the electrons jump into greater orbits by the absorption of definite quantities of radiant energy, and into smaller orbits with the emission of definite quantities of radiant energy. In such theories, however, since the element of mental construction enters largely, we may wonder whether man is not studying his own mind. What we find in the atom may be some reflection of ourselves. If we find levels, and if we find that nothing can ever be predicted accurately in atomic phenomena, it may be that these 'facts' are related to the mind itself.

Now the older views, like those of Erigena, regarded man and the universe as quite inseparable. Man was held to be a little world, *an image of the greater world*. Nothing that he discovered about himself did not apply to the world, and nothing that he discovered about the world did not apply to himself. He is microcosmos in macrocosmos.

70

Such a view entitles us to say that from one angle *every man is the centre of the universe.* Let us look for a moment at this idea, which we will study later. Sometimes the world produces an overwhelming impression, perhaps particularly today, when everything is so abnormally linked up owing to the discoveries in electrodynamics. We hear one another speaking at immense distances. This velocity of radiant energies through which we are put into instantaneous communication with every part of the earth, is obviously incommensurable with man, i.e. it is out of all proportion to man's proportions. He is living, as it were, in a world *that does not belong to him*, and must necessarily feel loss of individuality and locality. He becomes over-whelmed, and emotionally dulled, lost in a clamour of outer things. Yet each one of us is at the *centre* of the world, because he himself sees the world and all that is in it.

·   ·   ·   ·

At the top of the scale of reality Erigena puts Mind, outside space and time. Scientifically, we put all original *causes* far back *in time*. From our natural thought, we cannot understand how cause can be regarded otherwise, for our natural ideas arise out of our experience of space and time. We find ourselves in the world passing in time from moment to moment – a world of opposites, of contradictions, and, as it were, of half-truths. Summer is followed by Winter, war by peace, and so on, and these opposites are separated by time. What was called our 'passive' reason argues from time and space as we know them. It tries to explain everything on this basis. But when we come to study systems like that of Erigena, we learn that our space and time are only particular *conditions*, to which mortals are subject. We know, in short, only a limited reality, which is characterised by passage in time. So we are told that the ultimate cause and origin of all things is not a million million years ago; it is *outside time – Now*.

·   ·   ·   ·

71

Erigena draws certain conclusions from the world-scale on which his system is based. Whatever is on the lower level cannot understand a higher level but can be fully comprehended and understood by what is above, and only finds its full meaning through seeking to enter the reality above it. Man's consciousness is capable of ascending this scale.

Since this scale is given as a representation of the true structure of the universe we are told that everything is in a certain relationship to everything else. We found the same idea in the Pythagorean scale of harmonic proportions. To a certain extent we know from experience that nothing lives of itself. We perceive that our vital life is drawn from the energy of the sun, which acts on the minute solar-machines in the leaves of plants and in the organisms floating on the surface of the sea. These build up, out of light, air, water and minerals, the food that sustains organic life in general. In this sense, we depend upon what is perceptibly greater and perceptibly lesser for our physical existence. Sun, man, cell, are connected. But these are of different orders. The sun is a body of vast energy with an interior temperature of forty million degrees. The cell is the microscopic watery element of life out of which all living tissue is built.

We exist in a *universe of relationships* in which everything is bound together in an *order*, so that the whole constitutes a unity. This order is in itself something actual. We find order in the atom, in the limited number of possible orbits surrounding the central proton. We find order in the constitution of man's body, in the inter-relationship of its organs and integrations of the nervous system. We find order in the world of stars and planets. We do not find only positive and negative electrical charges, or action and re-action, but a third principle, order.

Since all is related proportionally and bound together in a common unity of order, the universe for Erigena is throughout united. The lower is comprehended in the higher, and relative to it is less real. *Everything is real, but relatively less real than what is above it.*

In so far as man is a little universe in himself this scale of relative reality exists in him up to a point, so that he is capable of becoming more real, of reaching fuller existence, by ascending this scale in himself.

'The effect of this scheme is to make the world a complex system of degrees of reality, within which every single thing is from one point of view, real and existent, and from another, unreal and non-existent.... The lower existence is unreal in comparison with the higher right through the universe.... Unless the whole of things is a disconnected mass of particulars and therefore not a universe at all, it is impossible to think of every single thing as on the same plane of reality.... We secure the relative reality of every single fact and at the same time the absolute reality of the universe as a rational system when we hold the manifold appearances of the world to belong to successive orders of reality' (Henry Bett, *Joannes Scotus Erigena*, p. 123).

Because Mind is the ultimate reality and is greater than any *perceptible* thing, so every perceptible thing exists more in the mind of man than it does in itself, i.e. we can give one another more existence in our mental apprehension of one another. It is not surprising to find, in view of the enormous value that Erigena places upon man, that he goes so far as to say that everything perceptible to the senses is made for the sake of man's senses. The emphasis is upon man, not upon the outer world. But as a mere creature of sense man has no proper existence. He then suffers evil because of his own relative unreality, because he does not correspond to the reality possible to him. Hell is a *state* of being, a state not corresponding to anything real, a state of falsity.

·   ·   ·   ·

73

We have spoken of a higher level of consciousness being characterised by a larger synthesis. If many sides of a question are drawn together suddenly into unitary meaning, then the many are combined into one, and a new synthesis results. What, then, would a new experience of *oneself* mean in this connection? For we do not only have experiences of the outer world, or of relationships to one another, but also inner experiences that have to do with the feeling of *I*. We can feel ourselves differently.

In all those disciplines whose object was to raise people to a higher level of reality, an overcoming of 'oneself' was demanded. For example, a purification of the emotions was held to be necessary, as well as a different way of thinking, a different relationship to people, etc. A change in *oneself* was held to be necessary, because as long as one remained just as one was, one could not have different experiences. Only through new ideas and new efforts could any permanent change be produced.

But momentary changes sometimes occur. They indicate to us that there are *other states of oneself*; and while they last one is changed, through a new feeling of oneself.

All change in oneself comes through a changed feeling of oneself. We have what can be called a 'natural reality' in which we dwell. We move in a small orbit of meanings, of notions about ourselves, others, and the world. If this orbit is broken we are usually in a peculiarly helpless condition, having no idea of anything else. There seems to be nothing to fall back upon. What we actually lose is the *ordinary feeling of ourselves*. So we become frightened and lost, not so much because of what has happened but because we cannot recognise ourselves.

To become different means another recognition of one-self. We are told that this 'oneself' is capable of changing. But if it changes there will be another sense of oneself. There are completely new feelings of oneself to which, I believe, people sometimes come very close – without understanding what they are. A person may touch a much better feeling of himself (momentarily) without knowing what it is, and perhaps only be frightened of it. He may experience 'truth' in some form which makes everything that usually occupies his attention seem *unreal*, and merely think that something is seriously wrong with him.

We know that there can enter into all that we see, do, think, and feel, a sense of unrealness. Sometimes it takes the form of seeing the unreality of other people. We observe that some force seems to be hurrying everyone to and fro. We see transiently a puppet-world, in which people are moved as by strings. Sometimes, however, in place of unreality, an extraordinary *intensity of reality* is felt. We suddenly see some one for the first time, whom we have known for years, in a kind of stillness. We perceive the reality of another existence, or we perceive the existence of nature, suddenly, as a marvel, for the first time. The same experience, felt in relation to oneself, is *the sense of one's own existence, independent of everything else*, the realisation of one's invisibility, the perception of *I*, of duration without time.

These feelings surround our 'natural reality'. I think that they show us clearly enough that there are other meanings of oneself, or forms of conscious experience.

Let us consider an example of a changed state of consciousness and see whether we can regard it in some degree as an example of the reaching of a higher level. It is the familiar one that Tennyson recorded of himself: 'A kind of waking trance I have frequently had, quite up from boyhood, when I have been all alone. This has generally come upon me through repeating my own name two or three times to myself, silently, till all at once, as it were, out of the intensity of the consciousness of individuality, the individuality itself seemed to fade away into boundless being, and this not a confused state, but the clearest of the clearest, the surest of the surest, utterly beyond words, where death was almost a laughable impossibility, the loss of personality (if so it were) seeming no extinction but the only true life.... I am ashamed of my feeble description. Have I not said that the state is beyond words?'

We can understand that a higher level will make the lower seem unreal. Tennyson felt the unrealness of his usual state because he felt *another* kind of *realness*, which freed him from all that sense of himself that goes with the *name*.

Also he passed out of the *usual sense of time*. In the reality that we derive from our experience of passing-time, death confronts us. We are incapable of thinking of death, incapable of realising it as the inner perception of an *idea*. In the true idea of himself that he touched, *death was an impossibility*. But death as a visible *fact* (that we try to grasp with the outer mind) continually feeds the uneasiness on which most of our life rests; or if it has left a blank in our lives, keeps on dragging us backwards in a useless way. With the sensual conception of life we cannot meet these difficulties. Passing-time makes death an insoluble, incontrovertible problem, blinding our understanding; and from the natural sense we cannot comprehend time save as we experience it. *Death* is a *fact* in our natural reality – that is, in our sense-given experience of life – and as long as we cannot understand that we apprehend through the senses only a minute part of total existence and reality, we cannot escape from the violent effect of its suggestion.

The experience recorded by Tennyson shows that he touched an entirely new feeling of *I*. He says that he lost his ordinary sense of personality. This by itself would be a terrible experience; to feel one's ordinary sense of *I* disappearing would be like death. But in his case his whole life seems to have been gathered up into a larger synthesis, in which his existence became something quite new, above the level of ordinary consciousness and the familiar feelings of I that belong to it (the 'I-conceit' of Buddhist teaching). He knew *himself* behind himself, behind the sense of personality, by direct cognition; and descending once more to the ordinary level of consciousness (which does not know the higher level) he is unable to find words to describe his experience. He can feel only that his description is entirely inadequate. If we say, then, that this experience belongs to the noetic level we probably have some right to do so. Only the experience refers to a higher form of knowledge of *oneself* – it is confined to this – and perhaps we could say to the true *idea* or form behind the ordinary oneself.

.   .   .   .

The main difference between a standpoint such as that expressed by Erigena or Plato and the naturalistic or materialistic standpoint is that *greater reality* is posited, lying not ahead of us in future time but in some other direction independent of time. The reader will understand that all that has been said so far in this chapter relates to the existence of an *above* and a *below*, i.e. to *scale*. In man, as in the universe, there is an *above* and a *below*. From the standpoint of consciousness, a higher level of consciousness exists in man, whose quality is not comparable with that of ordinary consciousness. The realities belonging to ordinary consciousness are only relative realities, just as that aspect of the world manifest to the physicist is only relative reality. Just as we know one aspect of the world through the senses, so do we know only one aspect of CONSCIOUSNESS. To refer to the analogy of the schoolmaster and class mentioned in the previous chapter, we know only a form of consciousness comparable to a disordered class from which the schoolmaster is absent, or in which he is asleep. His awakening is not a matter of future time. We imagine that what we lack must lie in future time. But we have already seen that, according to Erigena's system, greater reality lies *above* us – not, so to speak, horizontally in the line of passing-time, the line of past, present and future, but vertically, on another level. This vertical direction does not belong to time. Our strivings have their full fruition not in the horizontal direction but in the vertical one. We must imagine this direction in reflecting upon Tennyson's experience. Apparently he awoke to another and *fuller* order of conscious experience.

In the philosophical system of Averroes (twelfth century) it is said that the fruition of all man's strivings is 'already and always attained'. This actualisation, which is, of course, incomprehensible to our reason, is achieved 'now and ever', *beyond the limiting conditions of time* to which we are subjected and from which our customary mode of thinking is derived. The full fruition of the universe and all that it contains, being already and always actualised (according to this and other thinkers), certainly cannot belong to the time-order as we know it. But since the direction of our thinking follows the time-order, we have great difficulty in understanding this quite different and singular point of view. According to Averroes man is constructed in such a way that he can understand *this other direction, and can indeed only attain happiness when he begins to discover it.* Above the passive understanding, it is said, lies an 'active' understanding which can grasp the nature of this direction. Yet, while all this remains incomprehensible, we can to a certain extent understand what it must mean. *It must mean that we are asked to think differently about time.*

.   .   .   .

As we shall see later on, it has been said repeatedly that we cannot understand anything rightly unless we overcome the 'illusion of time'. Some transformation of our natural understanding is requisite in order that another level of understanding can be born in us. So much importance was attached by the older thinkers to this higher level of understanding that, as I have already mentioned, we often find it said that no one can say he has real knowledge unless he has felt the influence of this higher degree, i.e. something very definite must happen to a man before he can begin to *understand* in any real sense. Speaking cosmologically, Averroes says of our ordinary understanding that it belongs to the sub-lunary world and is incapable of solving the problems that confront us, because it *understands* nothing.

Just as waking makes dreams unreal, so, we are told, does waking to another level of consciousness make all our ordinary problems, preoccupations and perplexities seem unreal. One of the best interpreters of the psychological ideas of Boehme has expressed this standpoint very plainly in the following terms: 'The Greatest Part of Mankind, nay, of all Christians, may be said to be asleep; that particular Way of Life, which takes up each Man's Mind, Thoughts and Actions, may be very well called his particular Dream. The Learned and the Ignorant, the Rich and the Poor, are all in the same state of Slumber, passing away a short life in a different kind of Dream' (William Law). This eighteenth century writer goes on to say, in theological language, that man has the possibility of some other state above the state of slumber which is the chief psychological idea found in religion. We must notice a connection that he makes. As we might expect, he connects this state of slumber *with time*.

In this he follows his teacher closely, for Boehme said that man 'fell asleep in time'. We cannot, of course, understand what this means. In order to begin to understand what this may mean we require a great many new ideas and conceptions. Law remarks that man can never understand what his life means unless he grasps that his constitution contains a higher possibility within it, which stands above the state of slumber and 'time'. Once a man realises this possibility (whatever it is) he comes to a new view of himself and of the significance of his life, and this realisation, we are told, is to *know oneself*, to know *potentiality*. 'Do but suppose a man to know himself, that he comes into this world on no other errand but to arise out of the vanity of time.... Do but suppose him to govern his inward thought and outward action by this view of himself and then to him every day has lost all its evil;

prosperity and adversity have no difference, because he receives them and uses them in the same spirit, etc.' (vol. 7, p. 1, of *The Works of William Law*, Fellow of Emmanuel College, originally published in 1749, and privately reprinted in 1893).

.   .   .   .

And the same notion – the notion that we are not awake, that we are not at a level of consciousness where we can understand anything rightly, and where it is impossible to know or have anything real and where we cannot be in control of ourselves because we are not conscious at the point where control would be possible – is found through-out Platonic, Christian and many other teachings. But consider how difficult – how impossible – it is for us to admit that we are asleep in life. It cannot be an admission. It can only be a gradual realisation. And such an experience can only be brought about by the influences of efforts and ideas belonging to the nearly-lost science of awakening.

The translators of the gospel could not have properly understood this idea for they translated the Greek γρηγορεω as *watch* ('Watch, therefore, and pray', etc.). And this word *watch* is found in many places in the New Testament, but its real meaning is *to be awake*. And the force of this meaning is incalculably greater than that expressed by the term *watch*.

Because we are told everywhere in the gospels to be awake, is it not clear that we are at the same time being told that we are asleep, and that self-knowledge is to realise that one is asleep? Heraclitus said: 'I sought myself.' The doctrine of self-knowledge, written over the porch at Delphi, is not what we imagine. Only when we realise that we have no self can we seek ourselves. Only through a flash of truth can one understand ignorance and falsity. But this kind of self-knowledge escapes us. Socrates found the first step in self-knowledge to consist in becoming aware that we do not know ourselves, and indeed do not know anything. We pretend to know everything. In realising our ignorance, in catching a glimpse of pretence, in ceasing blindly to believe in opinions, slogans, words, we *begin* to know ourselves, i.e. we begin to awaken out of a dream. Our consciousness begins to be increased, just in what we perhaps might suppose to be a direction leading to an opposite result. But if you know you do not know, you are more conscious. Oneself becomes thus the instrument for awakening. The more we lie to ourselves, the more we are asleep. Consider today the power of lies and the increasing lack of resistance to them, and so the increasing sleep of the world.

Man has fallen asleep in matter and in time and in himself. But let us note how it is put in the great allegory of creation. Man is tempted by the serpent, which crawls on its belly in the dust. Where our feet touch the earth is where the domain of the senses begins. Here man is a creature of sense, sense-minded, sensual. Here his wisdom is of the senses. To kill your enemy is wisdom of the senses, for your enemy disappears. Your senses no longer register his existence. All the cleverness of materialism enters here, to make man think he knows. And though every sensible object is a mystery and the senses themselves are a mystery, he feels he can take hold of the sensible world, not only to enjoy it as he pleases, but to mould it to his commands. In this sense he eats the fruit of the tree of the knowledge of good and evil. He takes good and evil into himself and decides himself what should be done. And this necessary step leads on, not to recovery, but to the idea that he can rule. He becomes much wiser than the universe in his own estimation. It seems to him he can conquer all things, although his inner weakness, ignorance and lack of control remain unchanged. The whole problem of mankind remains as before, but it is hidden under an embroidery of words – a new state, a new humanity, a paradise of material discoveries!

But who is going to start from himself to render himself fit for any possible paradise – and how to do it?

What is going to raise the sensual up? Who shall either reinterpret science or place it in its place? Nothing that is in its right place can be wrong if it keeps its place. Mankind can be dragged down by a surfeit of increasingly sensual interpretation, which does not either cover the facts or afford the right medium of presentation. Everyone has in him more functions, more capacities, more sides to himself than can possibly be satisfied by sheer materialism. The serpent must be lifted up – in the wilderness. Who shall raise it? What spark shall kindle the marvels of science and transform them into the marvels of the universe? Can science cease to be animated by the latent spirit of hostility and can it create in man the free sense of wonder and awe in place of the spirit of denial?

.   .   .   .

We are told that we are asleep and can awaken. And when, as Law puts it, we begin to grasp this we see that we are all living in a kind of dream – a fact we sometimes become aware of in moments of great danger or emotion. You must notice that this is not a pessimistic doctrine. If you tell a man who is lying in the mud that all is mud, the teaching will be negative. When the writer to the Ephesians says: 'Awake thou that sleepest and arise from the dead' (5.14) he means, by the quotation, that we are like dead people and live the life of dead people, and that our state of sleep is really death. Not beginning with ourselves we do not see ourselves. To awaken is to see more clearly. At such a moment one may see how people are dead. One can see the terrible emotions that govern humanity – written on their faces – which they nourish without clearly seeing what they are doing. The idea of the Christian teaching at its source, before it became externalised and organised into machinery, was about awakening from sleep through the light shed by the inner meaning of the teaching. Christ was one who had awakened and taught others one way of awakening. The whole idea of following certain rules, precepts and ideas was not for any moral end but in order to 'arise from the dead', to reach a possible inner evolution, and so that writer to the Ephesians says, 'Awake thou that sleepest and arise from the dead and Christ shall give thee light. See that ye walk circumspectly....' To notice where one is going internally is to be more conscious to oneself. In this way, the writer adds, 'you will redeem the time'.

.   .   .   .   .

To return to Law, whatever we understand in particular of what he says, it is obvious that he regards our ordinary degree of consciousness as being comparable to a dream-state, and that our entire life, career, profession, our actions, thoughts and so on, are dream-like. We live in a kind of dream, from which it is possible for us to awaken, and – again we must note the point – this arousal from slumber is connected with another sense of *time*.

If, then, we are willing to admit the possibility that there is a higher level of consciousness, or a further degree of experience inherent in our nature, we have to suppose that another understanding of time is connected with it. It is extremely difficult to see what is meant here. Let us say at present that our ordinary level of consciousness, which Law emphatically says is a condition of sleep, and therefore unreal relatively to a higher order, is bound up with our ordinary experience of time. Or rather, it is bound up with our notion of time and with all the deductions and conclusions that we make by taking time to be what it seems. Let us suppose that at the level of our ordinary conscious state all our thoughts and feelings, and our understanding in general, have a certain arrangement common to us all; and let us suppose that this arrangement is to a great extent due to the appearance of things, as conditioned by time. As long as we passively regard time as what it seems sensually to be (as a moment passing into nothingness) we necessarily inhabit this level, i.e. our ordi-nary level of consciousness is closely bound up with our ordinary view of time.

Let us go no further at present save to say that noetic experience — that is, conscious experience on a higher level beyond our state of slumber — is beyond time-sequence, so that we can understand a little how *a different view of time may open the way to the possibilities of new experiences*. Actually, we should say rather that an internal perception of the *meaning* of another view of time might bring about this result. We would not suppose it comes merely from theoretical thinking.

To be told that time is an illusion does not help anybody unless they have already caught a glimpse of another *idea* of time. But one can readily see that one's ordinary consciousness is very much dominated by time and that a great deal of our fear and anxiety is a matter of 'time'.

.   .   .   .

What do we think about time?

We exist in a world that we do not understand in the least. What is nature? What is time? What is space? What are we?

We take all for granted. We do not face any real issues in our thinking but catch hold of some ready-made opinion. Do we ever get used to the mystery of *time*, for instance? Is not the problem of time always in the background of our minds although we can never really think about it? Consider the strange experience that a person *was* but *is* no more. Consider our childhood and death. Where is all that which has become *was*, and all that *will be*? What is this strange *now* and *then*, which when perceived together cause the mind to tremble on the verge of new meaning?

We stand before ruins and wonder at the mystery of 'once upon a time'. We cannot grasp what it means. We feel close to meaning that is potential but which we cannot reach. Again, we may feel how strange it is that we live among people of every age, people whose 'time' lies in front of them and people whose 'time' lies behind them, all inserted into a common point of another time, crowded into what is called the present moment of the world – different 'times' meeting in the same 'time'.

Now for our ordinary understanding *time* is a sort of no-thingness. All that we know by direct experience is a hypothetical point of time which we call the present moment. In this present moment we see things ending and beginning, old and new, things passing out of existence and things coming into existence. And we know that this present moment is somehow moving and always turning into another present moment. No matter whether we are sitting still or walking about, this movement of time is always going on. But we cannot think about it. We cannot think about it in the same way as we can think about something we can see or touch. We do not *think* about time because we cannot grasp it with sense as we can a solid object lying in the three dimensions of space.

We grasp the three dimensions of space through the visible objects that exist in it. They have length, breadth and height. Each of these directions is at right angles to the other. We say that a box is a three-dimensional object. A shadow on the wall is two-dimensional. It has length and breadth but no thickness, in so far as it lies on the wall. It is merely a surface, and so two-dimensional. A line, in the geometrical sense, is one-dimensional. It has only length. But turning from space, what can we say of time save that it is a moment that somehow or other moves into the next, then into the next, in a manner which we cannot think about because we cannot see this movement and can only mark it artificially by the hands of the clock, which we regulate according to the movements of the earth? We think of time as minutes, hours, days, years, but our thought does not get much beyond this, for how can we think save from 'natural' ideas, derived from what we see? We cannot see time. Time is 'invisible'; and, naturally, we do not think of time as a *dimension*, to be added to the three dimensions of space. Yet any object has not only length, breadth and height; it has *time* also or it would vanish. It is extended in time as well as in space.

Until the beginning of this century the science of physics, which treats of the motions of bodies, the measurements of quantities, and the nature of the external world, took space and time *separately*. The, world, for it, was three-dimensional, and time was something apart, i.e. space and time were treated as if they were independent of one another.

The three co-ordinates of space, which correspond to rectangular lines drawn, in the dimensions of length and of breadth and of height (let them be called x, y, z) were taken independently of time (t). But the objects of our perception 'invariably include places and times in combination. Nobody has ever noticed a place except at a time, or a time except at a place.... A point of space at a point of time, that is, a system of values, x, y, z, t, I will call a *world-point*. The multiplicity of all thinkable x, y, z, t, values we will christen the world' (Minkowski, *The Principle of Relativity*, p. 76, Methuen, 1923).

An object must always be *in a certain place at a certain time, and to define its position in the universe in spatial terms only is not sufficient*. A motor-car passes a particular spot in the road, which we can define spatially by taking co-ordinates and measurements. A man passes over the *same* spot, and relative to our co-ordinates he will be in exactly the same place as the car. But if we leave out time in that case the car and the man must collide. A further co-ordinate, or value, must be added, for although both the car and the man pass the same spot, an interval of time separates them. Observe the result of adding this fourth co-ordinate of time. We enter, at once, the 'invisible' world, for to our visible perception the world is three-dimensional and the spot on the road that both the car and the man pass is the same visible spot in the three-dimensional world. *It is the 'same place' in the three-dimensional world but it is not the same place in the four-dimensional world.*

In Minkowski's language, the spot on the road with the car passing it, and the same spot on the road with the man passing it later, are two quite separate *world-points*.

Time is thus taken as an element of the four-dimensional world – that is, of a world quite different from that perceptible to our senses. Our senses do not inform us of the four-dimensional world but only of a world-point, which appears as a three-dimensional world (moving in time).

Now every object, in so far as it persists in time, is not to be thought of merely as the visible three-dimensional thing it appears to be, as for instance, my hand that I can see before me at this moment, but as describing a line in the dimension of time. My hand and my body do not describe the same lines. It would be better, perhaps, to say that they are not only extended in the three dimensions of space, but also in the fourth dimension.

Such *world-lines* lie in the four-dimensional world. Where world-lines converge or meet there is a point in the four-dimensional world which, if our conscious experience relates us to that world-point, we call our 'present moment' and discover in it objects in a certain relation to one another in a three-dimensional space. 'The whole universe is seen to resolve itself into similar world lines and I would fain anticipate myself by saying that in my opinion physical laws might find their most perfect expression as reciprocal relations between these world lines' (Minkowski). We shall see later on that Fechner had similar ideas of the 'world'.

We have, moreover, to think that our own lives are lines in the four-dimensional world, and that, psychologically speaking, these lines have existence, and presumably have reciprocal relations between them *as lines* not only as points. We will come to the idea of the extension of our lives in higher dimensions subsequently.

CHAPTER FOUR

PASSING-TIME AND TIME ITSELF

IF THE WORLD, beyond its natural aspect, is first of all four-dimensional then we must be in some way four-dimensional, if we understand that man and the universe cannot be taken separately.

How do we conceive ourselves? We seem bodies, having three dimensions, existing in the moment of time called present. This is the appearance of things. If we begin to conceive ourselves four-dimensionally we must leave this appearance of things and penetrate into a deeper realm of thought and feeling, which must inevitably change the feeling of ourselves – the ordinary feelings of *I*.

The point is that a different understanding of time and a different feeling of I are linked together. All that has been said so far about different levels of consciousness is connected with this view.

Let us follow some reflections made by Ouspensky on the question of a different understanding of life gained through a different understanding of time. He divides consciousness into four forms. He regards our ordinary consciousness as a particular instance of consciousness (which he connects with a particular feeling of *I*) and our ordinary conception of the world as a *particular* instance of the conception of the world.

The first or most elementary form of consciousness he terms latent consciousness, similar to the instincts. The second he terms simple consciousness, in which flashes of thought may occur, as in animals possessing complex organisation. A dog may perhaps touch our level of thought momentarily. Such a flash of thought would be a *higher* form of consciousness for it. The third he identifies chiefly with reasoning, our ordinary power of thought. The fourth he calls *self-consciousness*, the beginning of a higher consciousness (P.D.Ouspensky, *Tertium Organum*).

He connects the fourth form of consciousness – which is not necessarily the highest – with another perception of time. Referring to the passage in the Apocalypse (Revelation, ch. 10, v. 6) where the angel swears that there shall be time no longer, he observes that there are states of the spirit where time disappears: 'In this very thing, in the change of the time sense, the beginning of the fourth form of consciousness is expressed.'

We recall that Tennyson reached a new feeling of I, or another self-consciousness, and this was accompanied by a change in the time-sense. He was no longer located in that 'time' in which we feel ourselves ordinarily to exist.

If we say that he became aware of 'higher space', in which death does not exist and in which he discovered a new form of himself, we must attempt to grasp what is meant by this term. *A four-dimensional world is one of higher space.* Our customary consciousness establishes for us a lower space of three dimensions, *moving in time.* Theoretically, time is a dimension that it is necessary to add to the known three of space. But psychologically experienced, higher space means, to begin with, a complete alteration in the feeling of *what one is.* Tennyson no longer felt himself a momentary creature, running in time, but something timeless, permanent. He caught sight of the fact that there is something *above* the level of his usual state.

.   .   .   .

Can we say that there is anything new in the conception of an aspect of the world in higher space? Let us take one of the earliest definitions of *God.* He is defined as the 'beginning and end'.

Beginning and end for us are necessarily separated by the passage of time. The co-existence of beginning and end immediately introduces us to the idea of higher space, for if we take Time itself as a dimension, the beginning and end of any event or of any person, must exist in this dimension. We can, of course, understand that the 'beginning' and 'end' of a stick co-exist in the space of three dimensions. That is obvious to sense. But the Time-dimension is not obvious to sense.

This definition of 'God' does not refer to qualities, and I think that we are justified in saying that it deals with dimensions beyond those accessible to the senses. God, or higher reality, lies in the direction of dimensions above those known to us. The definition turns our thought in the direction of higher dimensions.

Let us take some examples. 'God', according to an ancient (Orphic) saying, 'holding the beginning, middle, and end of all existence' (Plato). 'God is withdrawn from both ends of time, for his life is not Time, but Eternity, the archetype of time. And in Eternity there is no past and future, only present' (Philo). 'I am yesterday, today, and tomorrow.... There is not a day devoid of that which belongeth to it.... The present time is the path which I have opened' (*The Egyptian Book of the Dead*). Coming to the Old Testament: 'I the Lord, the first, and with the last, I am He' (*Isaiah*, ch. 41, v. 4). 'Declaring the end from the beginning, and from ancient times the things which are not yet done' (*Isaiah*, ch. 46, v. 10). And in the New Testament: 'I am Alpha and Omega, the beginning and the end, the first and the last' (*Revelation*, ch. 22, v. 13). We find also God defined as that 'which is, which was, and that which is to come' (*Revelation*, ch. 1, v. 8).

An order of existence above our natural comprehension is clearly referred to – an order of existence of which Eckhart says: 'Both the first day and the last are happening at the present instant yonder.'

A great expansion of our understanding is demanded by these phrases. By no logical argument can I grasp the *idea* that the first day and the last have simultaneous existence, nor can I understand that the beginning and end of my life co-exist. To reach such a standpoint my ordinary time-sense must disappear and with it my ordinary sense of myself. For this reason we can understand how many writers, such as Kierkegaard, Eckhart, Swedenborg, and others belonging to far earlier periods, have divided men *according to their understanding of time* or have spoken about the necessity of overcoming the illusion of time in order to understand our lives aright.

.   .   .   .

Let us think again for a moment how we ordinarily understand time. We certainly do not understand time as a higher dimension of space. We associate time with movement, as the turning of the hands of the clock, or the apparent rising or setting of the sun; or we think of it as change in appearance, as the changing seasons, or the growth and decay of the body; or as something that splits life into past, present, and future.

Following the evidence of our senses we believe that the present exists, but that the past and the future are non-existent and incapable of existing. *Where could they exist?* In what room or space?

One of the peculiarities of our senses is that they work in this single moment of time called *now* (which is not any real *now* to our ordinary experience) in which you read these lines. The time in which I wrote them seems to you to have vanished into nothingness. What is this nothingness?

In this single moment of time called the present, in which you read this sentence, the visible world appears before you. You cannot *see* the existence of anything a moment ago or a moment hence, and because you cannot see it you do not believe in its possibility.

Therefore you confine the sense of your existence to this single moment of time and to this you limit your notion of the existing. You believe that you exist now and only now; and if you think that the souls of the dead remain alive, you believe that they exist in this now and only in this now, in this moment of time in which you find yourself existing, and you believe that they travel along with you in the *passing-time* that is our common experience.

Since it rarely occurs to any of us that the nature of our senses makes what we call the present moment and the world as we know it, we suppose that the only possible present moment is *our* present moment. We reason from this basis. To imagine that *our* present moment is only *one point* in an infinitely larger present seems absurd.

The term existence implies a 'standing-forth'. What stands forth to sense we call the existing. The term, however, implies that not everything stands forth, and we know quite well that the senses show us only a part of the totality of things.

As regards time they only show us the world standing forth in the present moment. We cannot see into Time itself. We cannot *see* into this fourth dimension. The world in other parts of Time – if we begin to think in this strange way – is beyond the reach of our senses.

What, then, is the nature of the reality that we believe in evidentially? Transiency is the main reality. We appear to live in an ever-perishing world. It seems that our life is confined to a single instant at a time. We see everything passing away – *for ever*, as we say, without having the slightest idea of what we mean by this expression. Where does everything go – for ever? Where do our lives go? Certainly they are not contained in a space of three dimensions.

We witness, apparently, events, people, and things disappearing into total extinction, into an absolute nothingness, as the result of passing-time. This is the reality of appearances as registered by our senses. There goes with it a particular understanding of life. For all this seeming loss of everything, and the fear of losing, the apparent uselessness of so much that we undertake and cannot finish, the confused sense of missed opportunities, the feeling of hurrying life and the thought of the impossibility of going back and altering anything, combine to create one distinct picture of existence and one way of understanding it. This is the 'sensual' picture, and with it are related certain feelings of *I*, a certain sense of things, a certain interpretation of everything, and way of taking everything.

.   .   .   .

The *idea* to which we are giving our attention is that Time is a truly existing direction – a containing dimension of the WORLD. We think of our world as a *ball* in space. It is so in a space of three dimensions, and in that fragment of time called this instant – this present moment.

But it cannot be so in a space of four dimensions.

Thinking of Time as a real but invisible direction, in which all things have extension, there must be another aspect of everything we see, contained in this direction.

From this standpoint the world does not only exist in the known space of the present moment but in the dimension of Time itself. There is a *Time-World*, or World in Time – that is, in a space of more dimensions than our senses record. We touch this higher space at a point – the present moment. But outside this momentary point, at which a visible world is so brilliantly obvious to sense, there seems, for our natural understanding, to be nothingness, nowhereness – no other space or place, or any sort of room for existence.

Into this pin-point of the present, events are entering. From which direction are they coming? Following this line of thought, they are coming from the direction of Time itself – which is moving through us, or we through it, and so producing the illusion of *passing-time*. So, in order to think of *Time itself* we have to

93

think of the direction in which events lie, the direction in which the events of yesterday and tomorrow are extended. We have to think of the world not only stretched out in space, but *stretched out in the dimension of Time* – in another, a higher space.

Everything, then, that we see in the world now is part of something in the Time-World. Everything is also a 'world-line' in higher space. No thing is merely the three-dimensional object in the present moment that it appears to be for our sensual understanding. Our lives are extended events in this higher space. Our perceptible existence is one aspect of our existence, a fraction of it, and our usual sense of ourselves only one particular instance of possible forms of this sense.

It is evident that the fitting of higher space over lower space reverses our way of thought. It relates us to another way of thinking. From its standpoint, the momentum of visible phenomena does not create new phenomena. New phenomena result from the entry of the fourth dimension into the three-dimensional world of our experience, of higher space into lower. We can think from the natural sense-given point of view, or from an entirely different point of view based on the existence of higher dimensions. One point of view will answer some things, the other, other things. One will relate us to life in one way – which is essential – and the other will relate us to life in another way – in an *additional way* that gives us standpoints that we could not derive from empirical experience. If we accept higher dimensions we will understand that truth cannot be one and the same thing in all states of consciousness. Something of that relative reality mentioned in the description of Erigena's system will be felt.

.   .   .   .

Let us try to conceive further how time can be a dimension. Let us suppose that we are travelling along this dimension as along a road. We travel from yesterday into today and from today into tomorrow along a distance which appears to us not to exist. We are separated from yesterday by this distance, which is a time-distance. Now we realise that distance in space does not mean non-existence. London is distant from Paris by a space-interval of so many miles. Along this distance land, sea, towns and people are extended, and if we travelled along this distance we would see them. Although we cannot see them now we believe that they exist. We believe that the known dimensions contain their existence. But we have not this belief of distance in time. We believe that this distance is synonymous with annihilation, non-existence. We cannot travel along this distance as we please. Today I am in my room and yesterday I was in the same room. But an interval of time separates me from yesterday. I am in the same room – in a different part of Time. I cannot again be in the same part of Time, and to my natural thought that part of Time called yesterday has not only disappeared but has vanished into some dustbin – into nothingness. If I reflect upon yesterday, upon that part of Time to which I now stand in a new relationship, and of which I think *was*, I will reflect upon it as if it were no longer existing, perhaps with relief and in any case with the certain feeling that my life is no longer there but only here – in today. All that was said and done yesterday I will no longer take seriously save in so far as my interests may be affected today, because I will give no quality of *is* to yesterday. Yet to all that exists in the space of three dimensions, however distant from me, I will be quite willing to grant the quality of *is*, because I know that my body can be translated in space to any part of the world. My mind can go back in time, yet if it does so I call it memory, to which I give the quality of *was*. The existence of the past and the restoration of the past do not seem possible. In consequence all my thoughts about the past are coloured by the unreality of *was*, by a certain impatience or by a certain sentimentality.

Now if I were suddenly translated into yesterday with exactly the same thoughts, feeling, and memory which belong to it, I would have no idea that anything unusual had happened. I would be in another part of Time, at an-other world-point, with all the experiences belonging to it. I would be living my life at that part of Time – the same life – 'again', as we say. Perhaps we have no right to say again, once we realise the existence of the fourth dimension.

If we could see into Time – if we could see into this invisible distance – we would see other parts of Time and all that was happening in those parts of Time. The prophets of old were granted this power of vision. They saw *Time*. They saw the WORLD in Time. They saw events lying far ahead. They had two 'sights' – not only that sight which perceives a three-dimensional world but another which perceived the fourth dimension. For if Time is a dimension that we touch only at a point, it gives a higher space *in which all world-points exist.* It means that just as things separated by a spatial interval still exist, so also do events or states of the world and oneself, which are separated by a time-interval or by distance in time. Applied to oneself it means that the life exists in Time.

.   .   .   .

In Ecclesiastes which, as regards the early chapters, is a book about time, the writer sees all that happens coming out of the dimension of Time. He says: 'to all things, Time; and to every event under the sun, season' (ch. 3, v. 1). Season brings war and peace, birth and death, finding and losing. He must mean that the quality of time is different from day to day. Events lie in Time and as we reach them they determine the issue of things like magnetic fields. According to the event and season so will things tend to fall out. Now we do not see life from this standpoint; we think man creates events. It means that there are tendencies in things that vary from time to time, and that therefore something in the nature of a law of synchronicity is probable, i.e. similar things tend to happen together. Nothing can happen unless the event is present. Ecclesiastes draws a picture of man as under the domination of time and for him time is not a nothingness, a void, but a *structure of events of opposite character*, through which man is passing. In the first three chapters he speaks of time, of the recurrence of things, and in an obscure passage refers to 'eternity in man's heart'.

But we can find clearer indications of Time being regarded as a dimension. In early Hebrew thought the extension of the world in Time was certainly recognised. The world was not confined to a space of three dimensions in the passing-moment. The American scholar Tayler Lewis, who lived in the last century, was never tired of pointing out that we completely misunderstand many passages in scripture because we have lost sight of the ancient conceptions of time. 'According to the Hebrew conception the future world does not come to us and acquire reality by being present but we are going into it.... The future has as real an existence as that through which we have passed. In the prophetic vision events *are there* even now.... Events which require the journey of ages before one can reach them are, to the Seer, long since passed and gone.' Undoubtedly the time ideas found in the scriptures are quite different from our natural conceptions.

Some illustrative phrases and expressions in the literature of scripture are as follows: in the New Testament we find it said that God created the *ages*. This is a very strange thought. Do we grasp what it means? An age is a period of time. This, at least, is one of the meanings of the Greek word (aeon). We probably imagine that if God created the worlds he created globes in space at a particular moment of time, long ago.

In the Esdras apocalypse the phrase occurs: praeparatum est futurum tempus – 'future time is prepared'. In another passage from the same source the creation of the world *in all parts of Time* is indicated: 'For there was a time in the eternal ages when I prepared for those who now exist.' In the Slavonic Enoch it is said that all humanity – all people who exist one after the other in succession in time according to our way of seeing things – are already created. ('Every soul was created eternally before the foundation of the world.') The souls are sown into the *Time-world* from beginning to end, for it was held that to the divine mind all is, at once – together, not successive. From this angle of vision, we catch sight of the strange view that the world is developing, or otherwise, *in all its Time-length*, from 'beginning' to 'end'. It is regarded as existing at every point. That would mean that history is alive – always living and changing. It would mean that an age is a living thing.

Blake saw the world in this way – building or destroying itself at all points of time, in six-thousand year extensions. The WORLD, he said, is not a globe. The 'ratio of our senses' makes it appear so. The Universe is not a number of points separated by immense distances.

Enoch sees in his vision 'everything from beginning to end'. He sees also where time (as we experience it) 'is no longer'. Here the 'times perish', and there is 'no year, month, or day, nor hour, nor shall they be reckoned'. All those emotions which belong to passing-time, and perhaps are solely due to the illusion of present-momented existence, vanish. We are told that there is no anxiety, sorrow, or violence.

It is extremely difficult to grasp this extraordinary *idea* about time. We cannot imagine existence in another part of Time – in *all parts* of Time. It does not seem possible to believe that what lies *for us* hundreds of years in the past may lie for some other beings hundreds of years in their future.

Such a view means that our *was*, is, and *will* be are relative. There is no absolute past or future. 'To God there is no time. All things are to him one consentaneous whole' (*Meykanda*, thirteenth century). All is present. We are living in this vast *present*, at one

98

point of it. We are not really living in the world of three dimensions, but in a part of *living* history. In one of the Upanishads the throne of Brahma is depicted as being surrounded by 'the days, months, seasons, years, and ages, and the indestructible wheel of time which governs all creatures'.

Sebastian Franck (sixteenth century) says that the true creation of all human beings is *timeless*. Since God is timeless – outside time – he creates all things timelessly. 'He surveys our whole life as present.' This writer says that we cannot understand the timeless order with our natural reason but refers to another principle in us standing above the reason, which he calls anti-human. It is anti-human in the sense that it goes clean against our ordinary understanding, and can comprehend the timeless order. We can connect this with *a higher level of consciousness.*

All these views point in the same direction, to another existence of things in higher space. Higher space is timeless. Our ordinary consciousness touches a minute portion of total reality in higher space, like a revolving mirror that reflects only one part of the surrounding landscape and sets it into apparent motion. The ratio of our senses sets Time into movement, and it becomes passing-time. Higher space becomes time. Such is the view that confronts us.

.   .   .   .

If we could halt at one moment of time everything would remain exactly the same. Nothing would move.

Such moments are not unknown in conscious experience. Even our ordinary consciousness of time is not always of the same order. There is an ancient description of the halting of time in which the present moment is expanded and felt as eternally existing.

'Now I, Joseph, was walking, and I walked not. And I looked up in the air and saw the air in amazement. And I looked up unto the pole of the heaven and saw it standing still, and the fowls of the heaven without motion. And I looked upon the earth and saw a dish set, and workmen lying by it, and their hands were in the dish; and they that were chewing chewed not, and they that were lifting the food lifted it not, and they that put it to their mouth put it not thereto, but the faces of all of them were looking upward. And behold there were sheep being driven, and they went not forward but stood still; and the shepherd lifted his hand to smite them with his staff, and his hand remained up. And I looked upon the stream of the river and saw the mouths of the kids upon the water and they drank not. And of a sudden all things moved onward in their course' (*The Apocryphal New Testament*, p. 46, Protoevangelion. Trans. by M. R. James. Oxford University Press, 1926).

This is duration without time. One of our human moments does not lead into the next moment. Consciousness does not step across from one moment to the next, but halts in one fragment of enduring Time.

Our human moment is a particular *measure of Time*. It might be different. All the history of the world might be *one moment* to some being. To God, scripture says, a thousand years are as one day. All that we see in passing succession might, to another being, be duration in which quite a different kind of change is going on from that which we see. We cannot see what the extension of every thing in Time is doing. A life, an age, may be changing, not in the sequence of present moments – I do not mean change of that kind – but as a whole.

Eckhart says that 'if someone had the knowledge and the power to gather up the time and all the happenings of the last six thousand years and all that is to come ere the world ends, all this summed up into *one present now* would be the fullness of time'.

All the history of one century might be a moment or a day for another kind of consciousness.

100

Think what this means. We have to get entirely away from the idea of time as something connected with the clock. We inherit a definite measure of time which makes us see things as we see them. We see the world in a certain way, due to our minimum of time. 'If there were beings whose measure of time and perception did not coincide with our own but were shorter or longer, it would follow that the world would be wholly otherwise presented to them than it is to us. This question has been examined by E. von Baer who has shown that the phenomenal world would undergo a powerful transformation were our measure of time and perception altered' (Du Prel).

If it were altered in one direction we would begin to see the world-lines of Minkowski, i.e. another form of the world would appear. 'We mark off a space of time according to the number of changes of Nature comprised in it. Their number for us, however, depends upon our subjective celerity of apprehension, that is to say, upon our congenital scale of time' (Du Prel, *Philosophy of Mysticism*). If our congenital scale of time were different the form of the world would necessarily change. If a thousand years became as one day to us, the surface of the earth might seem in continual wave-like motion which, with our ordinary celerity of time, would be the experience of earthquakes divided by long intervals.

Ouspensky emphasises again and again in his writings on higher dimensions (see particularly Chap. X, *A New Model of the Universe*) that we do not see a simple uniform world. In some cases we see the *time-lengths* of objects. He says that our present moment includes the time-lengths (life-times) of electrons, for which reason we see *solid* matter. The minute particles that constitute matter reach our consciousness 'only through their time-dimensions, the fourth, the fifth and the sixth; in other words, they reach it only by virtue of their motion and the repetition of their motion'. We see the *lives* of electrons, continually repeated. An electron is not in our three-dimensional world.

101

Du Prel says that if the process of nature were quickened, with a corresponding change in our measure of time, we should be unaware of the fact and would be unable to believe that our lives were either longer or shorter than they are now. But the quickness of nature and our congenital measure of time must really be one and the same thing. I mean that it is our measure of time that makes nature appear as she does to us. What she is to herself is another matter. Processes that take centuries, in our experience, may be merely moments in her life.

.   .   .   .

Plato spoke of the *reversal* of time. The reversibility of the temporal order has often been considered. One mathe-matician has suggested that the movement from past to present, as we know it, has some connection with the quantity of the past in relation to the quantity of the future. If the value of these quantities were different we might know an entirely different movement of time (Weyl).

What would this signify? It is interesting to consider what it would mean. Plato connected the *Golden Age* with the backward movement of passing-time. If time went backward our entire lives would be different and the meaning of events. For example, no one could kill another person. What for us is the carnage of war would be the raising of the dead. We would live in a world in which physical violence would be impossible. Bullets would spring out of the bodies of the dead and travel accurately into the barrels of distant rifles. Another science would explain it as action at a distance – some kind of magnetic effect – whereas it would be a world-line traversed in a new way.

Men would be born out of earth, fire, and water – the drowned, the burned, the buried. The sea would give up its dead. Quite another *causality* would exist. Everything would be related

102

in a new temporal order of cause and effect. All the material of our lives as we know them, with all the chains of cause and effect that we connect with them and invent, would be transformed into an entirely new story.

It would be like that vision seen by Ezekiel of the valley of bones: 'There was a noise, and behold, a shaking, and the bones came together, bone to his bone and sinews and flesh came upon them ... and they lived and stood upon their feet.' Suppose a man died in the desert and passes into dust. Reverse time, and what must inevitably happen? Every particle of him must come together, even though his dust had been spread over the entire world. Pour a glass of water on the carpet: there is no process whereby it can be recovered. Reverse passing-time and every particle of water will arise from the floor and enter the glass. Nothing could be lost.

If we understand that Time is, we will realise that nothing can be lost.

It is this thought of the existence of Time itself, of its reality, of the fact that there is no time, that can begin to change the feeling of oneself in relationship to one's life.

As long as we believe that only the present moment of our life is actual and all else non-existent or lost 'for ever', we are bound to have one particular kind of feeling of oneself. We can have no sense of the indestructible and *living life*.

.   .   .   .

Let us look at a form of analogy that has been used by many writers in descriptions of higher dimensions. Conceive a two-dimensional world, a world limited to a surface. For such a world, our world of three dimensions would be higher space. Let us suppose this imaginary two-dimensional world to have a very small extension in the third dimension. A sheet of paper can represent

103

it. A sheet of paper has length and breadth and, relatively, very little thickness, so that its extension in the third dimension is very small.

If a pencil is pushed vertically through the sheet, only a very thin slice or *cross-section* will actually lie in the thickness of the paper.

Imagine beings living in the sheet of paper, cognisant of nothing else but their paper world and what lies in it. They would know only the *cross-section* of the pencil, for this would be all the pencil that would lie in their world. All else would be invisible. They would not know anything about the rest of the pencil, because we are assuming that their relationship to the third dimension is limited only to the thickness of the paper.

In a somewhat similar way we can think of our relationship to the fourth dimension as one that is limited to the 'thickness' of the *fourth* dimension we experience naturally – that is, to what for us human beings is the measure of time called 'present-moment'. The thickness of the paper is the measure of the third dimension for the paper-being; and only what lies within it – all cross-sections of any three-dimensional objects penetrating their world – can form part of their present-momented visible world.

The rest would be invisible, non-existent; not in their world, though in our world; *not in their present moment, though certainly in our present moment.*

So the pencil itself, as an integrated whole, would exist in the invisible world for them. But they could never conceive it – as pencil. Only a cross-section (which has no resemblance to an actual pencil) could exist in their visible world, and *all the rest of it would be in their past or future.*

If the pencil is slowly passing through their paper-world successive cross-sections of it appear to them. What has already appeared will pass out of their world, be no longer visible and seem to them to be in the past – in the already-experienced. The part of the pencil that has not yet passed into their visible world will be in their *future* – in the not-yet experienced.

To us, with our higher dimensional vision, all the parts of the pencil co-exist simultaneously – *its beginning and its end* – and it exists as a whole, a unity, having a form and function absolutely inconceivable to paper-beings.

Suppose we could descend into their paper-world and assume the conditions of their existence, learn their two-dimensional views and habits of thought, and explain to them that their world is only a limited expression of an infinitely larger and *different* world. What would they say?

With their 'natural' minds they would never believe that the cross-section of the pencil was part of a much greater and more interesting reality – a pencil. It would seem merely great nonsense. They would not believe in the reality of our world, in comparison to which the reality of their world would be relative.

Now the reader will see that *our world would be outside their time and space*, yet everything visible in their world would originate from another world invisible to them – namely our world.

At every point their views (based on their senses and on their visible world) would collide with our more-dimensional knowledge, and since the feeling of being right is at the bottom of most violence, we would probably find ourselves in danger if we tried to alter their point of view, which would be right for them but only relatively right for us. Their 'truth' would not be commensurable with our 'truth'.

If we are justified in making this analogy, then for us, living in a three-dimensional world, our perception of things may be nothing but a relatively real one. The present moment may only show us something comparable to a cross-section, or what I would prefer to call a certain *minimum*, of a vastly greater containing world, extended in dimensions hidden to our senses and *existing* in these directions which are unknown and inaccessible to us.

For if we touch the fourth dimension – limiting our-selves only to this dimension of higher space – in some such way as the paper-beings touch the third dimension, we must widen our conception of the 'world', and feel that we do not really know our world. The senses show us a section or a minimum. But can we not suppose that mind potentially opens on what is beyond this minimum?

The paper-beings could only grasp the nature of our world by mind – above the mind of sense. What we see, directly and without effort, would be for them a matter of difficult mental grasping, not through logical reason but by means of *ideas* which they *did not naturally possess*. Actually our sense would be their mind: we would see what they would have to *understand*. Idea for them would be fact for us. From this point of view, it is quite possible to think that what illuminates us suddenly as *idea* is a perception of an order of life above us – an order of higher facts.

Now if the pencil passed right out of the paper-world, it would no longer exist to the paper-beings. They would speak of it as having passed into non-existence. They would say: 'it *was*, once upon a time.' It would be in their yesterday; to which, of course, they would not give any real quality of existence, just as we do not. But we would say still: 'the pencil *is*' for we would see it in another place, in what would be higher space for them.

One point of the analogy is to show us what relative reality means. All that was real in their world of paper would be the higher realities of our world passing through it, immensely distorted. With their convincing visible environment, they would regard such a view as highly improbable. A cross-section of the pencil in their world would appear to subsist convincingly out of itself and to be explicable in terms of itself – to be quite real as it appeared. If they sought to get to the root of the matter, they would study its minuter component parts or atoms and then they would feel they had exhausted the 'reality' of the object.

They would never seek a further explanation in an extension of that dimension (which for them would be passing time and present moment) out of which all movement, objects and events swarm into the range of their two-dimensional life. If the sharpened point of the pencil first entered their world and passed in, they would see a circle of lead slowly surrounding itself with a wooden coat. It would look like growth, arising from the point of lead. Growth in our world may be similar.

If we tried to convey another kind of knowledge to them, it could probably only be done by means of allegories, parables, or symbols.

.   .   .   .

I said earlier that all function in man is four-dimensional. Any intelligible process has aim or purpose, cause and effect contained in it, but the three can only constitute one whole in four dimensions. Any process such as breathing, digestion, etc., is in time as well as in space. Breathing is a cycle of inspiring and expiring, no part of which can be left out, otherwise it would be useless. The process, then, exists as a whole, if we think of it as four-dimensional and can only be understood as wholes, as complete cycles, that with a certain end in view proceed by a linkage of cause and effect in time-order. Process itself cannot be seen by the microscope, save in cross-section. It has often been said that man is composed of levers not of wheels. Seen three-dimensionally in the present moment of time he is composed of levers. His bones are levers operated by muscles and there is no sign of any visible wheel in him. But four-dimensionally is he not *full of wheels* and is not his life itself full of returning cycles?

The modern 'functional' point of view, whether in physiology, biology, or psychology, is unconsciously four-dimensional – just as physics is avowedly so. The 'world' the latter regards is not the three-dimensional world in which the separation between objects is evident, but another world *where relations can exist that are not seen in our sensory world.*

For the addition of a dimension necessarily gives entirely new relations. What appears to be separated and unrelated in a space of fewer dimensions may be connected or related in a space of higher dimensions. For example, we know that the sides of a right-angle triangle are not related directly but that the *squares* on these sides have a relationship. Or consider a crude analogy: the prongs of a fork entering the two-dimensional world of paper-beings would seem to them entirely unrelated and separate – as four points. They would see them, in their space, as having no connection with one another.

We see people in our space as separate. But man is not in space but in humanity. But we see this 'humanity' abstractly or sentimentally, not understanding that it may have continuity in higher dimensions, and exist as a whole, of which each of us is a cross-section or certain minimum.

All this means that according to the number of dimensions 'reality' must alter. Discrepant views such as the wave-theory of light and the corpuscular theory have their origin in this. (See *A New Model of the Universe*, chap. X.) The language of continuous waves and the language of separate light quanta are entirely different, yet each is applicable in certain cases.

.   .   .   .

It would be impossible to explain to paper-beings the relationship between stationary objects in our world. Our world entering their world would give rise to the phenomena of *movement* to them. Stationary objects in our world lying at different angles to one another would appear to them to be moving – that is, their cross-sections would appear to be moving.

An example of this is given by Fechner ('Vier Paradoxa' von

Dr. Mises, 1846, in the volume *Kleine Schriften* – 'Der Raum hat vier Dimensionen.' Gustav T. Fechner, 1801-1887), in a paper on the fourth dimension (not published under his own name) in which he imagines a vertical red beam of light falling on a sheet of paper, and a yellow beam falling sideways at an angle on to the same spot, so that the two beams coalesce on the surface of the paper. The result is an orange spot.

Imagine the sheet of paper to be moved vertically upwards a little way. The yellow and red components of the orange spot begin to separate.

The position of the red spot caused by the vertical beam remains unchanged, but the yellow spot begins to move away from it.

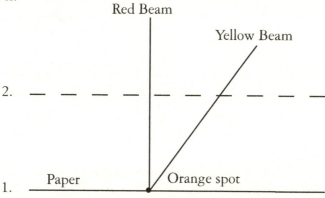

At the second position of the paper (in the diagram) the two beams of coloured light are separated. Move the paper downwards and the yellow spot moves towards the red on the surface of the paper. Move it upwards and the yellow spot moves further away from the red spot on the surface of the paper. Now imagine how this would appear to the paper-beings whose world is limited to the sheet of paper. At first they would see an orange zone which would gradually separate into a red zone and a yellow zone, and it would appear to them that the yellow area moved away *under its*

own force. We would see that the phenomena of movement in the paper-world were caused *by the entrance of the third dimension into their two-dimensional world,* and that through the curtailment in their third-dimensional perception the illusion of objects moving resulted.

If the red and yellow beams made a very small angle – if they are nearly parallel – the movement of the yellow spot away from the red spot would be very slow as the paper moved vertically upwards. If the yellow beam made almost a right angle with the red beam, the yellow spot would move across the surface of the paper with great velocity – *almost instantaneously.*

Regarded in this way, 'velocity is a dimension'. This thought occurred to Descartes, who was inclined to the view that the length, breadth, and height of bodies do not exhaust their dimensional attributes. Weight and velocity might be also dimensions in themselves.

So Fechner points out that velocity, as we experience it in our world, may be due to *the obliqueness of insertion of the four-dimensional into the three-dimensional.* He says: 'It all depends on the obliqueness of the yellow beam and the movement of the paper. The more obliquely the yellow beam is directed to the paper, the farther the yellow spot will remove itself from the red one by a given progression of the paper, the quicker therefore will its own movement appear. Naturally when something appears to move in our three dimensions, this only occurs because the beam that it projects into the space of the four is directed obliquely to the three dimensions, and therefore, by the progression of the plane of the three, these are always cut at different places. The more obliquely, the quicker the movement appears to be. If the movement is curvilinear, this only results from a curved aspect of the beam. This now leads to new food for reflection. First of all we see that the mathematician has no longer any reason to complain of the increase of work, because he is spared the whole science of mechanics. Everything stands as it stands, and he need no longer calculate the original movement of the world; it continues on its course. To calculate the aspects of space, he only requires to take his variable T as the fourth co-ordinate of space. On the other hand, the naturalist gains many new aspects of nature. Just to mention one briefly. If we see a planet revolving in a circle, this only results from the planet extending spirally or corkscrew fashion into the space of the four. As now the plane of the three, in which the planet finds itself at every moment, traverses this spiral beam in the same way as formerly the plane of the two, it appears as if the planet revolved in it. It is therefore evident that the universe must be considered as *a growth of spiral filaments*, and the whole science of astronomy as a microscopic part of botany. But the most important of all are the deductions for practical life. Only now will man recognise clearly that he gains nothing with his reduction of everything to ashes and his running about – in reality he does not move from the spot.'

Fechner conceived the invisible aspect of the world only in terms of a fourth dimension added to the three of space. But he saw in this fantasy that with the addition of another dimension our whole way of looking at things must entirely change.

.   .   .   .

Ouspensky observes that if the phenomenon of velocity is connected with the angle of insertion of the higher dimensional into our three-dimensional world, then we must know of some limiting velocity in our world, because angles themselves are limited. 'The sensation of a velocity may be the sensation of the penetration into consciousness of one of the dimensions of higher space unknown to us.... Velocity can be regarded as an angle ... an angle has naturally a limit in one direction and in another' (Ouspensky, *A New Model of the Universe*, p. 437). It is in this way

111

the limiting velocity of light, round which the theory of relativity is built, can be explained. Ouspensky approaches the question of velocity and angle from a standpoint that is different from Fechner's, and I must refer the reader to the entire chapter (chap. X) from which the above is taken. In connection with the view that we experience the properties of higher dimensions as phenomena of movement in our three-dimensional space, he remarks that animals may not live in the same world as we do. The third dimension may be for them in the nature of a higher dimension. When we walk past a house we see an apparent movement of it, but correct it with our reason. He thinks that animals may see this apparent movement as real so that 'a house turns about when a horse goes past it, a tree jumps into the road'. Animals would then attribute a mysterious power of movement to inanimate life, and thus live in a different world from our world owing to this lack of a clear apprehension of the third dimension in their consciousness. Ouspensky believes that we stand in exactly the same position in relation to the dimension of Time as animals stand to the third dimension of space.

CHAPTER FIVE

THE LIFE IN LIVING-TIME

WITH THE ADDITION of the fourth dimension the great Time-World emerges, living, where we thought it dead and gone.

Our lives are extended through a minute portion of it. In this world in Time nothing can perish. Passing-time makes things seem to perish, to pass away.

We think of the world as a ball in space. We imagine, if we believe that the world was created, that it was made as a round mass. When we read that the *ages* were created we do not grasp what is meant.

Creation in Time was meant. Imagine a *day* already created. Try to imagine a week as created and fashioned from beginning to end. The natural mind cannot do it. It can form no image of an already created day, still less can it do so of an already created age. It is necessary to get rid of the sense of passing-time and think of Time itself.

If we do this then the expression from the Apocalypse of Peter, 'Nothing perishes before God', becomes partly understandable. For everything stands in its place in Time and, though today replaces yesterday, yesterday is always today for itself. Our passage through the dimension of Time gives us the experience of succession. More than this, it gives us the impression of annihilation. We believe the past is annihilated. We believe yesterday cannot be anywhere. Where could there be room for it? How could there be room for yesterday today?

I think it scarcely possible to describe how deeply our experience of passing-time affects thought and feeling. It would be foolish to attempt to do so because we are psychologically built round the natural belief in passing-time. It might be better to say 'annihilating time'. So we seem to live the most fragile of existences, in an ever-dying sad environment; and our life seems only what we have at *this* moment or hope to get tomorrow.

We have no other conception of the *life*. It seems to be nothing but the body at this instant, the scene before us.

Yet the effects of the past on the present have been studied in the light of the *unconscious persistence* of early impressions. And the possibility of the effect of the future on the present has been inferred mathematically – taking the world as four-dimensional – for example, by the Austrian mathematician H. Weyl, who concludes that the future may overlap the past so that, in principle, 'it is possible to experience events now that would in part be an effect of my future resolves and actions' (H. Weyl, *Space, Time, Matter*, p. 275, Methuen, 1922).

The interconnection of the world as a whole in higher dimensions suggests such a possibility. Higher space sig-nifies possibilities, connections, inter-relations undreamt of in the narrower space and time familiar to us. The definition of God as 'beginning and end' has introduced us to this view; and we can recall here the definition in the New Testament which connects the idea of God with *all possibilities*. 'With God all things are possible.' In both of these definitions I believe the idea of higher space appears – that is, of another connection of all things.

Since the life is extended in *Time* itself, the effect of the *present* upon the *past* has also to be considered as a possibility. The effects of what we do now, from this standpoint, are to be thought of as spreading in two definitely existing 'directions' not apprehended by our sensuous contact with the 'world'. We call these directions 'past' and 'future'. From this point of view our past life, our present life, and our future life are always in *functional* relationship. There are three elements, or three influences, at work. The past is no dead thing nor the future a blank. The consequences of acts lying ahead of us and the consequences of acts lying in the past mingle with the consequences of acts lying in the present, and the determining point is *now*. Only, as we shall see, we do not know or possess this *now*, i.e. we have no determining point.

It is certainly strange to think that the past may be changing through the action of the present and future. But such thoughts belong only to the four-dimensional conception of man, through which all the *life* is made alive. Man is a living *world-line*. Let us conceive mankind as a network of these living lines in higher space. Let us suppose that the senses cut through all these lines at a point called 'present', showing us a cross-section, that is, a picture of *three*-dimensional bodies, a mass of perceptible people, in one moment of passing-time called 'present'. These living lines in four-dimensional space are, then, to be thought of as living 'organisms' of which every part influences every other part. This four-dimensional organism is not the perceptible body, but the invisible body containing the visible body. By sense, we are only related to the visible body itself, that is, as given perceptually through sight and touch and hearing.

Viewed thus, the *life*, rightly conceived, is not merely a local phenomenon in passing-time, confined to the point we call the present, and isolated in the visible three-dimensional world. As direct experience, it is so – but it is more. It is more because we are not regarding three-dimensional space as the *sole container* of things. It is the sole container so far as empirical experience – that is, the experience of our senses reveals the 'world' to us. We are trying to force our thoughts beyond the limits of sense, beyond that aspect of the total world rendered by sense, towards the realm of *idea*.

.   .   .   .

We actually find such an exercise recommended in a passage from the ancient Hermetic literature, which belongs to the earliest centuries of our era. To reach another state, another level of understanding, we are told to 'expand ourselves to the magnitude

of all existence'. Only in this way, the writer says, can the life become permanently unified ('changed into eternal substance').

What is 'the magnitude of all existence'?

The sense of existence throughout all one's Time is meant
– the sense of this living 'organism' in higher space which contains the little living organism of the temporal body. *Think that
you are not yet begotten, think that you are in the womb, that you are
young, that you are old, that you are dead, that you are in the world
beyond the grave, grasp all that in your thought at once, all times and
places'* (*Hermetica*, edited and translated by Walter Scott, Oxford
University Press, 1924. Vol.1, p.221). The perception of this idea
– that the life is extended in time – is a step towards the unification of life, because all the *life*, strange and incredible, appears.
The writer adds that only in this way can we begin to apprehend
God, whereas if we shut the soul up in the bodily senses – i.e.
think *sensually* – we can have no conception of *God*. Is not the idea
of *God* here definitely connected with dimensions beyond those
perceptible to sense and so with higher reality in ourselves?

Now if we are to grasp that we live at all points of our life, no
longer can the distinction between yesterday, today, and tomorrow be made. But something must yield in us before we cease to
make this distinction. We come here against some very strong
point of denial.

From one side, this denial originates from our belief in the
evidence of things seen – from our materialism. To perceive, inwardly, that the life lies in higher space, as a living process veiled
from sense, means that we must be prepared to seize hold upon
an *idea*; and this idea opens the life out, admits the life, draws the
life together, causes the entire sense of the life to change.

The illusion of passing-time begins to be broken through.
The relative *nothingness* that we give to yesterday and tomorrow
begins to disappear.

Speaking from another angle, Eckhart says that if we 'hold

116

fast to the distinction between today and tomorrow and yesterday, we hold fast to nothingness'. In higher space there is no time
as we understand it – nothing of our past, present, or future;
nothing of our yesterday, today and tomorrow. With the sense
of Time itself, with the sense of the magnitude of all existence,
would we not cease counting time as we do, cease making the
particular distinction that we make between yesterday, today and
tomorrow? For we make barriers between them, and think of
escaping into tomorrow. But it is really all the same – one 'today'
– the life itself. But we cut the life down to a little point, which
determines our weal and woe. Tomorrow is still one's life – all the
life makes a Today – and we cannot escape from our life. All my
life *is*. Of all my life, I must say is. Let the reader note the feelings
that begin to arise with this summoning up of the life apart from
this present moment of existence and the distinction between yesterday and tomorrow.

.   .   .   .

In contrast to these feelings is our present-momented
psychology, which is governed by self-love and the belief in passing-time. I am relating these two factors from the standpoint that
the structure of our 'natural' psychology is interlocked, one factor
depending upon another factor. Any alteration in this structure,
any change in the quality of consciousness, depends partly upon
a change in the *time-factor*. A change in the time-factor will mean
change in other directions as well. The Hermetic exercise is obviously designed to change the 'present-momented' psychology,
through a change in the time-factor and a consequent expansion
of consciousness – throughout *all the life*. It hints that 'self-deve-
lopment' is partly develop-ment into Time. So we can understand
that our *apparent* relationship to time gives us a wrong feeling of
self. Self-love is a wrong feeling of self: and to begin to alter it the
living life must first be felt.

117

This definite psychological effect of adding a dimension to the *sense of oneself* cannot be set aside. I say merely that the self-love is connected with our ordinary sense of time and the Hermetic exercise is designed to give us a sense of living Time. But the self-love requires a sharper environ-ment and a more constant pressure for its transformation than our own thoughts. It particularly concentrates itself in the sense of present-momented existence and the visible life of appearances, and in the related feelings of *I*.

       ·   ·   ·   ·

We seem merely bodies existing in the present moment. We connect with these bodies the customary feelings of *I*. As such, we respond to moment and event, having little or no background. The Hermetic exercise is to produce background, through making the *invisible* side of things real. It is only through our conceptions of the invisible that we can change our present-momented psychology. As it is, everything that happens to us at the moment influences us. And to every alteration in our present-momented psychology we give the feeling of *I*. So we have a *momentary* psychology, against which the Hermetic exercise is surely directed.

I maintain that this momentary psychology, into which the self-love enters so powerfully, rests partly, if not fundamentally, on the distinction between *was*, *is*, and *will be* – that is, on the belief in passing-time which makes only the instant seem to be the site of the life. The result is a point of reaction that is overstressed and shifting, and one that gives no starting-point for unity or integration – one, in fact, that could not possibly do so.

       ·   ·   ·   ·

It has been repeatedly taught in the past that man is in *division*, in a state of inner confusion. He is not one, but many. True philosophy has been defined as 'that which knows how to join him together', i.e. the integration of man was held to be possible. Integration means the binding together of parts into a whole and so to become whole or complete. It means to become unified, to become one; and for this unification *ideas* that are foreign to our disintegrated psychology are necessary.

Let us turn to some descriptions of man's multiple nature, bearing in mind that we make the greatest mistake if we suppose that we possess any 'oneness' or unity naturally.

Our ordinary state has been described by Synesius (fourth century) in these words: '... Man is not some simple object nor is he cast in one pattern, but God has made to dwell in the constitution of a single creature a host of forces mingled together and with full-toned voices. We are, I think, a monstrous animal more extraordinary than the Hydra and still more many-headed. For not with the same part of our nature, of course, do we think and desire or feel pain and suffer anger, nor is our fear from the same source as our pleasure. Again you will observe how there is a male element in these organs and a female, and that there is courage and also cowardice. There are, in sooth, all kinds of opposites within us and a certain medial force of nature runs through them which we call Mind' (Augustine Fitzgerald, *Synesius: On Kingship*, vol. I, p. 118. *The Essays and Hymns of Synesius of Cyrene*. Translated into English with Introduction and Notes by Augustine Fitzgerald. Oxford University Press, 1930.)

This multiple nature of man is described thus by Plutarch: '... each one of us is made up of ten thousand different and successive states, a scrap heap of units, a mob of individuals.' (See *Concerning the E at Delphi* in A.O. Prickard's Selected Essays of Plutarch. Oxford University Press, 1918.) Having no unity, Plutarch remarks, we never really *are*. Nor can we feel *now*. '*Now* is squeezed into the future, or into the past, as though we should try to see a point which of necessity passes away to right or left.'

It is well described in a recent article: 'A person is an assembly. This assembly consists of many dramatis personae who have come from different directions, animated by different inclinations and tending to different ends. Some-times one of them gets up, gives a discourse or accomplishes an act, then reseats himself and remains silent, motionless, while another in his turn speaks and acts. At other times several of these personages get up together, support each other in their discourses and combine activities. But often too, those who get up are not in agreement one with the other, they dispute fiercely, quarrel, and anathematize each other. Occasionally the assembly grows very tumultuous, all the members rise together and fight frenziedly. That is a person, and such is each one of us.'

Since we are an assembly, inner development and the reaching of unity cannot be taken separately. The one necessarily implies the other. 'Unless he attains inner unity man can have no "I", can have no will. The concept of "will" in relation to a man who has not attained inner unity is entirely artificial. The whole of life is composed of small things which we continually obey and serve. Our "I" continually changes as in a kaleidoscope. Every external event which strikes us, every suddenly aroused emotion, becomes caliph for an hour, begins to build and govern, and is, in its turn, as unexpectedly deposed and replaced by something else. And the inner consciousness, without attempting to disperse the illusory designs created by the shaking of the kaleidoscope and without understanding that in reality the power that decides and acts is not itself, endorses everything and says about these moments of life in which different external forces are at work, *"This is* I, *this is* I".' (Ouspensky, *A New Model of the Universe*.)

.   .   .   .

There have been many systems of thought, religious and otherwise, with corresponding methods, whose object was exactly to bring about unity of being. The systems differ, but the object is the same. All these systems are means to an end, not ends in themselves. They belong to different periods and different conditions of culture. To compare them with one another in order to prove by their discrepancies that they cannot have any truth is beside the point. In all these systems there is always much that is very difficult to understand, much that the natural mind cannot understand. This is necessarily so, for a system that does not stand beyond the natural reason that is based on the sensory world cannot open 'levels of reality' beyond that one on which we ordinarily dwell. A scientific 'religion', based on the logic of natural science and our *known* reality, is a contradiction in terms; for if we take *religion* as meaning 'binding-together again', it means that its true significance, long ago lost sight of, is the attainment of unity; and *unity connotes higher reality*.

The usual state of man is put in a somewhat different way in the following passage from the Hermetic literature: 'The real is that which consists of itself alone, and continues to be such as it is in itself; but man is composed of many different things and does not continue to be such as he is in himself, but shifts and changes from one form to another. Oftentimes men fail to recognise their children after a short interval, and children their parents. When a thing so changes that it is not known, how can it be real? Is it not an illusion inasmuch as its changes manifest themselves in varying appearances? You must understand that whatever is, and that alone, is real. But man is not a thing that ever is and therefore man is not real, but is only an appearance. We ought to call man appearances.... We ought to call a child the appearance of a child, a youth the appearance of a youth, an adult man the appearance of an adult man, etc.' (*Hermetica*, vol. I, p.387.)

We believe that there is something more, but what more is there *in a practical sense*? If we are capable of honesty with ourselves, we are very little more than creatures of the moment. But we think we are not. We imagine that we are merely resting, merely abiding our time. We believe that what is I in us never changes and that we could always be different if we wished. And just as we imagine that we act consciously and could behave differently if we wished, so we believe that we have one I, a unity, a permanent reality, that presides over all that we do. If we read that we are an assembly, or a monstrous animal more extraordinary than the hydra, and still more many-headed, we do not really believe it. To *know* that this is so is to begin to have a knowledge that does not belong to the natural sense-governed mind. Even to begin to know this is already to begin to have a changed feeling of oneself – a moment of arrest in the current of our illusions, a doubt – '*Who am I?*'

It is in *this direction that the possibilities of changing lie*. Ouspensky emphasises this psychological principle. For behind all *becoming* lies that which we cannot reach, cannot concentrate upon, just because we cannot turn the feeling of *I* toward it but are dragged back into the *I* of the moment, into the stream of passing-time.

It was mentioned previously that sometimes we feel the unreality of all that we do or see or say or think. And then it is really the illusory feeling of *I* deserts us. But since any other feeling of *I* is strange, we only feel fear, as if we were being dissolved away. We begin to move, say something, clear our throats, in order to get back to the familiar feeling of oneself.

So we can understand how distasteful at first we find ideas that threaten to dissolve this 'reality'. Indeed, all the natural mind fights against them.

Yet if we desire change it is necessary to escape from the power of these 'I's of the passing moment that mutually exclude one another and act as transient 'caliphs'. There must be another stimulus. All that belongs to passing-time will not help. But an idea about time can help. An idea about a thing puts us into a definite position in regard to it. It is in this that the power of an idea first lies. If we could feel the *idea* of Time itself, of all our life lying in Time, the momentary I of passing-time would not have the same hold over us. The idea gives us a certain power, even a certain freedom. This is where its value lies. Instead of saying 'This is I', we shall begin to realise this is not I.

What reason had the Hermetic writer to tell us to expand ourselves to the 'magnitude of all existence'? This power of vast combination was recommended as an *exercise* that leads towards the transmutation of a man into 'eternal substance'. When Eckhart tells us to 'escape from time', is he not saying the same thing? But no natural ideas, formed from what we actually see, will help us to do this.

Our senses imprison us in the present moment and make passing-time. The visible world, the senses, the *I* of the moment, all these unite to produce one effect, a pin-point of reality that we take as *all*. We are told to expand this pin-point into the magnitude of all existence. By being *all* the man himself is *none* of them. To know and to recognise all that is in one's life, to begin to know and remember all sides of oneself, to feel *all the life*, that is to begin to change and cease to be always only one of these little 'I's of the moment. And if we think of 'eternal' as meaning wholeness or unity, then we can understand that as long as we are only these little 'I's and as long as our consciousness enters entirely into them, there can be no possibility of any real being, no wholeness.

So against becoming and changing in passing-time we must first put the idea of the life extended in Time. This is the first *idea* that challenges our present-momented psychology. We have already noticed the connection between this idea and the unification of the life. The unification of the life depends on another understanding of time. Put in another way, our ordinary feeling of *I* does not enable us to reach unity. But we have already con-

123

nected a different understanding of time with a different level of consciousness. Unification of the life, the attainment of a new level of consciousness, a different understanding of time, and a new feeling of *I*, are thus all related. We shall see later that they are all included in the ancient idea of 'eternal life'.

.   .   .   .

What am I? I am my life. *All my life is my Time.* The present moment of my life is in the all-ness of my life, a point in the magnitude of my existence. And this all-ness is my only *Time*. 'Life in itself is *time* for man. For man there is and cannot be any other time outside the time of his life. *Man is his life.* His life is his time.' And that is *life* for him. There is no tomorrow for a man beyond the time of his life. 'Man dies because his time ends. There can be no tomorrow after death' – but only one's life. (Ouspensky, *A New Model of the Universe*, p. 476.)

Remember that the *life* itself is indestructible. Passing-time brings us to the end of the life beyond which there is nothing for us. It is an end, just as in the world of three-dimensional objects the end of a table is its termination in known space. There is no table beyond. The hand passing over the table no longer touches it, so that for the hand the table ceases to exist, but not for the eye. In the same way the life seems to be destroyed, to end. It does end. But four-dimensionally it is still there and is indestructible, just as the world is indestructible.

People imagine the world might be destroyed by the release of atomic forces. That is impossible. It may come to an end *in passing-time*, but that only means that its time-length, or *life*, does not extend beyond that point.

The real destruction of the world would be its destruction in higher dimensions from beginning to end, at all points of its time-length, and the force necessary for such destruction is not found in physical energies. No explosion or electronic bombardment could effect this. Its life could not be destroyed any more than a man's *life* in Time can be destroyed by shooting him *now*. We cannot shoot *into Time*. No bullet can shoot the *life*. And no act of self-destruction can destroy the *life*.

.   .   .   .

No one can change himself beyond his life, hereafter, beyond his Time, but only *within his life*. His attainment of unity is something that must belong to his life, this life, that is *himself*; and if we can equate unity and 'eternal life', it is something that cannot lie in some 'tomorrow' or 'hereafter' *beyond* a man's life. Its possibilities belong to us now, to something we have to do now. *It is this life that must be worked upon, be made more real*, by separating the false, by insight.

Now the idea of unity is not to be taken negatively. Although it is often connected with the process of getting free from certain things in oneself it is also anciently as often connected with the idea of growth, through which the different sides of man are brought into balance. Plato describes this harmony in terms of *justice*, i.e. a just balance, an adjusting. In the New Testament the same word is rendered *righteous*. Plato says, '... But in reality justice was such as we were describing, being concerned not with the outer man but the inward which is the true concernment of man: for the just man does not permit the several elements to interfere with one another, or any of them to do the work of others – he sets in order his own inner life and is his own master and his own law, and at peace with himself; and when he has bound together the three principles within him – which may be compared to the higher, lower and middle notes of the scale, and the intervening intervals, when he has bound them together and is no longer many, but has become one entirely temperate and perfectly adjusted nature – then he proceeds to act, if he has to act, whether in a matter of property or the treatment of the body, or in some affair of politics or private business – always thinking and calling that which preserves and co-operates with the harmonious condition, just and good action, and the knowledge that presides over it, wisdom; and that which at any time impairs this condition, he will call unjust action and the opinion which presides over it, ignorance' (*Republic*, IV, p. 443).

A real change in the internal state is meant, not an external modification of conduct 'to be seen of men'.

All we do now can be made of infinitely more consequence through *additional* interpretation. If rightly understood, the extension of the life in higher dimensions, with all the new thoughts and feelings that it can arouse if its truth is perceived, can make us think far more distinctly about our present situation and in a way that makes every thing and person more real. For we can then understand that it is about our lives that we have to think, about all that enters and lies in our lives – about which we are always trying to think, but wrongly, owing to the illusion of passing-time and the sense of the life being only in the present.

.   -   .   .

Let us approach some illustrations of experiencing of the life extended in Time that have been put on record. They are not remarkable at first sight, partly because inner experiences cannot be easily described. Yet, if we really begin to think about their meaning they are remarkable. They serve to show that *all the life* can be undoubtedly felt. It is quite wrong – and far too easy – to think of them merely as curious, abnormal or pathological. While the unification of the life as one whole or the sense of the eternal existence of *I* is not illustrated by them, the experience of the living existence of all the length, all the *Time*, of the life is shown.

In an essay on time and space Tayler Lewis says that we have

126

all heard of well-attested cases in which the entire past, even to its most minute events, have flashed upon the soul in the dying moments or during some brief period of imminent danger 'arousing the spirit to a preternatural energy: if there be truth in such experiences, then no former exercise or motion of the soul is ever lost'.

He points out that since such experiences undoubtedly happen it means that all the moments of our lives can be regarded as *present*. 'They belong to us still just as much as our present thought or our present sensation, and at some period may start up again, causing us actually to realise that conception of Boethius which now appears only as a scholastic subtlety – *a whole life ever in one*, carrying with it a consciousness of its whole abiding presence in every moment of its existence' (Tayler Lewis, *Article on Time and Space*). But I do not think that the feeling of the life as one integrated *whole* could ever be connected with an experience of the extension of *all* the life in Time, because it would necessarily be of a different order – a summing-up of parts.

The life is certainly experienced under special conditions as stretched out in consciousness throughout its entire length. All the incidents can be re-experienced, re-lived, in an actual sense, difficult to describe, but not merely as memory. But the feeling of the unity of the life, gathered into one simultaneous whole, cannot be the same thing. For the experience of oneness (which is associated with the feeling of eternity) is not merely an expansion of conscious-ness through the time-dimension of the life, in which the reality of *all the life* is unquestionably felt, but another kind of consciousness, similar rather to that described by Tennyson.

It is possible to understand that whatever is experienced in separate parts in succession may be summed up (at another level of reality) into a whole or simultaneous form. The experience of this whole and simultaneous form will not be commensurable with the running experience of separate parts. If our conscious-

127

ness expands along Time we will see and know our life in some sort of series – as we knew it – but not as gathered together into a new synthesis.

Our ordinary memory makes us think that the past has no living existence. It is memory. But in the following experiences there is no way of understanding them save by admitting that the past has a reality that we do not suspect, some substantial living existence. The past is lived, entered – not exactly *again*, for it is always there. Something transcending 'memory' is experienced. All is – nothing is lost. What was long ago forgotten appears. The childhood is, and all the faces that belong to it; the early books are, the fragments of poetry, the stories, the early scenes, the houses, gardens, the days themselves.

In one example it is said (this and most of the following examples will be found in Forbes Winslow's *Obscure Diseases of the Mind*, 1860): the scenes of his early life were in their minutest particulars revived. He was taken to the cottage in which he was born, interchanged tokens of affection with his parents, gambolled once more with the companions of his childhood on the village green. 'He renewed acquaintance with the friends of his schooldays, the remembrance of faces known when a child was restored. Every trifling and minute circumstance connec-ted with his past life was presented to him.' All this happened in the few moments, during the struggle with death from asphyxiation. Now the language of memory is used in such descriptions, but they are not cases of memory as we know it. It is not recollection, remembrance, or reminiscence. It is actually being *present* in the past. It is the experience of the *presence* of the past. We have no language for this.

Another example: 'Under the pressure of great feeling, the soul lives with a rapidity and intensity which disturb all its usual relation to time; ... it once happened to me to assist at the recovery of a man who nearly forfeited his life while bathing. He had sunk the last time, and there was difficulty in getting him to land and still greater difficulty in restoring him.... He said that the time had seemed to him of very great duration; he had lost the standard of the work of time. He had lived his whole past over again; he had not epitomised it; he had repeated it, as it seemed to him, in detail and with the greatest deliberation. He had great difficulty in understanding that he had only been in the water a few minutes. During these intenser moments of existence the life of the soul has no sort of relation to what we call time.' Certainly not to what we call time, but to Time itself.

We cannot call this memory, nor can we understand it unless we think of ourselves as at least four-dimensional beings. Memory epitomises. It makes a summary or abstract of the past and shows it as the past always, as something that *was*. In the above case the life is *restored*, as present.

All ordinary relationship to time was obliterated, all present-momented psychology. His soul, no longer conscious at that moment of world-time in which the visible, three-dimensional outer scene appears to the senses, ceased to share with others the common-point of material existence called by us the present.

Where did it go? What direction did it find in which to travel? It did not pass into nonentity, nothingness, nor into some tomorrow or hereafter. It passed into the dimension of its own life which the man only knew until then as intermittent, past-coloured memory. It passed into the *life itself*, into the man's Time, not forward into *time beyond*.

One writer says: 'The hints of scripture point to memory as the chief energy of the soul under the new conditions of its existence (that is, at death). The words of Abraham to the rich man in Hades were: "Son, remember." He was to survey the whole extent of that life in which he had received his good things and had cared for little or nothing else. And these words at least fall in with some of the known facts of consciousness in this life. To

129

many, it is said, notably to those who have been in the peril of sudden death by drowning, and have, as it were, tasted its experiences – there comes, as in a moment of Time, the unrolling of the scroll of their whole past lives. Their memory acts with a new intensity and with an almost inconceivable rapidity. It becomes (to borrow a phrase from the *Dream of Gerontius*) the "standard of its own chronology". Even under the conditions of a calmer death we note something of the same kind. The mind goes back to the remote past of its life, and the scenes of childhood and the old familiar faces come back with a long vanished distinctness. It is almost inconceivable that such a retrospect should not affect the soul in which there is a capacity for growth' (E. H. Plumtre, D.D., *The Spirits in Prison*, 1885, p. 40. Wm. Isbister).

Certainly such 'memory' could not but change our lives. But it is not memory. It is higher space apprehended. If such consciousness of the life entered into every moment of our existence *nothing could remain the same*. And this is precisely the exercise the Hermetic writer advises.

.   .   .   .

It is just because we do not have this kind of 'memory', just because our memory is very limited and largely invented, that we again and again act in the same way and are again and again in those recurring momentary I's of which Ouspensky speaks. The power of life is so strong, the hypnotism of the present moment so intense, the outer scene, pouring in upon us through the senses, so vivid, that we *cannot remember*. And which of us ever thinks that he is not merely this visible body in the present moment of time, but something else, in higher dimensions?

'I once asked Dr. Holmes (Oliver Wendell Holmes), toward the end of his life, the question, "What is a man?" He answered without hesitation, "A series of states of consciousness." The word "series" introduces the element of time, the relation of which to

130

states of consciousness is empirical and not essential. Broadly speaking, certain states of consciousness associated directly or indirectly with matter occur in sequence in everyday human experience, but the same states may occur simultaneously under exceptional circumstances. It is well known that in the sudden presence of imminent and apparently certain death, the accumulated states of consciousness [of a lifetime] sometimes revive simultaneously in a single flash. The events of the whole past are seen down to the most minute and remote details, like a landscape under a flash of lightning. Dr. Holmes himself had had this experience on one occasion, just before losing consciousness altogether while drowning, and the memory of the occurrence persisted after resuscitation'. (William Sturgis Bigelow, *Buddhism and Immortality*, 1908. Houghton, Mifflin & Co. The Ingersoll Lecture.)

Another example: 'From the moment that all exertion had ceased a calm feeling of the most perfect tranquillity superseded the previous tumultuous sensations.... Though the senses were deadened, not so the mind; its activity seemed to be invigorated in a ratio which defied description, for thought rose after thought with a rapidity of succession that is not only indescribable, but probably inconceivable, by anyone who has not been in a similar situation. The event which had just occurred [falling into the sea], the effect it would have on a most affectionate father, and a thousand other circumstances, minutely associated with home, were the first series of reflections that occurred. Then they took a wider range – our last cruise – a former voyage – my school – and even all my boyish pursuits and adventures. Thus travelling backwards, every past incident of my life seemed to glance across my recollection in retrograde succession, not, however, in mere outline, but the picture filled up with every minute and collateral feature; in short, the whole period of my existence seemed to be placed before me in a kind of panoramic review; indeed, many trifling events which had been long forgotten then crowded

131

into my imagination, and with the character of recent familiarity. The length of time that was occupied by this deluge of ideas, or rather the shortness of time into which they were condensed, I cannot now state with precision, yet certainly two minutes could not have elapsed from the moment of suffocation to that of my being hauled up.'

.   .   .   .

In connection with this restoration of the past, the power of smell to revive former scenes must not be forgotten. 'For odours have an extraordinary and inexplicable power of spontaneously and suddenly presenting a forgotten scene to the mind, and with such nearness to reality that we are translated bodily, being caught up by the spirit, as it were, like St. Philip, to be placed once more in the midst of the old past life, where we live the moment over again with the full chord of its emotions vibrating in ourselves and startling our consciences. There are, it is true, certain sounds which wield the same miraculous power over our being ... but I do not think they operate in this way so frequently as do smells' (D. McKenzie, M.D., *Aromatics*, p. 49. Heinemann). Baudelaire, in one of his poems, referred to the grain of incense 'which restores the past'. The use of incense may have been originally connected with this power of odours to bring the *living* past into consciousness.

.   .   .   .

We know that all living tissue is constantly undergoing changes. There is a continual assimilation and elimination, a constant interchange between cell, blood, and lymph. The material substance of the brain-cells is always being built up anew by this interchange. Let us face the question: Do we really imagine that the past is 'coiled up' in the *matter* of these three-dimensional brain-cells that are undergoing such constant changes? The trouble is that we never face such questions; we do not want to face them. Even if we were satisfied that the ordinary memory could be explained solely on a physiological basis, how could we understand *the restoration of the entire life* as shown in the above examples? The *psyche* must be more-dimensioned than the physiological *brain*. The brain can be regarded as reflecting at any one moment a small part of the psyche: and if the brain is injured the reflection will necessarily be distorted. *But we cannot limit the psyche to three-dimensional space.* The psychic life is in 'higher space' and its point of communication with the visible world at a given moment is through the brain. We cannot explain the psychic life of man merely by the study of the three-dimensional brain. *Thought* is not in apprehended space. We cannot explain the restoration of the past in terms of the brain alone. This *inner memory* in which there is such wealth of detail must have another explanation.

.   .   .   .

A division of memory into two kinds has been described by Swedenborg. He divides memory into *exterior* and *interior.* The former he connects with what he calls the *outer* man, the latter with *inner* man. 'Nothing,' he says, 'perishes, though things are obliterated to the exterior memory ... such is the interior memory that the very least details of what a man has thought, said or done from earliest infancy to old age are inscribed upon it. All his aims, which were in obscurity for him, and all that he has thought, said or done through them, are in that book which is his interior memory.' He observes that the *book of life*, mentioned in the scriptures, which is opened at death, is just this interior memory.

If we connect this interior memory with the extension of our lives in higher dimensions, we can understand that the book of life is the book of *the* life. It is the life itself, lying in Time itself as a long living 'organism', inserted at one point of itself through brain and body into the present moment of passing-time.

Ecclesiastes speaks of man at his death going to his 'long home'. ('Because man goeth to his long home and the mourners go about the streets', ch. XII, v. 5.) Tayler Lewis says that the Hebrew *beth-olam* might be translated as 'house of the life'. It certainly does not mean the grave. The body goes to the grave. The man enters his life, this long organism – his long home, his indestructible *Time*.

As I said, every part of this long organism must act and react on every other part because 'beginning and end' are coexistent. Whatever we do now must affect what we call past and future. We cannot understand how the past can be altered unless we comprehend our existences through the power of this *idea* about Time itself.

CHAPTER SIX

AEON

THE HERMETIC WRITER who advises the practice of thinking that we are living at all points of the life remarks that in this way a man begins to be changed into *'eternal substance'*. What is behind this statement? Why is the notion of 'eternity' – whatever that means – connected with thinking this all of the life?

We need to get rid of some false meanings that we give to the words *eternal* and *eternity*.

.   .   .   .

The psychological idea connected with *eternal life* cannot be limited to the view that man is changed into another state at death, merely by the act of dying. It would be far more correct to say that it refers, first of all, to some change that man is capable of undergoing now, in this life, and one that is connected with the attainment of *unity*.

The modern term psychology means literally the *science of the soul*. But in former times there actually existed a science of the soul based upon the idea that man is in an imperfect state but capable of reaching a further state. Man can 'perfect himself', to use the psychological language of the New Testament. He can reach another state of himself, not by ordinary education, however efficient, but by a special kind of education – one not given by life and not to be found in the ordinary paths of life. This second education was the original task of philosophy in its ancient and practical meaning. It had reference to the unfinished, uncompleted state of everyone in life, wherein we find ourselves in disharmony, onesided, and full of contradictions. '... man is no more a unity; the inward unity or harmony of his existence is disintegrated into a diversity of autonomous functions. No totality-act is possible;

135

the will is separate from knowledge, the feeling from intellect.... Empirical psychology has to do with this disintegrated man, never with the integral' (Emil Brunner, *The Word and the World*, 1931). (This modern writer observes that the re-integration of man into a unity requires ideas and efforts that lie outside the field which psychology ordinarily concerns itself with. I would express this by saying that the unity of man is impossible on the *level* of consciousness which he uses.)

Our natural state is, internally, one of confusion, even insanity. We do not notice this distinctly. Now while this internal condition of man, at the ordinary level of consciousness, has been clearly realised from earliest times, what particularly characterises the early standpoint of practical 'philosophy' was the view that there was a perfectly definite further state of a seed or a chrysalis. Man could not merely become 'better' – a better social being or a person more adapted to life – but he could become something quite different. We find this central idea running through all *esoteric* teaching, whether in the New Testament or elsewhere.

Man can perfect himself, become complete, become a *whole being*; and as we shall see later 'eternal' had this significance. 'To lay hold of eternal life' referred to some possibility in this life, to some change that a man could undergo here – or at least begin to put himself in the way of. From this deeper standpoint, no true psychology of man can exist without this goal being recognised as the aim; and all the various psychological findings about man, however contradictory, can only gain their proper relation and proportion when drawn together under this supreme head.

The end of man is the attainment of this further state of himself. *His real explanation lies in this fact.* He is only to be understood through this end. All the different parts of him, like the separate parts of a machine, are not understandable or relatable, unless the final aim and meaning of the whole is grasped. Otherwise one investigator takes hold of one part, another another part, and in each case gives the significance of the whole to the part, so that only contradiction and, what is much worse, a mal-interpretation of man, result.

This powerful idea about man's possible goal, concealed in his nature, dominated early religious and philosophical thought. A real, attainable goal was meant. The righteous man of the New Testament is not simply a kind, good man any more than is Plato's *just* man. Such terms, which are synonymous (the original word being the same in each case) refer to one who has attained *unity*, to one who actually possesses what other people imagine they already possess, to one who dwells in another relation to what I call psychological space – on another level – to a person who is internally *not like us* and not *where we are*. They refer to one who has generated himself, raised his entire nature and discovered his real existence; and in a unique sense become an individual, so much so that we, constantly doing and saying and feeling entirely useless and meaningless things, probably seem mad to him.

So definite a state was meant that it was called a new birth – 'from above'. Whatever this means we can at least say that this new birth denotes another *kind* of man – an attainment which remains an impossibility unless we come in contact with ideas *above* those that belong to our ordinary education. For how can a man become anything greater unless he has not only the firm belief in something greater, but *ideas* that come from something greater?

.   .   .   .

In the Greek the word that we know in translation as *eternal* is *aionios*. Literally, the expression in the New Testament translated as eternal life is *aeonian* life. The Greek word aion – aeon – is translated usually by *eternity*. Many writers have (in vain) pointed out that these translations do not render the original meaning of the words. They are words that cannot be easily translated because they refer to conceptions that we no longer understand. Such difficulties, indeed, have been encountered in translating aion and aionios in the New Testament that we sometimes find them rendered by such different words as 'world', 'age', 'never', 'forever', 'everlasting', etc., i.e. the significance given suggests either a thing, a visible form of existence, such as *world*; or endless passing-time, as in the translation 'for ever and ever'.

We already know that behind the changing world in time, behind the life of becoming, older thought put an 'unchanging' world, an invisible reality beyond the process of time. It is with this higher order of reality behind time that we must connect the word aeon (eternity). Aeon does not refer to the three-dimensional world in passing-time. It refers to an order of existence belonging to what we are calling *higher space*. Aeon is not time, nor is it *Time itself* but some overshadowing Totality that comprehends All in itself.

.   .   .   .

In the New Testament God is said to have created the aeons (translated *ages*). He is called 'King of the Aeons'. If we think of this word as meaning ages it has a time-significance, only a strange one — one that begins to turn our minds towards more than a three-dimensional world. The *ages* were created. Let us first look at one interpretation of aeon in a time-sense. We can understand that to dwellers in a plane-world like a sheet of paper, anything belonging to our world passing through their world will take a *certain time* to do so. A pencil will take a certain time; and this time will be determined by the whole form of the pencil itself, which will, of course, be invisible and unknown to the paper-beings but known to us, as higher dimensional beings. We might approximately think of the pencil itself (existing in what is higher space for them) as the aeon (to them) of that cross-sectional and defective form which manifests itself in their two-dimensional world. This illustration gives us a hint of one possible meaning of aeon, i.e. that which determines the form and extent of any existence in time: or the higher dimensional reality behind its expression in a world of more limited dimensions. The illustration is only approximate and ultimately inadequate. But it suggests a way of thinking how every object, visible in momentary passing-time, has its own higher 'aeonian' reality. According to many ancient passages, *it is this aeonian reality that is first created*, in the scale of creation (e.g. *God* created the Aeons); and any creature in time and space derives its origin from its *aeon* – but falls under the limiting conditions of time. It then undergoes a cycle of changes that constitutes its growth and decay. And following only what its senses depict, it derives from this sensory surrounding *another kind of life*, one in passing-time, which seems confined to each moment only. In this successively single-momented life into which it falls there is no sense of the life as aeon. It feels its existence only in a time-sense. Now every creature's life, in a physical sense, has a certain length of appearance in time.

I will quote from an article by De Quincey about the meaning of *aeon*. De Quincey is writing about the reference to *eternal* (aeonian) *punishment* in the New Testament, insisting upon the 'false interpretation given to the Greek word *aion*, and given necessarily therefore to the adjective *aionios* as its immediate derivative'. Aeonian does not mean *eternal* – that is, in our ordinary usage of the term. 'What is an aeon?' he asks. 'In the use and exhortation in the Apocalypse, it is evidently this, viz. the duration or cycle of existence which belongs to any object, not individually for itself, but universally in right of its genus.

Kant, for instance, in a little paper which I once translated, proposed and debated the question as to the age of our planet, the Earth. What did he mean? Was he to be understood as asking whether the Earth were half a million, two millions, or three millions of years old? Not at all.... What he wished to know was simply the exact stage in the whole course of her development which the Earth at present occupies. Is she still in her infancy, for example, or in the stage corresponding to middle age, or in the stage approaching superannuation? The idea of Kant presupposed a certain average duration as belonging to a planet of our particular system....

Man, again, has a certain *aeonian* life; possibly ranging somewhere about the period of seventy years assigned in the Psalms. This period would represent the *aeon* of the individual Tellurian (inhabitant of the earth) but the *aeon* of the Tellurian Race would probably amount to many millions of our earthly years.'

He goes on to say that nothing throughout universal nature can for a moment be conceived to have an accidental life period. Whether bird or tree or plant or man, each has its own *aeon*, the period of its life-cycle. He observes that the most thoughtless person must be satisfied, on reflection, that every life and mode of being must have hidden within itself the secret *why* of its duration, i.e. it is impossible to believe that any duration of anything is determined capriciously. 'The period or duration of every object would be essentially a variable quantity were it not mysteriously commensurate with that object.... Everything in this world, possibly without a solitary exception, has its own separate aeon' (from an article in *The Wider Hope*, Fisher Unwin, 1890). De Quincey's article was written in 1852. Compare with this one of the propositions of Proclus: 'Every intra-mundane soul has its proper life periods and cyclic re-instatements' (*Prop. 199 of Proclus*. E. R. Dodds, p.175 Oxford University Press, 1933).

De Quincey brings out only one significance of aeon. There is something that determines the length of life, and the stages of growth and decay, of everything in the visible world; and this is its aeon. A thing cannot be at any stage it wishes or extend its life indefinitely. The cycle of any life is determined by aeon. The illustration of the pencil passing through the two-dimensional world assists us to understand what is meant. Any cross-section of the

140

pencil manifest to the paper-beings is not an independent thing although to them it will appear to be so. It is a partial manifestation of a higher-dimensional form and one stage of that form; and its location in any point of time is not haphazard. As regards the life of the earth being something definite, there are many references in the apocryphal literature of the Old Testament – which at one time was valued by many more highly than the canonical – which refer to *stages* of its life. [In the Ezra Apocalypse: 'For the World-Age (saeculum; aeon, in the time sense) is divided into twelve parts: nine parts are past already, etc.... Therefore lay aside thy burdensome cares and hasten to remove from these times.' Also: 'I disposed the world which I created by definite periods of time.' The secret tradition of measured periods of time in which only certain things can happen is based on the idea that the aeon or totality of the life of the earth in manifesting itself serially in time, follows certain stages, as does the life of man. 'I showed to him the secrets of the times and declared to him the end of the seasons.' The same view is met with in the ancient idea of successive 'ages' of the earth – the golden, silver, bronze and iron ages. The same idea can be made to apply to civilisations. However civilisations start, they appear to pass through definite stages, like other organisms, and just as there are people who attain maturity early or late so does it perhaps happen with civilisations. In any case, the fact that there are similar stages in the life of civilisations cannot be overlooked. Paracelsus applied this idea to disease. A disease runs a certain course and passes through certain stages. He called every disease an organism – ('a man', an entity) – that is related to the body as a parasite to a plant, and which causes it to run a certain course and pass through certain stages. This is not the same explanation of disease as that given by the germ-theory.]

.   .   .   .

Aristotle defined *aeon* (of the universe) in these words: 'That which constitutes the enclosing limit of the whole universe, and embraces the infinite period and the infinity of all things is *Aeon*.' In a fragment attributed to Plato the definition runs: 'Aeon carries all. Long time knows how to change name, shape, disposition, and fortune', i.e. time means for us continual change, from one thing to another, from one state to another, but aeon is not time, (or Time itself) for it carries all simultaneously realised – as altogether. Paul speaks of the 'aeon of this cosmos', i.e. presumably that which lies behind the visible cosmos moving in time. In the Hermetic literature we find the statement that 'Aeon is the *soul* of the cosmos'.

I must remind the reader of the definitions already given of *God* – as 'beginning and end', and as 'all possibilities' ('with God all things are possible'). Let us now set aside the consideration of aeon in its time-sense. I regard the definition of 'beginning and end' as referring to Time itself – everything is extended in Time, in the fourth dimension of the WORLD; and the other definition as referring to *aeon* itself. *Aeon contains all things, all possibilities* – 'the infinite aspect of everything'. It is already evident enough that time and moment limit us to *one thing* at a time. So far as we experience time – which is one thing, then another, then a third, – it certainly does not contain all possibilities.

It is necessary to perceive that time, taken only as one dimension above space, is *a line*. Seen thus, our lives are lines. But if we imagine there are further dimensions, then they are lines through a higher-dimensional world – for we must now begin to approach the idea of a higher space of further dimensions beyond Time itself. What we know as 'time' is merely *one* track through this higher space, and different in every person, i.e. no individual's time-line, or track, is the same as another individual's. Everyone meets his own obstacles, his own experiences; everyone follows, or even forms, his own time-track, sometimes close beside another person's, sometimes widely divergent. *This track in higher space is the life.* It may be comparable to a zig-zag line drawn through known space, like a lightning flash. Actually, however, we are conceiving it as drawn through 'higher space'. Now we have to imagine that this higher space contains everything – all possibilities, all possible events, all possible experiences, the sum-total of reality known and unknown. It contains the infinite expression of all things. Consider one thought, one act of your own. Imagine this thought or act developed into the fullest ramification, like a tree – into every possible result and every conceivable form. This full development would be the infinite expression, the infinite form of this thought or act. But, of course, it cannot exist in time. For in time we only know one form, one expression, one result. Now imagine the world realised *in all its possibilities*. With this thought we will approach the conception of *aeon*. It takes us entirely away from any relation to time.

.   .   .   .

The equivalent to the Greek word *aeon* is in Hebrew *olam*. *Olam* has not a physical significance, although it is often translated merely as *world*. But much more than the physical universe is meant by the term. We have already met this word in the passage from Ecclesiastes where it is said that man goes to his 'long home' at death. He goes to the house of his *olam* (aeon).

If we try to grasp that the world in higher dimensions gives origin to the curtailed world in fewer dimensions, we can see that nothing can be *added* to the lower world that is not already in the higher world. (The paper-beings can add nothing to the pencil itself.) In this light we can comprehend some of the meaning of the following passages in which the term *olam* is used. 'For the Holy One hath weighed the world and with measure hath he measured the times, and by numbers he hath numbered the seasons, neither will he rest nor stir until the number be fulfilled' (*Esdras*). Here 'world' is *olam*. 'I know that whatsoever God doeth it shall be done for ever: nothing can be put to it nor anything taken away from it' (*Ecclesiastes*). 'For ever' in this passage is, literally, *olamic*. God creates on the olamic or aeonian plane, i.e. behind Aeon is God, and behind phenomenal reality is Aeon. 'God makes the Aeon, the Aeon makes the Kosmos, the Kosmos makes Time, and Time makes Coming-to-be. The essence of God is the Good, the essence of the Aeon is sameness, the essence of the Kosmos is order, the essence of Time is chance, and the essence of Coming-to-be is life. The workings of God are mind and soul, the workings of the Aeon are immortality and duration, the workings of the Kosmos are re-instatement in identity and re-instatement by substitution, the workings of Time are increase and decrease, and the workings of Coming-to-be are quality and quantity. The Aeon then is in God, the Kosmos is in the Aeon, Time is in the Kosmos, and Coming-to-be takes place in Time' (Walter Scott's Translation, *Hermetica*, vol. I, Libellus XII. Oxford University Press, 1924).

This is causation in terms of rank or scale; or, as it was called, order of excellence. Everything is contained in something greater and what is greater is *soul*, i.e. what gives origin and meaning to what is lesser. This something greater does not act from the horizontal line of past, present, future, but meets us 'vertically'. Where this vertical and horizontal line meet, in the point of *now*, stands man: and into this *now* of man (if it be realised) enter causes and effects from the line of time, from past and future; and influences from the vertical direction, from what ranks above the order of time. Seen in this way we need not only be products of the past. The 'cause' of our existence does not only lie in the generations of the past. Along the horizontal time-line are parents, grandparents, etc. – one source of causes. But along the vertical line is cause coming from another direction – from *aeon* – and entering every moment into the present: 'God, then, is the source of all things; the Aeon is the power of God; and the work of the Aeon is the Kosmos which never came into being, but is ever coming into being, by the action of the Aeon, and that which holds the universe together is the Aeon' (Hermetica).

.   .   .   .

'Let us lay down two classes of being, the seen and the unseen: the unseen, eternal *in their relations*; the seen, never the same but ever-changing' (*Phaedo*, 77, A). We know those changing relations that belong to the changing order of time. In ourselves we can know the kaleidoscope of changing *I*'s. We know nothing of another form of relations, another existence and arrangement which Plato here calls eternal (aeonian), quite different, for example, from the linked chain of apparent causes and effects in the phenomenal world. Cause and effect in time is one order of things but only one order. The aeonian order demands a form of thinking that is 'opposed' to the contemplation of the world by the senses, acknowledging nothing higher than the connected chain of things in the world of appearances' (Neander). Now understanding is certainly more than sense. 'All the primal forces from which come the things seen lie entirely out of the field of sense either as perceived or conceived under any of the forms of sense' (Tayler Lewis).

Plato means that the order and relations that are 'aeonian' by their very nature do not belong to time and sense but are governed by principles which are 'fixed, unchangeable, and necessary', not in the sense that they give a dead immovable order of existence but one of infinite harmony. All that belongs to time is a weak reflection of this perfect order of things. All belonging to time Plato calls a *moving image of eternity*. This moving image is that in which we live. In his allegory of creation, referring to the order of scale in the universe, Plato says that God 'thought to make a moving image of the fixed eternity (Aeon); and as he arranged the heavens, eternity itself always remaining in unity (i.e. without succession) he made an image of eternity to proceed by number (i.e. by succession) the same which we call time' (*Timaeus*, 37, D).

The reader will understand that all references to eternity as being fixed or unchangeable do not mean a static or frozen condition of things. On the contrary they mean a perfect expression of all things – a state in which all possibilities, interblending and interpenetrating, are in harmonious accord, a state of infinite richness and diversity and *fullness*, obeying unchanging principles which bring every part into relationship with the whole. If man could reach a state of harmony, he would have *being* corresponding to this eternal world. Aeon, as a thought of God realised to its full, is developed in every direction; and *time* is a moving image, a trace of aeon, limited to our imperfect understanding, one expression of this full form.

If we think of it in the language of dimensions, it means that time, as we know it, suffers from insufficiency. It has not the dimensional capacity to contain aeon (just as the paper-world cannot contain a pencil). Let us note in passing that this inability of time to embrace aeon was held to be the cause of a circular movement, i.e. time is curved and keeps coming back on itself. To this we will return, when speaking of *recurrence*.

.   .   .   .

The aeonian order is *full* form, unknown to us in time. Limited form is time; for it is like a single note of a composition in which we do not hear the remainder, but hear only another note (in succession in time) derived perhaps from another composition. The 'word' of God (*logos*) expressed in aeon is the full form, the full proportion and all possible ratios, the full *meaning* and relations of things; having infinite diversity within its form – for we must not think of form (idea) as fixed, as we think of three-dimensional form, but rather as musical form, ever-blending and transforming itself within its own proportions, combining variation within variation, without departing from its essential being – from what it is – and so remaining 'ever the same' – or 'ever in one'. And time, by contrast, is a fragment, a succession of bits, a patchwork. What comes next in time (for our experience) is not necessarily *variation within form*, for what comes next in time may be quite unrelated to what preceded it.

So contiguity in time is largely mere change, from one thing to another. Our consciousness is incapable of remaining stable enough (owing to its lack of unity) to apprehend *form*, i.e. the infinite working out of *one* thing, the expansion of one motive into all possible transformations. In this sense I understand how time is an imitation of eternity and how *logos in aeon*, as the infinite meaning of everything, cannot enter the natural level of consciousness. Even the greatest art can only make copies of the invisible centre of full meaning round which we are set. And we can understand how transformation of meaning – the seeing of new meanings within those meanings we already know – is not a process of logical thinking. For logical thinking deals rather with cross-sections of meaning and is capable of bringing into juxtaposition things that are entirely unrelated in their true meaning and quite incommensurable, but which look as if related – as a two-dimensional picture, drawn without any sense of depth or perspective brings things into apparent relationship which are really far apart and unrelated.

In this world of meaning, of *meaning within meaning*, everyone is a point of reception and stands in relationship to infinite meaning according to what meanings he has opened in himself. And in thinking of the universe as meaning within meaning, as something ultimately experienced in the soul, we must not blame the senses for giving us a wrong picture of things or for making us see as outside us that which is within us. It is not the senses that

147

are at fault, but our use of them. It is what is *behind* the senses, the perceiving mind, the understanding, that is at fault, for the senses cleansed see all as 'infinite and holy'.

.   .   .   .

Let us reflect for a moment on what are our ordinary natural notions of *eternity*. The terms eternal and eternity are bound up with our time-psychology. Since we understand, naturally, everything in terms of our time and space we cannot help imagining that eternity means *eternity of time* – a vast *quantity* of time, time going on and on (in a straight line) beyond calculation – 'for ever and ever'. And we probably think that eternal life means only something following on death, an infinite perpetuation of oneself in endless time. We bring the same kind of thinking, the same level of mind, to bear upon the notions of eternity as we do upon the things of space and time.

In older thought time and eternity were thought of as being incommensurable, inalienably dissevered. (Plato speaks of the incommensurability of dimensions.) They belong to totally different levels in that scale of reality that is truly Universe: actually, to different dimensions. All that has to do with eternity, eternal life, the soul or world in eternity, was put in contrast to everything belonging to time, temporal life, the flowing world as we know it, and our customary thoughts and emotional life in it, when untouched by the sense of intenser meaning.

Eternity was connected with the world of *being*; time with the world of becoming – where 'nothing ever really is' (*Timaeus*, 27). In time 'nothing ever is but all things are becoming' (*Theaetetus*, 152). We cannot hold on to any thing or person in time, because what it or he or she really *is*, is not there, *in time*. All things are changing in time, some slowly, as the contour of mountains, some more quickly, as our bodies, some very quickly, as a house on fire. Time is change – on all sorts of different scales;

and the phenomenal world is made up of this continual changing, at different rates, of everything, like an enormous clock full of wheels. Outside, there is this stream of becoming; and within, a stream of ever-changing thoughts and feelings, a succession of different *I*'s, of fragmentary bits of ourselves – an inner world of becoming in which nothing *is*, in which we possess nothing and do not possess ourselves.

We think of all this changing in time as *progress*; and not only do we have this extraordinary and absurd illusion, but we imagine that the stability that we all secretly crave can be sought for in all this machinery of change, in the turning wheels of this enormous clock. But we know that what is stable was always put beyond time. In man, it was said, there is something behind his 'time-psychology', some definite possibility of *being* called 'eternity' or eternal life. Ecclesiastes says that while all things are governed by time in the visible world and man is under the dominion of time, 'he hath set eternity in the heart of man' (ch. 3, v.11). Here the word is *olam*, merely rendered as 'world' in our usual versions, but signifying the *macrocosmos*, i.e. the apprehension of higher space is a possibility in man. It is only natural to the thought of that period that Ecclesiastes after speaking of that order of reality belonging to passing-time should refer to another order outside time. He says that the heart of man can comprehend higher reality – up to a point.

The real distinction, therefore, between time and eternity is *qualitative* and so must lie in the realm of psychological experience. Considered abstractly, no *quantity* of time can produce eternity, just as no matter how far we extend a line we cannot produce a square or a cube. Considered psychologically, no quantity of temporal experience can constitute a moment of eternal experience.

'Eternity cannot be defined by time or have any relation to it' (Spinoza). We must clearly get rid of all associative connections with time before we can begin to understand what is meant by eternity. Especially must we cancel the expression 'for ever and ever'. When glory is given to God 'for ever and ever', *aeonian* existence is meant, the imagination being lifted to another order of reality above time ('unto the aeon' or 'unto the aeon of aeons'). God is *pre-aeonian* in order of dignity (scale), an idea that we meet with long before the New Testament was written. We have also seen the order *God, Aeon, Time* in the Hermetic quotation. But because we have, particularly nowadays, no sense of scale, the language referring to eternity and the language referring to time are continually mixed together.

    .   .   .   .

Psychologically, then, eternity was connected with a possible state of man, a *full* state of being. Cosmologically, it referred to a perfect form of the world behind the perceptions of man.

Let us turn to some thoughts and definitions. 'Allsoever where the "was" is one thing, and the "shall be" is another, is begotten but never is. It marches with time by which it is measured in "becoming-to-be".' In contrast to this flux 'all that is eternal is *whole at once*' (Proclus). The distinction is clearly *qualitative*. Karl Barth observes: 'If I have a system it consists in this, that to the best of my ability I always keep in mind what Kierkegaard has called "the infinite qualitative distinction" between Time and Eternity, alike in its negative and positive meaning.' He remarks that man *loses himself in himself* by confusing time and eternity (and therefore eternity with time) i.e. he attempts what cannot be attempted owing to this confusion of thought (W.G. Hanson, *Karl Barth*, p. 14. 1931). Hanson points out that the lack of perception – due to the lack of recognition of scale in the universe – of the difference between time and eternity gives man a sense of being able to *achieve*, that is entirely false. He quotes the almost forgotten lines 'doing is a deadly thing, doing ends in death', etc. Today, for example, we have the idea that we can conquer nature.

Psychologically, this wholeness or completeness which is connected with the word eternity is compared to a state in which a man 'abides in one'. It was said (at the beginning of this chapter) that the idea of unity and the meaning of eternity are connected. The expressions *one, single, unity, wholeness,* are all related, in this sense. And in contrast to this idea of one, all that belongs to time was said to follow 'number', i.e. it did not abide in one but ran away into time, into succession, into 2, 3, 4, 5, etc.

The idea of wholeness, and its meaning in its relationship to eternity, is given in the beautiful description by Boethius. I give it here in full because it is so often marred by being quoted in part. Boethius, a Roman senator of the fifth century, was in prison, faced with death, it is said, when he wrote his *Consolations of Philosophy* in which the following passage occurs (the italics are mine): 'That God is eternal, is agreed by all who possess reason. What then is eternity? ... Eternity is the complete and simultaneous possession of endless life *in a single whole.* The meaning of this will be clearer if we compare the eternal with the temporal.

Everything that lives in time moves onward through the present from the past to the future; and no being that is situated in time can grasp all the extent of its life together. Such a being has not yet reached tomorrow; it has already lost yesterday; and even in your life today, you live only in one fleeting and transitory moment at a time. Thus that which is subject to the conditions of existence in time, even though it has never begun to be and never ceases to be (as Aristotle held that the universe is without beginning or end), yet is not on that account a thing that can be rightly deemed to be eternal. For though its life is endless, it does not grasp and embrace the whole extent of its life together; it does not yet possess the future, and it has ceased to possess the past. That which grasps and possesses together, in a single whole, all the contents of endless life – that from which nothing of the future is absent, and nothing of the past has fled away – that is rightly called eternal. *Such a being must hold itself in its own grasp, must be ever present to itself,* and must possess the endless course of fleeting time as a thing present to it.

There are some who, when they are told that Plato held that this universe has had no beginning in time, and will never have an end, suppose that it follows from this that the created universe is co-eternal with its Creator. But they are mistaken. It is one thing to traverse the course of an endless life (and this is the mode of existence that Plato ascribed to the universe); it is another thing to hold *the whole extent of endless life grasped together in one present*; and to do this is clearly a peculiar property of the mind of God. It must not be supposed that God's priority to things created is a matter of length of time; he is prior to them rather in virtue of the peculiar quality of his indivisible nature.

The unending movement of things temporal is an imitation of the unchanging presence of the life that moves not. The temporal world, since it cannot adequately reproduce the model, falls away from immobility into movement, and declines from an indivisible present to an endless extent of time future and time past. It is unable to hold all the contents of its life in its possession together; but by never coming to an end, it seems to make some attempt at rivalling that which it cannot fully realise in its own being. It binds itself to such a present as the fleeting moment supplies; and that present, since it is a sort of copy of the abiding present, bestows on all beings which possess it an appearance of existence. But since that momentary present could not abide, it hurried forward along the endless path of time; and so it came to pass that it made continuous by its movement a life the whole contents of which it had not power to grasp together by abiding.

If then we seek to call things by their right names, we

shall use the words of Plato, and say that God is *eternal*, but the universe is *everlasting*. Now inasmuch as the way in which the judgment apprehends its objects must always be determined by its own nature, and God lives ever in an eternal present, his knowledge transcends all movement of time, and abides in the indivisibility of his present; he grasps the past and the future in all their infinite extent, and with his indivisible cognition he contemplates all events as if they were even now taking place.'

The full fruition of the universe is 'now and ever' in eternity, and this is *aeon*. We have already found this thought in Averroes. I said in an earlier chapter that the aspect of the WORLD which is manifest to the physicist is merely one aspect. As presented to sense the world is a ceaseless process of change, in which matter assumes one form after another, searching, as it were, for a finality which is unreachable in time. But Averroes says that the realisation of all strivings and their full fruition 'is already attained'. This actualisation, invisible to sense and beyond time, is achieved 'now and ever' – *now* and *ever* being the same. *The fruition of all man's strivings is likewise 'already there'.* This full fruition of the universe and of all that it contains was called the *fullness of all things.*

There is a form of consciousness that opens on this fullness – a light of the mind (which, Averroes says, man is capable of receiving, as does Ecclesiastes). In the New Testament and elsewhere the *fullness of all things* was called the pleroma (that which fills up, full measure). This is constantly referred to by Paul. He exhorts his brethren to be strong to apprehend 'what is the breadth and length and depth and height' so that they may be filled with the *fullness* of God. In the Hermetic literature the good is defined as the *pleroma* of God. By contrast, evil is littleness, clinging to one thing. Is not this *time*? Paul also speaks of the pleroma of God as that wherein he fulfils all things in all. ('The fullness of him that filleth all in all.' *Ephesians*, ch. 1, v. 23.) We have the idea of insufficiency (hysterema) often mentioned in contrast to the fullness (pleroma) of things in gnostic literature. The material world in time is regarded as a world of *defect* — a world of frustration, as Paul termed it, *where nothing can ever be right*. The pleroma is apart from the material world, attainable only internally.

Our own insufficiency is that we live in a fraction of ourselves, in a narrow *I*, in a narrow vision, *in time*, in a belief that the material universe of the moment is *all*. The perfecting of oneself, the attainment of unity, is connected with grasping the idea of pleroma, with a full-filling which must mean, to begin with, an overcoming of our narrow temporal vision — so that now we can understand better why the Hermetist advises the exercise of thinking of the life *as living at all points*, as a movement towards 'eternal life'. But time — life — is only one track through the fullness of things.

.　　　.　　　.　　　.

Psychologically, our position is determined by our internal states. A state is a place, psychologically. When Boehme was asked where the soul went to at death, he replied that it had no need 'to go' anywhere. Heaven and Hell are in us, in this inner space, that is the true site of our mental and emotional existence. Is not this inner space just that wherewith we are in relation to 'aeon'? Are not all those exercises of faith, of transcending time, of getting beyond our natural reason, designed to admit new *meaning* and so more of the world of infinite possibilities? Let us remember how we are in the moment, how our momentary will always goes into what is partial. As I said, we cling to one thing and this is one meaning of *time*. We think of ourselves as separate, unconnected, and self-existent. We hold to one set of ideas. We see in one way. We live in minute particulars, details. To embrace more reality, *to grow into that which is already there*, necessitates the giving up of this form of the momentary will, to resign something belonging to every moment of existence.

154

Speaking of the resignation of the *momentary* will, Boehme observed that man, in his own will (self-will), can only possess a minute particular – 'but in the Resignation he gets into the Total – into the *universal*, into ALL; for ALL is.' This indefinable process, here called *resignation*, is always mentioned in the literature referring to the transmutation of man. A tremendous devaluation of the self-will of the ordinary I is demanded. The notion of *higher* space gives this.

This resignation is not an end in itself. Above all it is not a *moral* end. It is a means toward an end, through which a man 'comes into the ground wherein all lies in eternity, and from being poor he becomes rich'. All things are in eternity, apart from visible creation: and he that does not see that time and space are fixed for us by the nature of our organs cannot move from the situation in which he is.

    .   .   .   .

We know that there are an infinite number of directions across a field, but have no idea of there being an infinite number of directions in 'time'. In the world beyond sense, in higher space, we must put all possible directions as *psychological directions*, just as in the space that we know we can imagine all directions of bodily movements. If the actualisation of all possibilities or the fruition of all strivings are conceded to this higher space, then not only are all possible forms of our own histories, but all possible forms of the histories of the world, realised. What *we* know as history is not only living in Time, as was said before, but is only one track in aeon, a line through *all possibilities*, which may be growing or degenerating at every point. From this point of view all manner of forms of the world are already realised and are always being realised and we know only one of these, just as we know only one track or one form of our own lives. The track which we are following is one of the realisations of our lives, surrounded on all sides by other realisations. To follow another track would mean that we realised, as ordinary beings, another set of possibilities, which are always realised, only we are not conscious of them.

In this respect we put the idea of 'another world' too far away. We think either of this known world or a *next* world – a world *hereafter*. We should think first rather of another direction, close to us, that always starts from *now*, of which we continually catch glimpses, for often we stand on the edge of new meaning. There is no other real starting point but *now*. But we start always from imagination. Eternity enters into *now* – and of *now* we will speak later – and it is with eternity that we must connect all other real possibilities. But living in imagination we regret yesterday and look forward expectantly to tomorrow. So we run in time, seeking completion. We make no attempt to create any horizon above time. We have no idea of an already-existing ALL. To struggle out of time, out of the flow of becoming, some point beyond it must become so real to us that we begin to see other orders and possibilities of existence. None of the ordinary knowledge that we train ourselves in will assist us in this.

.   .   .   .

That all possibilities exist, only we follow one line through them, is put in the following way by Ouspensky: 'Time does not exist! There exist no perpetual and eternal appearance and disappearance of phenomena, no ceaselessly flowing fountain of ever-appearing and ever-vanishing events. Everything exists always! There is only one eternal present, the *Eternal Now*, which the weak and limited human mind can never grasp and conceive. But the idea of the Eternal Now is not at all the idea of a cold and merciless predetermination of everything, of an exact and infallible pre-existence. It would be quite wrong to say that if everything already exists, if the remote future exists ... it means that there is no life, no movement, no growth, no evolution. People say and think this because they do not understand the infinite, and want to measure the immeasurable depths of eternity with their weak and limited finite minds. Of course they are bound to arrive at the most hopeless of all possible solutions of the problem.'

The *real world* is a world of infinite possibilities. 'Our mind follows the development of possibilities always in one direction only. But in fact every moment contains a very large number of possibilities. *And all of them are actualised*, only we do not see it and do not know it. We always see only one of the actualisations, and in this lie the poverty and limitation of the human mind. But if we try to imagine the actualisation of all the possibilities of the present moment, then of the next moment, and so on, we shall feel the world growing infinitely, incessantly multiplying itself and becoming immeasurably rich and utterly unlike the flat and limited world we have hitherto pictured to ourselves. Having imagined this infinite variety we shall feel a 'taste' of infinity for a moment, and shall understand how inadequate and impossible it is to approach the problem of time with earthly measure. We shall understand what an infinite richness of time going in all directions is necessary for the actualisation of all the possibilities that arise each moment.... We shall feel that the world is so boundlessly large that a thought of the existence of any limits in it, a thought of there being anything whatever which is not contained within it, will appear to us ridiculous' (*A New Model of the Universe*, 1st edition, p. 139. 1931).

With eternity, Ouspensky connects a *fifth* dimension, calling it a second dimension of 'time'. Ultimately, he sees the universe as six-dimensional – as having *three dimensions of 'time'*, and three dimensions of space. The line of fulfilment of one set of possibilities is a *line in time*. Now a surface is infinity for a line, because a surface can contain an infinite number of lines. But a surface is two-dimensional, so that, thinking in this way, eternity in comparison with time is as a surface to a line. 'Everything we know,

157

everything we recognise as existing lies in the line of the fourth dimension, the line of the fourth dimension is the historical "time" of our section of existence. This is the only "time" we know, the only time we feel, the only time we recognise. But though we are not aware of it, sensations of the existence of other "times", both parallel and perpendicular, continually enter into our consciousness. These parallel times are completely analogous to our time, and consist of before – now – after, whereas the perpendicular "times" consist only of now, and are, as it were, cross-threads, the woof in a fabric, in their relation to the parallel lines of time which in this case represent the *warp*' (*New Model*, P. 428).

In order to understand how from every moment of time possibilities branch off in every direction it is necessary to add a sixth dimension, that is, a third dimension of 'time'. 'Time' then *becomes a three-dimensional space above our known space*. Ouspensky explains the hieroglyph of the two superimposed triangles in reverse, called the seal of Solomon, as a representation of the six-dimensional universe, one triangle representing the three known dimensions of space, and the other the three invisible dimensions of 'time'. Every object we perceive in space extends into the three dimensions of 'time' apart from its visible extension in space. In some cases we see the *time-bodies* of things, e.g. electrons, as *solid matter*. The complete figure of everything is six-dimensional.

'We live and think and exist on one of the lines of time. But the second and third dimensions of time, that is, the surface on which this line lies, and the solid in which this surface is included, enter every moment into our life and into our consciousness, and influence our time.... In thinking of the *time-solid* formed by the lines of all the possibilities included in each moment, we must remember that beyond these there can be nothing. This is the point which we can understand as the limitedness of the infinite universe.' From this point of view full *space-time* is a higher space of *six* dimensions or the space of the actualisation of all possibilities.

The six-pointed star, or seal of Solomon, is the representation of this space-time or 'period of dimensions' – the three-space dimensions and the three-time dimensions in unity – 'where everything is everywhere and always'.

CHAPTER SEVEN

ETERNITY
AND THE RECURRENCE OF LIFE

MOST PEOPLE HAVE experienced that sudden sense of familiarity which makes them ask: Where, when, did this happen before? We see a place for the first time and yet know that we have seen it before, 'long ago'. But when? We cannot reach the answer. If a scent restores the past we recognise the far-away scene. We have the sensation of living momentarily in another part of our lives, as if we re-entered the past. But the strange feeling of familiarity or consciousness of a previous existence is not the same. It remains unsatisfied; we cannot trace it to its source. The past is not restored to consciousness, yet we feel certain that we have been in that place or done that thing before. Sometimes, in some crisis, the soul becomes detached from what is happening precisely through the feeling that 'all this happened before'.

It was an ancient idea that 'time' is bent in a circle, and that all things come round to the same point again. Up to now we have taken the life as a line in Time. Now we come to the further idea of the life being a circle, and to the question of the repetition or recurrence of the same events.

.   .   .   .

I will begin with some experiences of the life being seen in terms of recurrence – and not only the life, but the universe, regarded as a series of repeating events. These experiences were obtained by the use of anaesthetics, which can sometimes induce a special state of consciousness. After studying these experiences we will pass to some general views about recurrence, ancient and modern.

If all process in time is 'curved' everything will come back to its starting-point. *The life will recur*. The life is a circle. We will come once more to the same points in the life, to the same experiences. But we cannot believe that the realisation that this is so belongs to our ordinary level of consciousness any more than does the feeling of the living existence of all the life, or the pure feeling of *I*. Let us remember that the knowledge-value belonging to higher levels of consciousness cannot be the same as that which characterises our ordinary level. What is merely theory to our ordinary consciousness can be the direct cognition of real fact on a higher level. Now the *idea* of recurrence is a very old one, and I would explain its persistence, in a historical sense, as due to its being cognitive *fact* at a higher level of consciousness.

Many anaesthetic experiences have been put on record. They are broadly divisible into two classes. In the first, the dream-level is touched, underlying but very close to the ordinary conscious state: in the second, degrees of consciousness above the ordinary level are experienced. In taking ether, for example, a man dreams that he is rushing in a train through darkness, or in the hands of torturers (personification of sensations). Such experiences belong to dream-states, and spring from the tendency of dream-consciousness to find analogies. But there are recorded experiences of quite a different order, that are not connected with ordinary images or analogies.

One of these records was made by a scientist of recent times, William Ramsay, from which I propose to quote. Not only did a changed feeling of time and a sense of eternity (everlastingness) enter into his experiences but also the feeling, or rather the direct perception, of the *recurrence* of things (*Partial Anaesthesia* by the late Sir William Ramsay, published in the Proceedings of the Society for Psychical Research, vol. IX, 1894). We must recall here the general rule that *a change in the time-sense characterises higher degrees of consciousness*.

161

In the following experiments small quantities of ether were inhaled successively and the changes in consciousness noted. Sometimes the observer described his sensations at the moment to an assistant who made notes, and sometimes he recorded them himself. In the initial stages [when the effect of ether was lightly felt] Ramsay first noticed a heightened perception of the outer world. 'Two states apparently supervened; one of attention to minute details, furniture, surrounding objects, etc.; and the other of complete subordination to idea of Theory of Universe. The transition from one to the other was well-defined and instantaneous.' He passed from 'outer' to 'inner' abruptly. We shall see that when he was subordinated to the inner, *the universe appeared to be within him*, and he was at the centre of things. Yet in this state he often retained the power of seeing outside things, only whenever his glance fell on any object he saw it in a new way, which will be described. After attaining to the inner stage 'an overwhelming impression forced itself upon me that the state in which I then was, was reality; that now I had reached the true solution of the secret of the universe, in understanding the secret of my own mind; that all outside objects were merely passing reflections on the eternal mirror of my mind; some more, some less transient. In later experiments with anaesthetics I have tried with success to recall events of the day; how I was occupied in my laboratory; how I walked down Oxford Street in the morning; what I saw, and whom I met; and with success; but they impressed me as a fleeting vision; something quite trivial and transitory. The main and impressive fact for me was that I was self-existent, and that time and space were illusions. This was the real *Ego*, on whose surface ripples of incident arose, to fade and vanish like the waves on a pond.'

The emphasis of this stage is plainly upon the reality of himself, upon *I*. Before this stage set in, the emphasis was upon the outer – as when, at the commencement of the inhalation of ether, he notices how a more comprehensive perception embraces what he looks at and he sees objects in certain new relationships, e.g., his eye catches sight of the bars of the grate or the cross-pieces of the window-sash and the 'idea of a harmonic arrangement suggested itself, as if the bars of the grate were arranged so as to form gaps corresponding to the fundamental note, the fifth, and the octave'.

In one experiment [begun with nitrous oxide] he wrote down his impressions himself. 'Singing in ears, slight difficulty in focussing, etc.', [he continued with ether]. '... became unusually sensitive to outside things; heard water dropping from cistern ... tingling in spinal cord of neck, beginning of consciousness of previous existence.' He swallows, and marks this stage of swallowing as important – as a definite stage in the whole range of sensations. He allows himself to recover slightly and writes: 'This refers to feeling that same stage always recurs and to feeling of eternal existence.'

It is this feeling of previous existence and recurrence that I will now trace in further experiments which were recorded in notes made at the time by his woman assistant. A particular feeling about the nature of the Universe arose in his mind owing to the nature of these experiences.

In one experiment four doses of ether were inhaled [over a period of five minutes]. After the second dose the mental state was clear but Ramsay begins to be aware of what he calls the *recurrence of events*. 'Everything has occurred before.... Trace of beginning sense of having been here before ... feeling of recurrence, e.g., table, mantlepiece, etc., having been *always* there.' After the fourth dose, following a period of silence lasting two minutes, the eyes being open and motionless, Ramsay exclaims: 'This, one little piece of enormous coherence of universe – utterly ridiculous in its smallness.' [More complete recovery.] 'Every bit of these events recurred – except fact of woman instead of man as observer

– cycle of events recurring bothers me greatly, because I expect each stage to go further – i.e., stage in evolution of universe.'

The main feeling is that everything has happened before and that in some way everything always is. The idea is two-fold. With this *always-ness* of things is a continual *re-experiencing* of them. This re-experiencing of things within this always-ness of things makes a cyclical process, i.e., there are cycles of events constantly recurring. Amidst all these cycles of events [that here he hints as constituting the *Universe*, and, in another experiment, definitely so states] he discerns *stages*. It is possible to get beyond a particular cycle; and it is obvious that at the moment of the above experiment he understood that getting beyond recurring cycles of events is connected with a feeling of *evolution*. The sense of previous existence and the sense of re-experiencing what has happened before [not in exactly the same way for he mentions a woman observer being present instead of a man] together with the feeling that all *is* always and all is always recurring, that it is possible to reach further cycles of experience only by escaping from those in which we turn, and that this further stage of experiencing would be the experiencing of a further stage in the 'evolution of the Universe' – all this insight is contained, I maintain, in these brief notes and results from bordering on a higher degree of consciousness.

Now let us turn to further confirmation, found in the notes of further experiments. Four doses were taken over a period of six minutes. After the third dose the assistant notes that Ramsay is in 'the stage of repetition' and close to unconsciousness. Ramsay then exclaims: *'This* is the scheme of the Universe and my being here – but I have never reached the point of having taken ether before.' After the final dose he says: 'I see you think I have had enough. I will stop short to explain. In the ordinary work-a-day world this is an untenable theory – I mean the sense of "myself alone" – of what affects me – there is a series of precisely similar events. I believe, as far as I can comprehend, that this is the Universe. At a certain point the order of reason alters – this time has brought me a stage further. That is wrong.' The notes are fragmentary. But I think that the last sentence refers to some uncertainty in his mind as to whether he had ever taken ether before or not, in the cycles of recurrences. In the first experiment he had the strong impression that every detail of the events that he was in had happened before. In the above experiment he feels that he had never reached the point of having taken ether before. But in both experiments the sense of recurrence and of the Universe being made up of cycles of events is the same. This experiment ends with the note: 'Here I have recognised the ultimate scheme of the Universe, as far as I am concerned, up to a certain stage. It will probably be worked out when I die. Yet that is not the end – I shall go on after that, but – to what?' ... 'I will take ether again.' It is difficult not to conclude that Ramsay saw [during the experiments, certainly not after] some special significance, as regards himself, in taking ether. It gave him some insight or knowledge that he connects with the evolutionary process of his life. He sees [during the experiment] clearly enough that his life repeats itself and that he will come back to the same point again – and perhaps get beyond it.

The notes on the third experiment which lasted for over ten minutes, eight doses being taken, are as follows. After the fourth dose he says: 'It is one or the other Theory of the Universe, and mine must be the most probable.... I may be the central person in the Universe – I don't mind, I can't help it.' After the sixth dose: 'The Universe is in our brain. Is this a big thing? Do you hear the man sawing – more or less quickly? Now I breathe hard. Now I note appearance of a particular man there [pointing to fireplace] whom I never asked you to note before nor will now, but he appears as part of the Universe.'

.   .   .   .

Let us piece together Ramsay's impression of the nature of the Universe. He has seen the Universe under the aspect of *cycle* and *stage*. In the above experiment he sees a man as part of the Universe. Of course, in our ordinary state of consciousness, we do not see anything as part of the Universe. We see merely a small portion of the world in three dimensions, in which everything seems separate. In one experiment Ramsay wrote: 'With the consciousness of writing, sitting at this table; with a handkerchief at my mouth, a door on my right, a window on my left, a cigarette on the table [I am wearing striped trousers and there is a caned-bottom chair on my left], a ticket before me and a book open at page 8. All these and other things convince me [as I have been convinced before by seeing a piece of crumpled paper] that this is a stage in the cycle of the Universe. The notion is that I alone am privileged to see all this.... It is a place in my development.' Now in all that he says about sitting at the table, wearing striped trousers, etc., he is, of course, describing nothing ordinary. He is aware of a new and tremendous significance entering into familiar objects. They are all 'part of the Universe'. He perceives that each object must be just like that at that time, just where it is, and in just that state, because it is part of the *always-ness*, i.e. part of the higher-dimensional world.

For example, he says in another place: 'My eye caught sight of a Bunsen burner – a common object in every laboratory; and here again I knew it had been there through endless ages. Some noise – the emptying of a cart of coals in the street, perhaps – struck my attention. I not merely knew that it had happened before but I could have predicted that it would happen at that particular moment.' His consciousness had expanded so that every-thing he saw and heard contained an echo created by the Universe itself. He saw the Bunsen burner outside passing-time, in Time and Eternity. Seen ordinarily, it is where it is because someone happened to put it there. The coal-cart is outside the house, because

166

someone brought it there, because coals were ordered. Ramsay saw another order of *cause*. To perceptual consciousness the cart might just as well be in another place, or come earlier or later. But under the aspect of higher space it is necessarily where it is, *just then*. That coal-cart is always emptying coals at that point in Time and the moment is always recurring to any consciousness apprehending it. It is the *event* of the coal-cart emptying coals that is always repeating itself to the mind perceiving it, as a book will always repeat itself to the consciousness that reads it. So, to the experiencing mind, it is part of a cycle always recurring [but only sensed as recurrence when consciousness is exalted] and for itself it is always existing. Therefore, to the exalted consciousness, into every experience there enters the feeling of *eternity*, not in the sense we have spoken about in the previous chapter – namely, the sense of fullness and infinity of possibillties – but in the sense of the everlastingness, indestructibility, or eternity of each moment of time.

The arrangement he describes of things on the table – the ticket, the book open at page 8, etc. – are seen in the same strange light. Even the book *open at page 8* is 'part of the Universe'. It is possible to come to the conclusion, theoretically, that everything happening at this moment is necessarily a stage in the cycle of the visible Universe. But this is not knowledge as *seeing*. We do not *see* a piece of crumpled paper as rooted in the Universe as an essential part of it, always in that state just then. We cannot exclaim with Ramsay – 'This, one little piece of the enormous coherence of the Universe – utterly ridiculous in its smallness.' We do not see this invisible interconnection, for to see it we must be aware of immense background – a back-world, a world at the back of the visible world – a world of higher space. It was quoted in the first chapter (p. 15) that 'if the senses were eliminated the world would appear as a unity'. This is, I think, what Ramsay understood in the state of consciousness induced by ether. In our ordinary state,

167

when the senses alone govern us and work in their customary way, we see and feel nothing of the enormous coherence and unity of the universe. Nor do we realise anything of a like nature about our own lives. We are confined to the pin-point of an apparently momentary existence. Nothing is added to our perceptions. The 'real' is what we see; and we see only multiplicity on all sides, without clear connection or meaning.

While Ramsay sees everything in its place, necessarily just where it is – apart from the ordinary reasons why we think a thing is where it is – he perceives that in this Universe of *always-ness* and *recurrence* there is the possibility of getting beyond the repetition of the same experiences. Seen from within, from the *inner*, the Universe is made up of cycles of recurrence, which represent for us, stages or states.

.   .   .   .

Let us think of these stages as corresponding to degrees of understanding, each of which gives a standpoint that implicates both inner and outer. We can take an illustration. Ramsay reaches a certain stage of understanding which he describes, and with which he becomes quite familiar. At this stage [he says] 'it looks to me as if the Universe were the creation of a demon', i.e., this is one possible way of viewing the Universe, one state of understanding it. He feels that he can get beyond this stage or standpoint and that the getting beyond is connected with the *evolution* of the Universe [again understand that the inner is meant – the Universe in man's mind or *as* man's mind]. He says: 'This is a stage in the development bound to recur.' I ask the reader to particularly notice this part. If, in our growth of understanding, we are bound to reach successive stages and eventually one of seeing everything as the work of a demon, how are we to get beyond this stage of complete denial? Ramsay says the stage is bound to recur: '... but each time I can stop and anticipate it. Now, I want to go on a stage further, if you will let me.' By realising that it is a state of mind that is bound to come, and that it always recurs, Ramsay feels that he can get beyond it. He sees the state objectively, and does not fall under its power [in the experiment].

Once again, we must clearly understand that Ramsay is seeing the Universe as a *mental* process and not as a *sensible object*. He inhales a further dose. 'Now I am beginning to get into a new dose. There are two Theories of the Universe. One individual undergoes a series of mental transformations. People choose to imagine there are worlds – that is to say, build mental cosmogonies.' I take this passage as meaning that the two theories of the Universe, 'inner' and 'outer', are as follows: (1) The Universe is 'in our brain' and thus everyone is at the centre of the Universe. The evolution of the Universe is then a series of mental transformations and stages of understanding *in the man himself*. According to one's level, so one sees the Universe; and so it is, at that stage of understanding, or level, i.e., the Universe must be all things, to make our growth possible. (2) The other view is that we imagine that *external* visible worlds – planets and stars – constitute the Universe, and that is all that we understand by the term. Then we form cosmogonies in our minds, following the evidence of the senses, and speculate about nebular hypotheses, action at a distance, gravitation, a four-dimensional continuum, receding star-islands, etc.

The first view of the Universe, *as a series of mental transformations*, makes oneself and the Universe identical. The Universe is given, as it were, to everyone as seed or *microcosmos* within him – to develop as he pleases. As *microcosmos* in man it can evolve or not. Our own inner struggle for light then becomes *the evolving Universe*. It constitutes the Universe, in evolution – or devolution. And as regards this individual evolution of the Universe in a man there are *stages* or states of understanding that must be passed. There are recurring cycles of precisely similar *mental events*, identical standpoints and experiences. Just as in a journey in outer space, people must pass through the same areas, so in this inner journey (in psychological space) the understanding reaches definite stages; and of these, one is the stage at which one *must* see everything as meaningless, evil or useless – everything as 'the creation of a demon'. This attitude develops in the inner life at a certain point – even, mark you, when one has already seen and understood the world differently. Why does this point of negation meet us sooner or later? Negation means saying *no*, the attitude of no, the fascination of denial – a certain very powerful poison. I will only say that it is possible to reflect that such a stage must be reached by everyone before any *individual* solution of the meaning of existence can emerge and before what I will call the active understanding can awaken fully. In the darkness of *no* a man must fall back entirely on himself, on all he has ever felt and understood, and struggle *for himself* [that is the point] to get beyond this stage – so that all getting beyond can only be done through what is most genuine, profound and sincere in him. Previous enthusiasms will die because they are intrinsically false; the first flush of hope that all new understanding brings must fade; all collective things, outer devotion, faith as ordinarily understood, and dependent belief in others, must depart; because one is confronted by an internal obstacle that only *I myself* can pass, as through my own gate, that will open to nobody else's key: my *individual* mark will be on that key.

We can imagine the barrier that Ramsay reached under artificial conditions will not seem so easy to pass when it is encountered in the path of a normal development. But to see it as a stage in those mental transformations that mean development robs it of something of its power. Only, to see it internally in this way is one thing; to recognise and meet it in everyday life is quite another thing.

. . . .

Let us turn to a corresponding idea about the Universe as inner experience or *state*. We are studying viewpoints gained from what we are taking as higher degrees of consciousness. We must grant to the poet the power of vision above the level of our customary conscious outlook. Blake taught that man is in touch inwardly with a world of *states*, already existent. Man cannot be taken separately from these states. Man is not simply a body. The creation of *man* is not merely the creation of a visible body of legs, arms, head, etc. Man, his *psychology*, his possible history, all his potentialities, all his emotions, thoughts, moods and attitudes, constitute his creation. *All this is man.*

We imagine, of course, that any state that we are in – sorrow, resentment, joy, suspicion, anxiety, etc. – is something quite unique to ourselves. This makes it splendidly attractive. It does not occur to us that we are touching one of the 'already-made' *states* common to Man and belonging to his creation. More than this, Blake saw all possible human situations as part of the creation of Man. He saw every aspect, every plot and drama of human life, as already worked out – as 'mere possibilities' as long as we are not in them, but as over-poweringly real when we are in them. He saw them as designs, patterns, or what he called *'sculptures'*. (In the following quotation *Los* (sol) is his personification of *Time*.) 'All things acted on Earth are seen in the bright Sculptures of Los's Halls, & every Age renews its powers from these Works with every pathetic story possible to happen from Hate or Wayward Love; & every sorrow & distress is carved here, every Affinity of Parents, Marriages & Friendships are here. In all their various combinations wrought with wondrous Art, all that can happen to Man in his pilgrimage of seventy years' (*Jerusalem* I.16). A similar idea is found in the Slavonic version of *Enoch* where the seer is shown the entire world in Time from beginning to end 'and everything relating to man and the lives of men' (XXIII.2).

Blake penetrates the illusion of passing-time. He is not a

171

poet of passing-time, a singer of regrets. All his thought is im-
bued with the sense of a higher-dimensional world. 'I see the Past,
Present, and Future existing all at once before me' (*Jerusalem* 1.1
5). He views: 'All that has existed in the space of six thousand
years permanent and not lost, not lost nor vanished, and every little act, word, work, and wish that has existed, all remaining still.'
Again: 'Everything exists, and not one sigh, nor smile, nor tear,
one hair, nor particle of dust, not one can pass away.' And of his
figure, Los: 'Both time and space obey my will. I in Six Thousand
Years walk up and down; for not one moment of Time is lost, nor
one Event of Space unpermanent, but all remain; every fabric of
Six Thousand Years remains permanent, though on Earth ... all
things vanish and are seen no more. They vanish not from me...'
(*Milton*, Book 1.24).

At *all points of Time* things are being re-fashioned. But
whereever a man may be inserted into the Time-World, he is
in touch (at his ordinary level of consciousness) with these *states*
which Blake sees in vision as a hall of sculptures. On this point,
Blake's psychological teaching, as I understand it, is that ordinarily *man is nothing but states* and has no proper separate existence.
The states are permanent. Man passes temporarily into one or
another; and when in any one state, it is quite real and all other
states are shadowy. We are always in one state or another state,
in one human situation or another. All these are 'already created'.
Every possible situation is fully worked out. Only we cannot see
it in this way.

We cannot see our daily situations objectively, as: 'This is
called thinking one is misunderstood – this is called losing something valuable – this is called being ill – this is called being angry
– this is called self-pity – this is called blaming others – this is
called being deceived, etc.' We have not sufficient power of insight or detachment, and consequently *are merely the state itself*; yet
the state is not us any more than are the I's that make up the psy-

172

chological kaleidoscope in us. The *individual* (the *I* of Tennyson) is not his states; but not having any contact with this individuality we are always merely ready-made state. Blake taught that what he called *divine imagination* in man – which he connects with the individual identity – is separate from state. 'The Imagination is not a State, it is the human existence itself. Affection or Love become a State when divided from Imagination.' The individual identity is *eternal* – i.e., not in passing-time, not in the momentary *I*'s. But if man is nothing but his states and the imitation of other people's states, and confounds *himself* with these states, he never attains *existence in himself*. He acts from state, not from himself. He thinks that state is himself, and does not understand that there is something in him that must be separated from state – and that towards every situation that life can produce (every 'sculpture of Los') he must be *more* than that situation or state. Unless we know, grasp, and seek to transcend *states* they will always recur, as Ramsay saw. He saw that the state in which one sees the universe as the creation of a demon is *merely a state* – as something that could be got beyond; by recognising it as *state*, by seeing what it is. There is a dialogue between Christ and Peter which seems to belong to this question of state. I have quoted Blake as saying that all love and affection, when divided from 'imagination' are nothing but state. Christ asks Peter three times if he loves him and Peter replies in the affirmative. But Christ uses the word *agapein* in his first and second question and Peter replies always with the purely emotional word, *philein*. It is obvious that the quality of love is the question at issue. Is your love mere *state* or more? 'Ye must love beyond yourselves. So ye must learn to love.'

.   .   .   .

What kind of *ideas* help us to change our relation to *state*? We have seen that the sense of *I*, as Tennyson and Ramsay experienced it, is accompanied by another feeling of time, or by the entry of the feeling of eternity and recurrence. There may be *ideas* at a still higher level than these. But these ideas about time, eternity, and recurrence bring about a definite result. The ordinary preoccupations and anxieties of daily life are weakened by a new knowledge, by a knowledge that is over and above our ordinary knowledge. New perception, new knowledge, a new sense of I, a new understanding of the universe, a change in the time-sense – and as we shall see shortly in some further examples, a new power and ratio of thought – characterise a higher conscious level, above that one given to us naturally – which we take as *consciousness.*

We are already familiar with the view that perceives the universe in the light of a scale of reality, i.e., everything is 'real', only relatively so – the lesser reality being transformed or absorbed by contact with the greater. Any heightening of consciousness must therefore transform, or do away with, problems that seem very real at the ordinary level. Even on the scale of ordinary experience we know something of the truth of this. In our better states we cannot imagine why we acted as we did in our worse states. The latter seem unreal. Yet when we were in them they were real enough. Now an *idea* which belongs to a level above us must have more 'reality' than any of our ordinary ideas that we derive from natural, three-dimensional life. It must therefore have the power of *drawing energy* out of our ordinary states.

An *idea*, in the sense in which I am endeavouring to use this term, has the power of altering our standpoint and changing our sense of things. I mentioned that the Hermetic exercise of thinking of the idea of the life, as living at all points, has this significance, psychologically. The exercise is to *imitate* a direct cognition at a higher level. The idea itself can only become direct cognition in another state of consciousness, as in the recorded experiences of partial drowning, when all the life is seen.

Apart from the idea of *Time* itself, the idea of recurrence, which Nietzsche called the *thought of thoughts*, alters us. Why? Because this idea, which belongs to a cognition at a higher level, draws energy out of our ordinary thought. Nietzsche says: 'This mightiest of all thoughts absorbs a lot of energy which previously stood at the disposal of other aspirations, and in this way it exercises a modifying influence; it creates new laws of motion in energy, though no new energy. But it is precisely in this respect that there lies some possibility of determining new emotions and new desires in man.'

.   .   .   .

But before continuing with the subject of recurrence I wish to digress in order to give some further examples of higher conscious states which illustrate their cognitive value – and also how the energy which ordinarily flows into the small and petty things of our life is absorbed into a new sense of reality.

In the first example, one given by William James, the emphasis of the description is laid upon an increased power of the thought – thought of a higher order, 'eternal' in the true sense of being much fuller and more comprehensive. He describes how he had: 'sudden and incomprehensible enlargements of the conscious field, bringing with them a curious sense of cognition of real fact. All have occurred within the past five years; three of them were similar in type; the fourth was unique. In each of the three like cases, the experience broke in abruptly upon a perfectly commonplace situation and lasted perhaps less than two minutes. In one instance I was engaged in conversation, but I doubt whether the interlocutor noticed my abstraction. What happened each time was that I seemed all at once to be reminded of a past experience; and this reminiscence, ere I could conceive or name it distinctly, developed into something further that belonged with it, this in turn into something further still, and so on, until the

175

process faded out, leaving me amazed at the sudden vision of in-creasing ranges of distant fact of which I could give no articulate account. The mode of consciousness was perceptual, not concep-tual – the field was expanding so fast that there seemed no time for conception or identification to get in its work. There was a strongly exciting sense that my knowledge of past (or present?) reality was enlarging pulse by pulse, but so rapidly that my intel-lectual processes could not keep up the pace. The *content* was thus entirely lost to retrospection – it sank into the limbo into which dreams vanish as we gradually awake. The feeling – I won't call it belief – that I had had a sudden *opening*, had seen through a window, as it were, distant realities that incomprehensibly be-longed to my own life, was so acute that I cannot shake it off today.... I have treated the phenomenon under discussion as if it consisted in the uncovering of tracts of *consciousness*. Is the consci-ousness already there waiting to be uncovered? and is it a veridical revelation of reality? These are questions on which I do not touch. In the subjects of the experience the "emotion of conviction" is always strong and sometimes absolute.'

In the next example the writer describes how all the pro-blems of ordinary life vanish (as Ramsay saw) in the light of hi-gher consciousness. The experience was produced under an anaes-thetic. '... I was all at once awake and fully conscious in a different world. It gave no sensory impressions yet I immediately recogni-sed it was being far more real than the other world out of which I had just come ... since my waking there have arisen a score of mental problems which I have felt (still feel, indeed) would sim-ply vanish could they be looked at in the light of that world, yet when I seek to picture it, it escapes like water from every form of words I fashion and in telling of it, I realise not simply that I fail to enlighten my individual hearer but that the words themselves are such as could not be expected to carry any clear impression ... all of us feel that there ought to be a world different from and better than this one. My feeling is, that for a moment, I stood on the borderland of such a world: it was *there*' (Frederic Hall, *An Ether Vision*, Open Court Magazine, Dec. 1909).

The triviality of what ordinarily concerns us, when seen in the light of a higher level, is also described by Ouspensky. He formulates the psychological view *that it is our ordinary feeling of I that causes us to understand everything wrongly*. The first sensation of approaching a higher level of consciousness (he says) is the disappearance of our ordinary feeling of *I*. (We must recall here how much *Buddhist* teaching concerns itself with the wrong feeling of *I*.) This may produce a sense of fear. Just because we associate the feeling of *I* with so much that is worthless and relatively unreal, so when we approach greater reality, we seem to be disappearing, turning to nothing. This was his first sensation. But in subsequent experiences the disappearance of the ordinary feeling of *I* produced an 'extraordinary calmness and confidence, which nothing can equal in our ordinary sensations. I seemed to understand at that time that all the usual troubles, cares, and anxieties are connected with the usual sense of *I*, and result from it and constitute and sustain it. Therefore when this "I" disappeared all troubles, cares, and anxieties disappeared.' It then seemed to him that it seemed strange that we could take such a terrible responsibility on ourselves by bringing *I* into everything, and that our ordinary sense of *I* 'was something almost abnormal, a kind of fantastic conceit which bordered on blasphemy, as if each one of us called himself God. I felt then that only God could call himself "I", and that only God was "I"' (*A New Model of the Universe*, p. 334). As a result of his experiences he perceived that the reaching of higher reality was only possible through a change in the feeling of I. Now, in the above records of higher conscious states we find no mention of recurrence, whereas in Ramsay's experiences the fact of recurrence was strongly felt. Yet much in Ramsay's experiences corresponds to what we find in the above descripti-

177

ons. In the lifting of consciousness, in other words, different cognitive levels are touched, into which the perception of living time, the changed feeling of *I*, the increase of mental grasp, the sense of everlastingness, the feeling of self-existence, the perception of recurrence, etc., do not equally enter.

CHAPTER EIGHT

RECURRENCE IN THE SAME TIME

TO RETURN TO the idea of recurrence: Nietzsche saw the universe 'as a circle consisting in a definite number of changes which continually recurs ... activity is eternal, the number of the products and states is limited' (*The Eternal Recurrence*, VI). His argument was that no incalculable number of states could evolve out of a given quantity of energy [the quantum of energy that is the Universe] or a system of limited forces, so that repetition was bound to happen sooner or later. 'The whole process of Becoming consists of a repetition of a definite number of precisely similar states ... everything has returned; Sirius, and the spider, and thy thoughts at this moment, and this last thought of thine that all these things will return.'

The dust at our feet is formed from the ashes of innumerable once-living creatures. It will live again *in these creatures*, in the circle of Becoming. 'Fellow-man! your whole life, like a sandglass, will always be reversed and will ever run out again – a long minute of time will elapse until all those conditions out of which you were evolved return in the wheel of the cosmic process. And then you will find every pain and every pleasure, every friend and every enemy, every hope and every error, every blade of grass and every ray of sunshine once more. This ring, in which you are but a grain, will glitter afresh for ever. And, in every one of these cycles of human life there will be one hour where for the first time one man, and then many, will perceive the mighty thought of the eternal recurrence of all things – and for mankind this is always the hour of Noon.'

Ask yourself the question, with the thought of recurrence in yourmind: 'Is what I am doing now what I am prepared to do an incalculable number of times?' Before this thought is effective it is necessary to know and understand a great deal.

In connection with the idea of recurrence Nietzsche asks a pertinent question. How can we give weight to our inner life [to the thoughts which powerfully affect it] without making it appear evil and fanatical towards people who think otherwise? The difficulty is that people do not want to think, to arouse themselves. Even when we are discontented with life we do not want to make the effort of thinking or finding new outlooks. A man wants momen-tary enjoyment; he does not want to be disturbed; he prefers to cling to the opinions he has, and to make everything as easy as possible for himself. The idea of recurrence is painful unless *understood*. Most of us look for rest at death or annihilation. How often does the physician hear the dying say: I want only rest, oblivion – even amongst those who have appeared to have held the strongest religious opinions? How few of us truly wish to meet anyone again, or at least how few are those we could ever deeply wish to meet. We need to find new reasons for meeting again. And how strangely the doctrine of recurrence affects us here, for the 'next' life is this life. We meet everyone again. Have we lived this life in such a way that we desire to live it again? Have we unfinished things that we long to finish, and have not time? 'Ye fancy that ye will have a long rest ... 'twixt your last moment of consciousness and the first ray of dawn of your new life no time will elapse – as a flash of lightning will the space go by, even though living creatures think it is billions of years, and are not even able to reckon it. Timelessness and immediate re-birth are compatible, once intellect is eliminated!' Stamp, he says, the impress of eternity upon your life, for this thought contains more than all religions which teach us to despise life. 'This life is thy eternal life.' Of course, this statement is incomplete – as any statement about recurrence must necessarily be. Nietzsche takes *eternity* in the usual sense. Also he does not comprehend the dimension of Time itself. He does not grasp the idea of the living life.

But the idea of the life standing through all its length in

Time is completed by the idea of the recurrence of the life. *The life is and the experience of the life in some form returns.*

As Nietzsche says, such ideas by themselves can alter us. He sees the idea of recurrence as the supreme idea for the future, one that will lead to a state of life on earth of which the imagination of no Utopist has ever dreamt. But he puts this very far distant. He apparently believed that *passing-time* brought man to a certain point of understanding – that the transformation of man lies always in the future of passing-time. This mightiest thought, he says, will require many millenniums. But is this not just what we always think about the action of time? Are we not always in the state of believing that the mere passage of days will bring something new and wonderful? It is strange that he did not see that the comprehension of such ideas as that of recurrence lies 'at right angles' to time – and that all growth of man lies in that direction.

.   .   .   .

Let us turn back to a study of older sources. As I said, *the idea of recurrence is ancient.* It is an idea that has lurked in the background of man's speculations about life from the beginning of our European thought. But it is an idea that has so much latent content that we cannot expect any clear formulation of it. It is too deep. If we say that it probably comes nearer the truth about 'another life' than any other view, we must not expect that a logical statement concerning it must therefore be possible. It is above logic. In a sense, at a time when 'other-worldliness' has become too weak a concept for the modern mind, the *idea* of recurrence brings with it a new worldliness, a new 'materialism' that relates itself both to this life and another. For now we exist no longer in a world of *solid matter* but in a world of energies, dimensions and relations; and we must connect all these with the concept *life*, going beyond three dimensionality, present moment and solid body.

181

The life is a circle. The image of the circle of the life is found in the New Testament. In James 3.6, the revolution of a man's life is spoken of – the wheel of becoming. 'The tongue ... setteth on fire the wheel of nature (margin: birth).' 'Setting on fire the whole round of our lives' (Weymouth's translation). In the Old Testament the spiritual Universe is seen in the form of *wheels*, in the vision of Ezekiel (chap. 10). 'Now as I looked upon the wheels they were very high, so high that they were dreadful to behold, and they were full of eyes all round about. And their appearance and their work was, as it were, *wheel within wheel*. As went the living creatures so went the wheels; and when the living creatures rose, the wheels also were lifted up in correspondence with them. For there was a *living spirit* (a spirit of life) in the wheels. Wheresoever the spirit was to go, there they went, and where the living creature stood, there they stood. For there was a living spirit in the wheels.' This is the translation given by Tayler Lewis. In another place (*Six Days of Creation*) he remarks, in speaking of the cyclical law (repetition) as the law of all natures, that the early rabbinical writers regarded the vision of the wheels of Ezekiel as representative of the *whole* system of nature. The wheels are cyclic processes, not to be seen in three-dimensional space but in the supra-sensible world, i.e. in higher space.

Aristotle says: '... For men are wont to say that all human things are in a circle: and in the same way they speak of all things that have a physical genesis. The reason of this is, that all things are *measured by time*, and have their beginning and their end, as it were, in a period; *for time itself seems to be a wheel or cycle*' (*Phys. Ausc.* Lib. IV, 14.5). We do not find the wheel in visible living structure. The time-wheel belongs to higher dimensions. The life in time is a circle – but is it complete? We die. 'Man dies', says the Pythagorean physician Alcmaeon, 'because he cannot join his end with his beginning.'

Now to our ordinary sense of things the beginning and end

of life seem furthest apart. This is because we think of passing-time as a movement along a straight line extended between birth and death. So, with our ordinary conception of time, it seems nonsense to say that *yesterday* can be the *future* of today. But if we take a circle and mark points on it, and imagine a movement around it, we can see how any point may be either regarded as 'future' or 'past' in relation to any other point. It is impossible to speak of any *beginning* in such a circle. If we arrange the days of the week round the circle we cannot say that any one day begins the cycle of days. The whole cycle is one thing. Its points lie 'together so that you can find no place in which the movement can be said to begin: for it is evident that all parts in the movement both precede and follow one another for ever and it is in this manner that time revolves' (*Hermetic Literature*).

Regarding everything as arranged on a recurring time-cyde, the philosopher Cardanus (sixteenth century) observed that no one is a mere successor and heir of his predecessor, but also the converse, owing to the *periodic recurrence* of all things, i.e. a man comes both *after* and *before* his father, grandfather, etc., in the circle of time.

The circular movement of time was regarded as a perfecting process by some ancient thinkers. Others saw in it only an ever-lasting process without comprehensible object. 'But is not time the image of Eternity because it effects the perfecting of earthly natures just as Eternity is the container and preserver of being? ... Things which proceed from Eternity and are not able to share in a stable perfection, whole and unchanging, are under the dominion of time' (Proclus). The idea is that incomplete natures, as ourselves, must live in time and succession, not having the strength or *being* to live in any other state, i.e. we live in *becoming* because we have no *being*. Proclus thus gives a cause for the existence of passing-time, it being designed in such a way that 'through it all things should be stimulated to their own appropriate energies, by which they are enabled to receive the end adapted to them, through certain *apocatastatic* periods'. *Apocatastasis* means recurrence. This positive conception of the universe moving in time relates it ultimately to the highest possible meaning, i.e. a return to perfection throughout all its parts. Proclus says that the operation of time is 'to confer perfection on things imperfect and a circular *apocatastasis* in things that proceed (apparently) in a straight line (of time)'. And this, he adds, does not appear 'to fall short of an invention or contrivance'. Observe that this contrivance consists in the bending of time round so that a continual return is possible.

We must study different views about this bending of time. First of all, there is the idea of a *general apocatastasis* according to which the whole history of the universe moves round in one single and immeasurably vast circle. Nietzsche spoke of recurrence from this standpoint. But we have already seen that Proclus spoke of 'certain *apocatastatic* periods'. We will return to Proclus subsequently. The idea of general apocatastasis, of a single vast circle of return, especially belonged to Stoic thought. The Stoics conceived one great time circle, comprising the entire universe throughout all its history. Note again that only one circle is indicated – not circles within circles. The period (time of going round) of this circle, was called the *Magnus Annus*. During its passage the universe passed through certain transformations. One state was that of fire. In the New Testament it is stated that the universe will 'end' in fire (2 *Peter* 3.12,). For the Stoic there was no end. The circle, not the straight line, underlay their thinking. Everything in the universe eventually returned from complexity to simplicity. The simplest state of matter was called *fire* (or aether). But once the universe had reached this state, then, by successive combinations and condensations, it was again restored. As the same laws were always at work the successive worlds were held to be exactly similar, so that the same persons, the same situations, and the same events appear again and again, i.e. 'after the conflagration the same things will come to pass by number so that the separate peculiarities will be the same as before' (*Alexander Aphrodias*, Anal. Pr.).

Tertullian, the early Church Father, explains the phrase 're-surrection of the dead' in terms of recurrence of this kind. Everything must be restored to life as the wheel of passing-time turns. The body will again come into existence. There can be no end, no cessation, no annihilation – no death, as we see death. He writes: 'Let me say it once for all: Every creation is subject to recurrence. Everything you meet had a previous existence: whatever you have lost will come again. Every-thing comes a second time: all things return to a settled position when they have gone away, all things begin when they have ceased to be. They are brought to an end in order that they may come into being: nothing is lost except that it may be recovered. All this revolving order of things, therefore, is evidence of *the resurrection of the dead*. God ordained it in works before He commanded it in writing, He proclaimed it by strength before He proclaimed it in words. He first sent you nature as teacher, intending to send you prophecy also, in order that having learnt from nature, you may the more easily believe prophecy. . . .' And again: 'Thou, man of nature so exalted, if thou understandest thyself, taught even by the Pythian words ["Know thyself"], Lord of all these things that die and rise – shalt thou die to perish evermore? Wherever your dissolution shall have taken place, whatever material agent has destroyed you, or swallowed you up, or swept you away, or reduced you to nothingness, it shall again restore you.'

In a letter written in the first century A.D., the Roman Stoic Seneca observes: '. . . if you are possessed by so great a craving for life, reflect that the things which vanish from our gaze ... are not annihilated: they merely end their course and do not perish. And death, which we fear and shrink from, merely interrupts life but does not take it away. *The day will return when we shall be res-*

tored to the light. Many would object to this, but they are returned without memory. I mean to show you later that everything which seems to perish merely changes. Since you are destined to return, depart with a tranquil mind.'

The world comes into existence, waxes, grows old and dies, and again comes into existence, waxes, grows old and dies, and everything belonging to its life repeats itself. This *palingenesis* (again-becoming), or *apocatastasis*, the restoration or recurrence of all things, was regarded by some of the older Stoics as an exact repetition. In this sense we might understand a remark of Ecclesiastes – that there is no new thing *under the sun*. He adds: 'There is no remembrance of former things.' One ancient writer says of the *gods* that they are those who *remember* the whole previous cycle of events (Nemesius, *De Natura Hominis*, p. 38).

But some of the later Stoics believed that there was variation at each repetition. The Church Father, Origen, gives an account of the Stoic point of view in the following passage: 'The disciples of the Porch [the Stoics] assert that after a period of years there will be a conflagration of the world and after that an arrangement of things in which everything will be unchanged, as compared with the former arrangement of the universe. Those of them, however, who evinced their dislike for the doctrine, have said there will be a change, although exceedingly slight, at the end of the cycle, from what prevailed during the preceding cycle. And these men maintain that the same things will recur, and Socrates will be again the son of Sophroniscus and a native of Athens; and Phaenarete, being married to Sophroniscus will again become his mother.....' And, in reference to *Pythagoras* and the doctrines of his school, Origen (writing about six centuries after Pythagoras) asserts that 'as the planets, after definite cycles, assume the same position and hold the same relation to one another, all things on earth, they [the Pythagoreans] say, will be like what they were at the time when the same state of planetary relations existed in the world. From this point it necessarily follows that when, after the lapse of a lengthened cycle, the planets come to occupy toward each other the same relations which they occupied at the time of Socrates, then Socrates will again be born of the same parents and suffer the same treatment, being accused by Anytus and Melitus, and condemned by the Council of the Areopagus again.' In the same passage Origen states that the Egyptians held views of a similar nature (*Contra Celsum*, Bk. V).

It was sometimes said that Pythagoras taught that the soul of man passed through every possible form of life, vegetable, animal, human. But Burnet definitely states that this doctrine of *metempsychosis* has only very late authority and is based upon a confusion of ideas. He says that the original Pythagorean teaching was *palingenesia* or again-becoming. The point that we must notice is that the doctrine of again-becoming appeared *at the dawn of our European culture* – and was apparently not a doctrine of metempsychosis. Man lives his life again. Now in what sense *again*?

A pupil of Aristotle, Eudemus, is reported as having said at one of his lectures that if the teaching of the Pythagoreans was to be believed then he, Eudemus, would again lecture to them as he was doing at the moment. 'You will be sitting there and I shall again be giving you my lecture with this (professorial) *baton* in my hand and everything will be exactly the same.'

This passage has been commented upon by many different writers. It is sometimes taken as meaning that following on the destruction of this world will come a new one in which everything will be the same – that is, it is taken in the Stoic way.

In such a case repetition is *in future time*, much as if having eaten food today I eat similar food *again* tomorrow and so repeat the process.

The passage from which the extract comes is found in the commentaries of Simplicius on Aristotle's Physics. 'The Pythagoreans said that the same *things* come numerically again and again. It is not out of place here to call attention to the words of Eudemus, contained in the third book of his physics, where he says: "Whether the same *time* comes, as some say and others deny, is open to question".'

That the same things, the same people, the same events, come again in the repetition of the vast cycle of the universe is comprehensible. But are we to think that *the same time* can be 'again'?

    .   .   .   .

We cannot think of time save as passing-time unless we grasp the idea of the fourth dimension. If we think of something happening *again*, we ordinarily think of it happening in the same *way* but only at *another time*. If we think that all history happens *again*, we think of it happening in some future time. We cannot help thinking *'again'*.

Our mode of thought, which is moulded on phenomenal presentation and the sequence of before, now, and after, cannot escape from treating the doctrine of apocatastasis as a recurrence of the universe in some far distant epoch which has, as yet, no kind of existence. How can we escape from this word *again* in thinking of repetition? How can repetition be in *the same time*? How can we escape from saying 'it was – and it will be, *again*'?

I have already said that if the actuality of the fourth dimension is grasped, all history becomes alive. All *is*, in this dimension, not *was* and *will* be. Every moment is. Every moment is *living*. The world extended in Time *is*. The creation of the world *is* in Time. It is all *present*.

Once we have passed to another moment, the previous moment seems to be gone for ever. But if we could re-enter the moment again we would live in it, be conscious of it. Our experience of it would be 'again'. But the moment itself would not be 'again'. it would be the same *time*. Would it not be *recurrence in always-ness*, as Ramsay saw it?

To return to the passage from Eudemus: the question is whether not only the same *things* come again and again but whether the same *time* comes. The writer says that it is obvious that the same *kind* of things come over and over again. He observes that summer is followed by winter and winter by summer. The movement of the sun produces the phenomena of solstice and equinox.

This is repetition in sequence in passing time. But the Pythagoreans held that there was another kind of repetition. There is another kind of 'again' in which the *same time* is re-experienced. 'If we are to believe the Pythagorean notions that the same things *numerically* happen again.... Then I will talk to you again (as now) sitting like this, holding the professor's staff like this, and everything will be just the same and *the time will be the same.*' Commenting on this passage A. E. Taylor says: 'That is, if all events recur, the moments at which they occur must recur too, and the numerically same moment is endlessly repeated' (A. E. Taylor, *Commentary on Plato's Timaeus*, p. 176 [footnote]. Oxford University Press, 1928). That is, I would add, repeated as regards our experience of it.

This latter kind of repetition – repetition of the same moment – is called by Ouspensky *repetition in eternity*. The moment is indestructible, ever existing, and so in this sense, ever eternal. In his comments on the Eudemus passage he says: 'These two kinds of repetition, which Eudemus called repetition in the natural order of things and repetition in the number of existences, are repetition in time and repetition in eternity. It follows from this that the Pythagoreans distinguished between these two ideas, which are confused by modern Buddhists and were also confused by Nietzsche' ('Eternal Recurrence' in *The New Model of the Universe*, p. 469).

The number of existences in the same moment is the repetition of the life in that moment of time. The moment itself is always in existence, and all that belongs to it – all the thoughts, emotions, spoken words, actions, sensations – are re-experienced, re-lived, i.e. the moment is re-entered.

.   .   .   .

To return again to the Stoic point of view – which is, so to speak, the most elementary view of recurrence. Their *Magnus Annus*, or Great Year – the period of the complete cycle of the world from beginning to end – was estimated as being 365 x 18,000=6,570,000 years. But several other estimates of the Great Year existed in ancient times.

Since the Stoic view of recurrence is limited to the recurrence of the world on a vast scale, according to it all the course of history repeats itself *once* with every revolution in time, so that every person, thing and event recurs once with every revolution. After a vast lapse of time and after a cycle of vast changes, Columbus again discovers America, Napoleon again marches east, Belgium is again invaded. The same things are again said, the same things done – *once* [more] with every revolution of the cycle. All reappears in its due season, in the World-Time. The Stoics had no clear idea about Time as an actual fourth dimension. The world as it exists in the present moment was for them, I think, its only existence.

All the effects of the future lay in the tensions existing in *matter* in the present moment. The idea that man could recur *more frequently than the cycle of the world's history* was, therefore, not conceivable to them. Man is – from the Stoic view of recurrence – nothing but a creature of World-Time, brought into being and destroyed by the vast processes of cyclic repetition of the universe.

His 'time' is a function of world-time – an infinitesimally minute part of all *Time*, from our point of view.

With this view the nightmare sense of infinity paralyses the

190

imagination. The Medusa appears. Man, the minute, is overwhelmed by the immeasurably vast.

What is man's life compared to the life of the whole Universe?

If man's life is nothing but a minute part of the life of the whole world, if he is inserted into the cycle of all the Universe so that his appearance and reappearance is dependent upon the gigantic cosmic processes that belong to the Universe, what chance has he of altering anything in his destiny?

.   .   .   .

A hint that Plato appears to give rescues us from the power of this false conception. The life of man is not *commensurable* with the life of the world. Just as the conception of time as a straight line, endlessly going on, produces wrong forms of thought (and emotion), so the confounding of man's life with the life of the whole world has the same effect.

Everything in time moves round in a circle, but man's time is not the world's time. *Man's time is his own* and his recurrence is in terms of his own circle in time and his aeon.

The aeon of the World, and man's aeon, though related in manifestation in time, are separate and distinct and man repeats his *period* independently of the period of manifestation of the aeon of the World.

It is obvious that unless there is a higher dimensional WORLD – unless Time itself is – this will be impossible. If the present moment contains all existence, this present moment must be shared by all creation equally. There will be nothing else, no other 'place'. It will be impossible to conceive of different scales, different periods, different fourth dimensions; and if there be such a thing as recurrence, the Stoic view will be the only possible one.

In a description of the creation of mankind given by Plato in the *Timaeus*, each soul is connected with eternity, but is sown in time. Plato uses the following allegory. When the Creator had mixed the substance out of which souls were to be made – 'when he had wrought the whole mass, he divided it into souls of equal number with the stars, assigning each separate soul its separate star. Mounting them on these, as it were in chariots, he displayed the universe before them.... They were to be sown each in the *instrument of time* assigned it.'

They had been made on the model of the soul of the universe itself, but on being sown into bodies and appearing in time, the impressions coming through the senses produced disorder in them. 'When sensations from without break in upon them, and draw the whole volume of the soul after them', the inner structure of man is disturbed, and the ratios and proportions existing between body, soul and mind are interfered with. This is comprehensible.

Now, if man could readjust these, he became balanced, that is, having right proportions, or righteousness. 'If they should master these, their life would be righteous ... he that should live his appointed time well, should return to the abode of the star belonging to him, and live in felicity in harmony with it.'

Otherwise, each succeeding life in time tended towards a degradation of the individual. The knowledge that the soul gained before it was inserted into the 'instrument of time', when it was in contact with its 'star', was forgotten in the body.

But it was possible to reach it again. 'The soul of man is immortal and at one *time* has an end which is termed dying and at another *time* is born again, but is never destroyed ... the soul, being immortal, and having been born again many times, and having seen all things that exist, has knowledge of them all.... If a man is strenuous and does not faint,' he can reach all knowledge (through mastering his soul). This he must be taught how to do; but from another aspect 'there is no teaching but only recollection', i.e. the soul, freed from the excessive impact of the senses, can recall knowledge that is already in her.

Now let us proceed to the hints that Plato seems to give about recurrence. I mentioned that he insists upon the necessity of understanding incommensurability in order to get a right view of things (*Laws* 7.819). Speaking of what is behind his attempts to awaken his listeners to a different understanding of existence he says: 'I shall leave nothing untried until I either persuade [them] ... or achieve something that will help them in their life when they come into being again and meet with similar discussions.' His interlocutor exclaims ironically: 'You certainly have a short time in view.' The reply is: 'Nay, the time is merely nothing in comparison with all time.' Plato seems to be thinking of a different cycle of recurrence as belonging to the individual – one that is independent of and incommensurable with the world-process. (See *Republic* 6.498D.)

What is meant by '*all time*'? I think that the period of recurrence of the entire universe is all time – a certain period which includes within it all other periods, like a great wheel containing smaller ones within. In his commentary on the *Timaeus*, Proclus says that 'all souls ... have different periods, greater or less'. The soul of the world and the soul of man have different periods (*period* and *soul*, be it noted, are very closely related ideas). Over and above all these smaller periods is a great period which comprehends them all. 'All time exists in the one period of the universe ... *apocatastasis* is different to different souls, some being shorter, some being longer.' The *apocatastasis of the universe* 'has for its measure the whole extension of time and the whole evolution of it, than which there is no greater except by the "again" and the "again".'

The soul, whether we think of man's soul or the soul of the universe, is thus connected with the *period of time* that belongs to its cycle. 'The soul of the universe alone energises through the whole of time, but other souls in a part of this whole, conformably to which their *apocatastasis* is defined' – i.e. within the wheel of recurrence of the universe are smaller and smaller wheels, which have their own period of revolution. This is like the vision of Ezekiel.

Now if a man's life can repeat itself again and again in a particular part of Time, this part of Time *must always exist*. If the life of Caesar can repeat itself and is repeating itself, the part of 'history' in which it repeats itself must always exist.

It is plain that at least a four-dimensional world is necessary for this view. If only the present moment of the world has existence, the independent repetition of each individual time-circle would be impossible.

The repetition of the individual life would then be one belonging only to the repetition of all the World in passing-time.

But Plato seems to imply that his hearers may meet the same discourses in a period of time very short in comparison with 'all time'. If the historical world is extended in the dimension of Time, then all *is*, there, fitted into the *part of Time* that it belongs to, and our present moment that we experience now is merely one out of an infinite number of present moments that *are*, and numerically, are the same.

It is only in this way that we can understand how the life of every human being can repeat itself in that part of historical Time to which it belongs, more frequently than once in the circle of all time.

In another place, speaking of the great rewards that man can receive if he searches for truth, Plato appears to dwell upon the same idea.

'Such great rewards,' he says, 'cannot be obtained in a short time, and the life of man is very short. How can anything great be contracted into a small space of time? The whole time between childhood and old age is brief in comparison with all time. Rather describe it as nothing' (*Rep.* 10.608). He seems to mean that man has not enough time in one single revolution of his life to reach 'individuality'. He may get nothing more than a glimpse of what has to be done. If death ends all, of what use is this?

It must be remembered that the thought belonging to the period from which we are drawing this material had not yet been weakened by the idea that man perfects himself, or is perfected, in some state after death. It is *in life* that we have to 'perfect' ourselves. If we limit 'this life' to one single journey between birth and death there is not enough time. People give up trying, just because of this appearance of things. They do not bend the life round in a circle, but leave the whole matter to the 'hereafter'.

We cannot grasp that beyond the 'end' lies the *beginning*. Natural understanding will not conceive this. It can only conceive that beyond the end lies either nothing-ness or something entirely new.

Beyond our life we meet – our life. We cannot turn in any other direction!

· · · ·

It is obvious that Plato thought of recurrence in the light of possible development, and not merely as an incomprehensible process of eternal repetition. The circle of the life need not be traversed endlessly without change. We have seen also that Proclus regarded time as a perfecting process. Every living thing had its individual period of *apocatastasis* and moved towards its possible perfection.

Now if the same time recurs and one re-enters the same moment and changes something belonging to one's former experience of that moment, must it not follow that one changes what has been done in the former experience of that moment, *because the time is the same?* It is extraordinarily difficult to catch a glimpse of what this means. An image may assist our thought. I think, however, that the image is not satisfactory and that the crux of the matter lies in understanding what *the same time* means.

Regarding the life as a fixed circle, this figure by itself will not represent the possibilities of growth of that life. It will represent only the constant going-round of the life. But supposing a person begins to leave a trace of himself in his life, one that accumulates – what effect will this addition have on the circular process? We find in ancient thought that time is sometimes connected with the image of the *spiral*. For example, in the Mithraic religion, which so closely rivalled Christianity at the beginning of our era, *Boundless Time* was deified. In the existing representations of this god, the spiral appears as a snake wound round the body. Was recurrence a secret teaching of Mithraism? Proclus refers to people, 'who celebrate time as a god, eternal, boundless, young and old, and of a spiral form. And besides this, also, as having its essence in eternity as abiding always the same, and as possessing infinite power. For how could it otherwise comprehend the infinity of apparent time, and circularly lead all things to their former condition, and renovate them, and also recall things which become old through it, to their proper measure, as being at once comprehensive both of things that are moved in a circle, and according to a right line. For a spiral is a thing of this kind' (Proclus, *Timaeus*, p. 207). Now it is plain that a time-spiral requires three dimensions for its representation. A circle requires only two dimensions. If we think of time as a straight line, then we add one dimension above the three of space. But if we think of all lives in time as being curved and returning on themselves we need to add two dimensions over and above the three of space. And if we replace this time-circle by the figure of a spiral we require to add three dimensions of 'time' over and above the three of space.

'The three dimensions of time can be regarded as the continuation of the three dimensions of space, i.e. as the fourth, the fifth and the sixth dimensions of space. A six-dimensional space is undoubtedly an "Euclidean continuum", but of properties and forms totally incomprehensible to us. The six-dimensional form of a body

196

is inconceivable for us, and if we were able to apprehend it with our senses we should undoubtedly see and feel it as three-dimensional. Three-dimensionality is the function of our senses. Time is the boundary of our senses. Six-dimensional space is reality, the world as it is' (Ouspensky, *New Model of the Universe*, p. 426).

Six-dimensional reality, the world as it really is, 'we perceive only through the slit of our senses, touch and vision, and define as three-dimensional space, ascribing to it Euclidean properties. Every six-dimensional body becomes for us a three-dimensional body, *existing in time*, and the properties of the fifth and sixth dimensions remain for us imperceptible.'

According to Ouspensky, the three dimensions of time enter into every moment. If we picture a straight line along which past, present and future lie, this is the line of the fourth dimension. At right angles to this line is the fifth dimension and the perpetual existence of every moment is established by this dimension. The life regarded only as a circle lies, as it were, on the *surface* formed by these two dimensions. But entering this surface, and at right angles to it, is the third dimension of 'time'.

The circle of life can now be turned into a spiral. 'The fifth dimension is movement of the circle, repetition, recurrence. The sixth dimension is the way out of the circle. If we imagine that one end of the curve rises from the surface we visualise the third dimension of time, or the sixth dimension of space. The line of time becomes a spiral.'

The figure of the spiral, Ouspensky observes, 'is only a very feeble approximation to the spiral of time. It is merely its possible geometrical representation. The actual spiral of time is not analogous to any of the lines we know, for it branches off at every point. And as there can be many possibilities in every moment, so there can be many branches at every point.... A figure of three-dimensional time will appear to us in the form of a complicated structure consisting of radii diverging from every moment of time. . . .'

All these radii, taken together, form the three-dimensional continuum of time. This represents *every possibility*. If we could experience, follow, be conscious in every one of these radii, we would realise 'every possibility'.

But we only realise one possibility at a time and the line in time that our lives make is 'the line of the fulfilment of one possibility'.

'We live and think and exist on one of the lines of time. But the second and third dimensions of time, that is, the surface on which this line lies and the solid in which this surface is included, enter every moment into our life and into our consciousness ...'

We may in our dreams sometimes glimpse possibilities that belong to the moment, the directions of other branches of radii that exist but which we do not follow – this time.

All these radii, or lines of possibilities branching from every moment, form a three-dimensional continuum which Ouspensky calls the *time-solid*.

.   .   .   .

In recurrence, the same line of time will be followed that has been followed before by those people whom Ouspensky calls 'types of absolute recurrence'. The life in such cases is the same each time. But at each repetition it becomes more easy, more certain. No new events enter into the life. No other possibilities are realised.

The sameness of the lives creates in such people a kind of certainty and inevitability. They have 'a kind of ironical contempt for people who are restless and are seeking for something'.

The stability of their lives is grounded in the unchanging nature of their recurrences. They always do the same things again and again, and must do them. They think the same things and say the same things, over and over again.

Those people who rapidly attain fame and success, who rise

very quickly, are also, in Ouspensky's view, people of absolute recurrence. While they endeavour to explain their fame and success by pointing to their hard work, shrewd judgment, simple fare, etc., the real reason is that they have followed the same line life-time after life-time, and that each time success has become easier to win. What they attribute to intuition, business instinct, application, wisdom, etc., is really unconscious memory.

Ouspensky describes two other types or forms of recurrence, *descending* and *ascending*. He conceives the world of humanity as divided into three groups. The first group is that of absolute recurrence which consists of people whose lives are 'always' the same. The second group is composed of those whose lives are descending in recurrence. 'With each new life they "fall" more and more easily, offer less and less resistance. Their vital force gradually weakens. . . .'

Such lives that are descending at each recurrence cannot be stayed. The whole tendency of the accumulated past presses them down. Try as one will to help them, they slip beyond one's reach.

The third group is that composed of people whose lives are ascending. These people are those who are not hindered by their success in life. Nor are they hindered by repeated failure, or increasing weakness or violence in the life, which so often characterises the descending type. An ascending life connotes *inward change*. Unless there is capacity for such change, the life cannot change. People may be so fixed in life, so attached to their interests, sufferings, cares, anxieties, reputation, position, prestige, etc., that there is absolutely no possibility of inward change.

.   .   .   .

Ouspensky gives us two images to assist thought about change in recurrence – the spiral and the branching off of lines at every point of the spiral. Some of these branches or lines must be on the same level as the life itself, some must rise above the life and some below it. If the life changes for the worse, it must follow the descending branches and so becomes a descending spiral, and *vice versa.* If it follows branches on the same level it must remain the same quality although with variations. At every moment of the life these branches enter and I think that we have to conceive of the life as being not rigidly confined to one point, but as simultaneously following several different directions from which a resultant direction arises.

As a result the life either evolves or degenerates. Ouspensky speaks of the absolute destruction of souls that follow the descending spiral. It is, of course, impossible to know whether this is so. I do not see how it can be possible, for everything must sooner or later meet its turning-point and therefore it seems possible to think that a descending life reaches some nadir and once more enters on a spiral of ascent. The annihilation of anything in the more-dimensional world is impossible for me to imagine.

The views on time and recurrence expressed in this volume show us that we belong to our own period. Every person belongs to his period, to his part of Time which is the 'place' of his experience. He dwells in that particular part of the total fabric of living mankind extended through Time. He traverses and re-traverses this section, which is the 'house of his life'. He returns, and re-turns again, revolving in his life, in the part of Time which is its position. Here is his field of experience and here lie all the elements for his experience, realised and unrealised. The question is *how he lives* in this given field of experience, to which he returns and where he finds what he has left behind, what he has done – as when we enter a room next day and find it as we left it the previous day. But we cannot know exactly what form recurrence will take. I will meet my life again and I will meet my problems again *in some form.* I will meet the effects of what I have done and what I have not yet done. But I cannot say in what form. In the light of higher space I can understand that I will escape from nothing.

But I do not know what constitutes *payment* for what I have not done or what effect action at one point of my life in Time will have on another part, either in 'past' or 'future'.

.   .   .   .

Two apparently irreconcilable teachings about the *hereafter* reach us historically – some form of repetition of the life on the earth, and the idea of a 'beyond' – that is, a world of spirits, *another* world, a world of heaven and hell. In both these teachings the idea of judgment exists.

In the Buddhist teaching, where the idea of the repetition of the life is stressed, the form of repetition depends on whether one has lived well or evilly in the previous life on earth. But in this teaching there is also the idea of a beyond, attained through the overcoming of all the grasping desires belonging to us in life. In the Christian teaching there is only a hint of the idea of 'again becoming' (*palingenesis*) and the emphasis appears to be laid on a hereafter. Lazarus, the man who has nothing, passes to heaven. The 'rich' pass to the place of torment. Christ speaks of the wicked, those who cling to what hinders them, being cast into hell.

Swedenborg insisted that at death man became a spirit and found himself in a world exactly like this, at first sight, so much so that the man did not know that he was dead. Then according to his state of understanding, he gravitated little by little in the direction of his 'ruling love' and so passed either toward heaven or hell. If a man is sick in his soul when he dies, and has tried to do nothing to cure his sickness, he remains sick in his soul after death and gravitates to that level of the world beyond that is the objective expression of the inner state of himself.

Is it not possible that both these apparently contradictory teachings may express different sides of the truth? May not the repetition of the life on earth be one aspect of truth and the idea of the spirit of a man dwelling apart from the earth be another?

Our 'existence' may be a far wider and greater existence than we grasp. Must we confine *existence* to the present moment of time in the visible world? The idea of the fourth dimension, of higher space, changes our view of existence. We may have more existences than one existence, though our senses make us believe that we only have one existence, and a very minute one. All that we have done so far may be gathered into some spiritual existence, into a kind of spiritual sum-total, and all that we are doing now, in what we take as our sole existence, may be effecting, and may be effected by, this spiritual sum-total of existence. In that case the idea of the repetition of the life will not contradict the idea of a spiritual state following on death. The whole thing is interlocked, *one system*, beyond our logical minds and beyond any visual image by which it can be represented.

It is difficult to reconcile oneself to the view that a single life determines our lot. We seem to come toward the end of our life just when we begin to get some insight. The illusion of passing-time makes us think that we cannot change the past and that it is not worth while trying to change anything now. We may just begin to realise that we were never taught anything about how we had to live life or about what we really had to do. We probably thought that education taught us how to live, and after a long period of perplexity began to realise that we had to find out things for ourselves. Then it may seem too late. There does not seem to be time for anything and we easily give up trying to think. The whole impression of the life is a confused one. We do not think we are only *beginning* something, but merely coming to the end of something. If we believe in a judgment and a hereafter, if we believe that our final lot is determined by this single confused life we have led, the idea seems so inadequate that it tends to make us merely shrug our shoulders and turn aside from all such thoughts. It is surely here that the idea of the repetition of the life *necessarily* comes in. Death then means that we come to the end of our *Time. Life is a day.* If we thought that we had only today, and not tomorrow, would we think it worth while to undertake what we are doing at this moment? Can we not realise that we must have a *future* – that our whole being is constructed to have a *future?* Without some form of the idea of future how can we understand life, how can we possibly interpret it, save in the most negative way? And why should we confine our idea of future only to a disembodied state which many of us find difficulty in accepting? Remember that we do not live only in this little visible moment but in a world extended in every direction, visible and invisible.

      ·   ·   ·   ·

We can only understand the evolution of man in terms of recurrence. We carry with us 'no remembrance of former times' because we leave no trace, because we let everything drive us hither and thither, because we are creatures of the moment – and so do not evolve. We do not understand that evolution of ourselves is to get beyond ourselves – how little we know what this means! – and that this depends upon *memory* of ourselves.

For this reason Ouspensky connects the evolution of man with *recollection*. He says that every evolving individual *remembers* and that with this kind of remembering is connected a mysterious quality which distinguishes it from ordinary memory. But such memory is not enough in itself. 'As evolution means escaping from the wheel of the fifth dimension and passing into the spiral of the sixth dimension, recollection has importance only when it bears an active character in a certain definite direction.' It must create a definite longing for something different and lead to definite inner work – that is, inner change. Ouspensky believes that a man can complete his evolution in a particular part of Time, and that when this happens he can go *back* in Time and appear at some point in 'historical time'. Remember, that with the view of higher space in mind, the *living* past is understood. History is alive at every point.

For us, it is merely history. For us, it seems unalterable – though, of course, our estimates of it are constantly changing. But for itself it is living. It is part of the world, part of the living Age. 'We cannot leave behind us the sins of our past. We must not forget that nothing disappears. Everything is eternal. Everything that has been is still in existence. The whole history of humanity is the "history of crime", and the material for this history continually grows. We cannot go forward with such a past as ours. The past still exists, and it gives and still gives its results, creating new and ever new crimes.... Man must go back, seek for, and destroy the causes of evil however far back they lie. It is only in this idea that the hint of the possibilities of a general evolution can be found. It is only in this idea that the possibility of changing the karma of humanity lies, because changing the karma means changing the past.... There will be no possibility of thinking of *evolution of humanity*, if the possibility did not exist for individually evolving man to go into the past and struggle against the causes of the present evil which lie there' (493-494). This going into the past, and appearing in another part of Time, is not recurrence. It is re-incarnation; and this is the only re-incarnation which Ouspensky teaches, i.e. people existing now are not re-incarnations of past historical figures but some people, in what for us is the historical past, may be re-incarnations of people who existed in our part of Time.

Such as we are we can only know recurrence, and *to change our lives we must change ourselves.* Every effort towards inner change lies as a point of force in the circle of the life, affecting all the life both 'past' and 'future'.

·   ·   ·   ·

The original Orphic-Bacchic teaching, which lies beyond the dawn of our European civilisation, contained the idea of the repetition of our earthly existence and the necessity of freeing the soul from bondage to the experiences of life in order to escape from the wheel of existence. Pindar says that those who 'through three lives can stand fast under trial' reach the Isles of the Blest. Plato refers to a triple repetition, the soul being shown *samples of lives* before incarnation and making a choice.

Proclus, referring to this choice of lives says that the soul chooses the same kind of life *by habit*, because it does not retain any clear memory and judgment. But he adds that whatever the choice of life may be the soul may subsequently live well or ill within it.

Whittaker observes that the most distinctive thought of Proclus is that for the perfection of the universe and of each soul all possibilities must be realised 'and that the possibilities can be completely realised in no one life even when it chooses and finds the best'. In the myth of Er, Plato shows that the idea of the repetition of the life and the idea of another world beyond this to which the souls go at death were both included in the same teaching. The soul has choice, but it chooses according to habit. ['Most curious,' he said, 'was the spectacle – sad and laughable and strange. For the choice of the souls was in most cases based upon the experiences of the previous life.' *Rep.* 620.] There is an Orphic fragment which refers to the incalculable value of memory, i.e. memory of the life. The 'impure and uninitiated soul' passes into *Lethe*. It passes into sleep and forgetfulness. It cannot remember what it is (just as we, in the little death of nightly sleep, usually lose ourselves). In the Orphic ritual the soul says: 'Give me quickly to drink of the cold water of the Lake of Memory.' The individual identity is then restored – the soul knows itself and remembers.

The doctrine of recurrence teaches that the moment of death

is the moment of birth. That the life is re-entered where it stands in Time, and choice for us lies *in this life*. Only by remembering can we make choice. The life can ascend through right choice and right memory – and, it must be added, right knowledge and right ideas. Such memory can eventually extend to memory of lives. The evolving man *remembers*.

CHAPTER NINE

TWO PSYCHOLOGICAL SYSTEMS
IN MAN

To think about time, etc., ideas are necessary which collide at all points with our ordinary notions. Actually, we think from a reversed direction. What does this mean and upon what grounds are we going?

We have seen that the truest feeling of self-existence is connected with a form of consciousness in which the time-sense is altered. Also, in this form of consciousness the universe seems to be 'in our brain'. Ordinary consciousness (which gives no true feeling of self-existence, of life in oneself) turns things the other way round. The world is outside us and our feeling of existence comes from the changing feelings of pleasure and pain, derived from our contact with it.

As Ramsay experienced these two states of consciousness they presented themselves as complete contradictions. It would appear that *two* psychological systems exist in us each starting from a different point and acting, as it were, in opposite directions – from *outer*, and from *inner*.

In that class of literature of the seventeenth century which deals with the inner nature of man we actually find diagrams which apparently refer to these two psychological systems. Let us look at a diagram made by Robert Fludd in a work entitled *Utriusque Cosmi* (1617).

Here are two triangles which represent something in man's constitution. In one the apex is downwards, in the other, upwards. We are at once reminded of the double triangles in the hieroglyph called the seal of Solomon, representing the three dimensions of space and the three dimensions of 'time' according to Ouspensky.

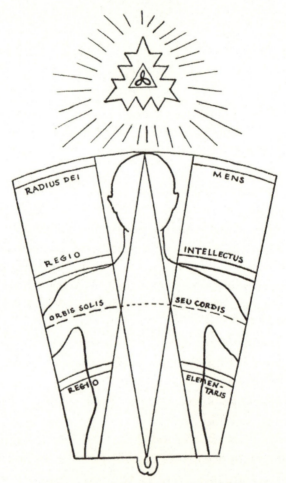

After Robert Fludd: Utriusque Cosmi, 1617

As regards the triangle with its base downwards Fludd (in another diagram) divides it from below into *body, vital spirits,* and *reason.* The reason touches the base of the upper triangle at a point in the level which Fludd denotes as *mind,* i.e. the highest use of a man's ordinary reason touches the level of mind (*mens*). It is, however, merely a *point* in 'mind'. The upper triangle terminates

208

in man's *sex* as a point. We might say, then, that there is a point in man's reason and a point in man's sex that connect him with a level of consciousness on a higher scale than his ordinary one. But each is a mere point or little door in the other.

Taking only the two bases of the triangles, upper and lower, we can consider them as lines representing two levels of consciousness. But it would be better to say that two *systems* of consciousness are represented by the two overlying triangles. With these two distinct psychological orientations in man I would connect Ramsay's experiences. Ether takes him out of one into the other. He then sees everything the other way round. He has a new feeling of *I*. In the same way can Tennyson's experience be explained, as well as all the experiences of new forms of consciousness described in this book. The triangle with the base upwards, ending below at the point on the level of sex, is related to the three time-dimensions of the 'invisible world'. When consciousness is situated in this system the sense of the life extended in Time, the sense of eternity and of recurrence, and the sense of self-existence, may all appear. They belong to the higher system which is concealed in man. When man is in his natural state he is in the psychological system represented by the triangle with the base downwards. So if we study 'natural' man we will find only this system in him. But, psychologically considered, man cannot be taken in terms only of one system. Some extraordinary *paradox* exists within his being. Another system is latent in him whose mode of action is in a reversed direction to the natural system, working from above downwards. If we are willing to follow this interpretation it means that *fully integrated* man must be some combination of these two systems. Man is the ground in which two systems meet. They represent a paradox, a cross, something extremely difficult to bring into union – above all something which must be roused into activity, because 'natural' man is adequate to life and need not know the action of this second system. The task is to *bring these two systems into relationship* – not to seek one at the expense of the other. All the experiences we have quoted merely show the existence of another psychological orientation. That is all. Ramsay finds himself in one system and then in another – and as such they appear totally contradictory. The integration of man must be the reconciliation of these two systems and this must mean the *gradual* awakening to the other system while remaining in contact with life. The principles belonging to the other system – the new sense of time, of I, of recurrence, must be related to life.

The highest point of 'natural' reason touches the level of such ideas, i.e. that which is best in our thought can touch another order of understanding. And similarly the highest point of sex opens in the same direction.

.   .   .   .

Plato says that when we start out on the path of knowledge we become more and more uncertain about all those things we were certain about, and more and more certain about all those things we were uncertain about. We begin to undergo some sort of reversal. At a certain point moments of illumination occur. 'Fire bursts forth' (*Epistle* VII). Let us call this the birth of the *active* mind, and connect it with the awakening of the second triangle or system in man. We understand so far that the attempt to grasp time differently has a clear purpose in view. It is to stimulate the activity of the second psychological system, for which it is necessary to think from the direction of *ideas*. We also understand that to awaken this system we must have new conceptions of 'reality'. It remains asleep in us as long as we take things for granted and are merged in the world of appearances. Since the two systems in man are respectively turned towards *visible* and *invisible*, we realise that the 'visible' will not fulfil us. It will never give us our complete significance. There must enter into us something from another direction. Our 'certainties' must become less matters of fact. Our fixed opinions must be loosened. It is especially the feeling we are right that we must suspect. We can imagine that such feelings confine us to the lower triangle. Also, since there are two systems in us, energies that should go in the direction of the higher system must cause some over-action of the lower system. As we are, we must be a *confusion* of the two systems.

Now all ideas that help us to conceive higher space touch the higher system. To grasp time differently, with the *individual* thought and feeling, brings us towards the higher system, because this system has not our time-sense, nor the notions that the lower system has. All the emotions and thoughts that belong to the upper system must be incommensurable with those of the lower. They are another world – yet one entering this world of the lower system. In a sense, one is discontinuous with the other, yet they are linked at two points. The *full* working of both systems would mean consciousness in ALL – in a six-dimensional world. The memory of all the life – or rather the direct knowledge of it – and the knowledge of recurrences would enter consciousness. Our present-momented psychology would be annihilated through being absorbed into something infinitely greater. Yet we would still be in life – but certain where before we were uncertain, and uncertain where we were before certain.

. . . .

Understanding the manifested world as only a *part* of an unmanifested world, it is then to be taken as that degree of *All* which appears to exist outside man as sensible environment. All that portion which remains unmanifested is that side of *All* with which man communicates internally.

The object of 'stilling the senses' is to awaken the interior perception of unmanifested realities, manifested reality lying outside us, in that portion of the *All* that our senses give us. A higher conscious level (or the awakening of the second system) will therefore mean that we include far more of the WORLD, i.e. Totality, and so of OURSELVES, than we do when in the ratio which the natural level of consciousness gives us between manifest and unmanifest. Regarded in this way we can think that the unmanifested degrees of the WORLD lie within man as a series of possible inward experiences (mental transformations) reached through fuller consciousness and perceived as 'internal truth' or whatever other term we prefer to call it.

Natural man, then, is defined by his conscious state. We, as 'natural', are a particular *ratio* between manifested and unmanifested, one common to the level of consciousness we have. But if there be higher degrees of consciousness, man is capable of striking new ratios, and of seeing and understanding things that we, as 'natural' men, will not comprehend, because this new ratio will only exist for himself and in himself. Thus, for us, his 'logic' will not be our logic, and his viewpoints will not be like ours; nor will his opposites be our opposites. He may therefore be easily incomprehensible to us, for where we see nothing he sees something; and where we see contradiction, because we are in parts, he may see harmony because, relatively to us, he sees *more* – more wholly, more of the WHOLE. All expansion of consciousness means a more comprehensive viewpoint, one that includes what for us, with our limited consciousness, will appear as opposites – and remaining opposites for us, hold us back. The opening of higher degrees of consciousness will not therefore be a process that will conform to our general ideas of things. There will always be something strange and difficult to understand belonging to it.

If all new understanding were *commensurable* with old understanding we could conceive that any right development of man, through which his sense of *I* gradually became connected with that *I* which belongs to the level of consciousness above our common one, would not involve any *reversal*. A man would not have to begin again, but would need merely to expand his natural understanding and knowledge little by little. But consider for a moment: will any continuous expansion of our natural understanding ever bring us to a new ratio, or to the idea of higher space? Do not all ideas that can create a new ratio reach us from a different direction from any that belong to our natural ratio, and so imply *reversal*? Reversal in what sense? In the sense of beginning to think from *ideas* that can grow in all directions in consciousness, altering one's standpoint in a thousand and one ways. Thinking thus we do not think from sensory evidence, or follow the logic that is turned outwards towards phenomena and is ever seeking to establish *one* chain of cause and effect in the shadow-life of temporal experience.

.   .   .   .

What exists in dreams at the sleep level ceases to exist in dayconsciousness. When we awaken the outer world is around us and the imaginary world of dreams disappears. Is there not discontinuity in this? Suppose that we could awaken still further – awaken out of this day-consciousness into the kind of consciousness that Tennyson awoke into. Would not our trouble vanish, actually cease *to be able* to exist? And would not this be discontinuity? Have we not some right to say that all increase of reality must necessitate what must appear to us as discontinuous steps, like the rungs of a ladder, and that there cannot be any gradual growth of our present knowledge and understanding, turning into a wider knowledge and a broader understanding, but rather something in the nature of sudden revelations of truth, sudden moments of insight which turn us right around and give us new and even quite *reversed* meanings?

.   .   .   .

Perhaps we do not realise how much was taught in the known historical past concerning the connection between greater reality of being and higher states of consciousness. I will give in the following pages some further material relating to the question of levels, beginning with a full account of Plato's myth of the Cave, which I referred to briefly in the third chapter. Let us remember that this belongs to the fourth century B.C.

'And now,' I said, 'let me show in a figure how far our nature is enlightened or unenlightened: Behold! human beings living in an underground den, which has a mouth open towards the light and reaching all along the den; here they have been from their childhood, and have their legs and necks chained so that they cannot move, and can only see before them, being prevented by the chains from turning round their heads. Above and behind them a fire is blazing at a distance, and between the fire and the prisoners there is a raised way; and you will see, if you look, a low wall built along the way, like the screen which marionette players have in front of them, over which they show the puppets.' 'I see.' 'And do you see,' I said, 'men passing along the wall carrying all sorts of vessels, and statues and figures of animals made of wood and stone and various materials, which appear over the wall? Some of them are talking, others silent.' 'You have shown me a strange image, and they are strange prisoners.' 'Like ourselves,' I replied; 'and they see only their own shadows, or the shadows of one another, which the fire throws on the opposite wall of the cave?' 'True,' he said. 'How could they see anything but the shadows if they were never allowed to move their heads?' 'And of the objects which are being carried in like manner they would only see the shadows?' 'Yes,' he said. 'And if they were able to converse with one another, would they not suppose that they were naming what was actually before them?' 'Very true.' 'And suppose further that the prison had an echo which came from the other side, would they not be sure to fancy when one of the passers-by spoke that the voice which they heard came from the passing shadow?' 'No question,' he replied. 'To them,' I said, 'the truth would be literally nothing but the shadows of the images.' 'That is certain.' 'And now look again, and see what will naturally follow if the prisoners are released and disabused of their error. At first, when any of them is liberated and compelled suddenly to stand up and turn his neck round and look towards the light, he will suffer sharp pains; the glare will distress him, and he will be unable to see the realities of which in his former state he had seen the shadows; and then conceive some one saying to him, that what he saw before was an illusion, but that now, when he is approaching nearer to being and his eye is turned towards more real existence, he has a clearer vision, – what will be his reply? And you may further imagine that his instructor is pointing to the objects as they pass and requiring him to name them, – will he not be perplexed? Will he not fancy that the shadows which he formerly saw are truer than the objects which are now shown to him?' 'Far truer.' 'And if he is compelled to look straight at the light, will he not have a pain in his eyes which will make him turn away to take refuge in the objects of vision which he can see, and which he will conceive to be in reality clearer than the things which are now being shown to him?' 'True,' he said. 'And suppose once more, that he is reluctantly dragged up a steep and rugged ascent, and held fast until he is forced into the presence of the sun himself, is he not likely to be pained and irritated? When he approaches the light his eyes will be dazzled, and he will not be able to see anything at all of what are now called realities.' 'Not all in a moment,' he said. 'He will require to grow accustomed to the sight of the upper world. And first he will see the shadows best, next the reflections of men and other objects on the water, and then the objects themselves; then he will gaze upon the light of the moon and the stars and the spangled heaven; and he will see the sky and the stars by night better than the sun or the light of the sun by day?' 'Certainly.' 'Last of all he will be able to see the sun, and not mere reflections of him in the water, but he will see him in his own proper place, and not in another; and he will contemplate him as he is.' (*Dialogues of Plato*, Rep.VII. 514: Jowett's Translation. Oxford University Press.)

In his comments on this passage, Robin says: '... Every degree in either scale is an "imitation" or "image" of the degree above. Between the absolute not-being of total ignorance and the absolute being and supreme knowledge, there is a whole ladder of intermediate stages – fictitious copies of ideal realities by sensible nature, the symbolical objects of science between these copies and their patterns and lastly the Good which rules the intelligible world and gives it life, the Good whose image in respect of the sensible world is the Sun.... All these relations are put in concrete form by the famous myth of the Cave. With our thought in bondage to conditions of birth and upbringing, we are the captives, unable to move since our infancy, with our eyes perforce fixed on the back of the cave. The steep, stony path rising to the entrance symbolises the difficulty of determining the nature and origin of our opinions. The great fire outside, which illuminates the cave with a vague light, is the sun, and the marionettes whose shadows are cast on the back are physical objects which are certainly artificial things. The real actors remain hidden behind the screen. The prisoners hear the echo of their voices, and take it for the language of truth, being chiefly intent on observing and remembering how the shadows on the wall appear together or in succession. When a prisoner drags himself or is dragged out of his cave, his dazzled eyes can make out nothing. To use them he has to be content with the "reflected image" of things. This symbolises the ascent of the soul towards truth.' (Léon Robin, *Greek Thought*, 1928. Translated by M. R. Dobie.)

Concerning the allegory, Plato himself says: 'The prison-house is the world of sight (of the senses), the light of the fire is the sun, and you will not misapprehend me if you interpret the journey upwards to be the ascent of the soul, into the world intelligible to the mind, according to my poor belief, which at your desire I have expressed – whether rightly or wrongly, God knows. But whether true or false, my opinion is that in the world of knowledge the idea of good appears last of all, and is seen only with an effort' (*Rep*. VII).

.   .   .   .

Let us turn to other conceptions of levels, not making any attempt to collate them, but seeking only the same general idea running through them all. There are some valuable remarks on levels to be found in Swedenborg's writings, which we can draw out of the mass of other material that does not enter into our discussion. He calls attention to two different kinds of degrees that apply to the inner psychical nature of man, remarking that we cannot understand a man's psychology unless we realise that these two different kinds of degrees exist. He calls them degrees of *extension* and degrees of *ascent*.

I remind the reader here of what was said about dimensions. We can extend a line as far as we like but it will never 'ascend' into a square or a cube. The gradual increase or decrease of heat or cold, light or shade, belongs, Swedenborg says, to degrees of *extension*. They are continuous. In the same way if we increase our knowledge of a subject, such as history or chemistry, we merely extend our knowledge by degrees of extension, but do not thereby strike into another order of knowledge. Degrees of ascent are *discontinuous*, i.e. inwardly experienced, they correspond to entirely *new* states of the individual. The perfecting of man, we are told, is a question of these degrees of *ascent*, not of extension. 'We are not speaking of the perfection of life, forces, and forms as increasing or decreasing according to the degrees of extension or continuity, because these degrees are generally known; but as ascending or descending according to the degrees of ascent, or discrete (discontinuous) degrees; because these degrees are not known. But how perfection ascends and descends according to these (discontinuous) degrees, can be but little known from things visible in the natural world.' The right study of things in the natural world, however, leads us only to the realisation that the more intimately they are examined the more wonderful their contents appear. 'From the former we learn only the more intimately they are examined the more wonderful their contents appear. Take for example the eyes, ears, tongue, muscles, heart, lungs, liver, pancreas, kidneys, and other viscera, also seeds, fruits, and flowers, and metals, minerals, and stones; it is well-known that the more these are examined the greater the wonders disclosed. Yet an ignorance of discrete degrees has concealed the fact that all these things have a still greater inward perfection according to degrees of ascent, or discrete degrees.'

The whole universe is constructed on the principle of degrees of extension and degrees of discontinuity. That part of the universe that is perceptible to the senses – the world in space and time, and that part of the universe that is outside space and time and so is not perceptible to the senses, are constructed of 'one only substance' which proceeding 'by means of atmospheres according to continuous degrees or those of extension, and at the same time, according to those of discrete degrees, or those of ascent, causes the variety of all things in the created universe'. This cannot be understood, he says, 'unless all idea of space be set aside, for otherwise appearances must necessarily give rise to fallacies'.

These discontinuous degrees upon which the universe is framed exist also in man regarded as a microcosmos and an image of the macrocosmos. In natural man, only the lowest degree is open, so that he understands everything in a certain way. Swedenborg asserts that there are three *discontinuous* degrees in man. This 'triple ascent of discrete degrees' also exists in the greatest and least things. 'They exist in every man by birth and may be opened successively. Each degree of ascent has also degrees of extension, or continuous degrees, according to which it increases by continuity.' When a man is born, he comes first into the state of the natural degree, and this is developed by *continuity* as he acquires various kinds of knowledge and so develops his intelligence 'until he reaches the highest degree of such intelligence which is called rationality. Nevertheless the second or spiritual degree is still closed. It can only be opened by a love of use derived from intellectual considerations, but this must be a spiritual love of use, which is the same thing as the love of neighbour.' This writer observes that: 'There is a difference between scientific truth (i.e. truth which is merely lodged in the memory, whether it relates to religion or to other subjects), *rational* truth, and *intellectual* truth, and they are successively attained. *Scientific* truth is mere knowledge, *rational* truth is scientific truth confirmed by the reason, *intellectual* truth involves an inward perception that the thing believed is true' (*Arcana Coelestia*).

As an example of what he means by discontinuous degrees he asks us to think of *end*, *cause* and *effect*. The *end* is the source of everything that exists in the *cause* and the end of everything that exists in the *effect*. The end, or aim 'must put forth something in which the cause may exist and, that it may be the source of everything that exists in the effect, there must be in the effect something derived from the end, through the cause in which it may be.... These three, namely, end, cause, and effect, exist in the greatest and least things.' He describes three levels of meaning or understanding – thinking from ends, thinking from causes, and thinking from effects. 'Take note, that it is one thing to think *from* ends, and another thing to think *of* ends, also it is one thing to think *from* causes and another thing to think *of* causes; and again it is one thing to think *from* effects and another to think *of* effects.... To think from ends is the method of wisdom, from causes that of intelligence, and from effects that of knowledge. From this it may be seen that all perfection increases in and according to the ascent to higher degrees.'

.   .   .   .

To turn back to older sources: in the Hermetic literature of the third century A.D. we find a passage in which three degrees of *knowledge* are spoken of – divine, cosmic and human. The divine mind is 'wholly filled with all things imperceptible to sense and with all embracing knowledge ... the cosmic mind is the recipient of all sensible forms and of all kinds of knowledge of sensible things. The human mind is dependent on the retentiveness of man's memory, that is, on his remembrance of all his past experiences. The divine mind *descends in the scale of being as far as man.* The knowledge which corresponds to the character and extent of the human mind is based wholly on man's memory of the past; it is the retentiveness of his memory that has given him dominion over the earth. The knowledge which corresponds to the nature and character of the cosmic mind is such as can be procured from all sensible (perceptible) things in the cosmos. But the knowledge which corresponds to the character of the divine mind – this knowledge, and this alone, is truth: and of this truth not the faintest outline or shadow is discernible in the (perceptible) cosmos. For where things are discerned at intervals of Time there is falsehood; and where things have an origin in Time, there errors arise.' (*Hermetica*, Asclepius III, p. 355.)

From this standpoint, there is an ordinary knowledge, with the meanings related to it, that man naturally possesses through his memory of his past experiences. There is a second kind of knowledge that he can reach by study of the visible universe in which he lives. There is a third kind of knowledge that reaches as far as man, which he does not make contact with in any ordinary way. So, according to this exposition, ordinary knowledge, scientific knowledge, and the third kind of knowledge form, as it were, three degrees, or levels, and the third kind of knowledge is not commensurable with the other kinds. It was called 'eternal' (aeonian). The other kinds of knowledge are connected with time and with the world as it is perceptible to our senses.

The third kind of knowledge, from this interpretation, is therefore not from the senses. It is from *mind*. It is not acquired from outside, though preparation for it comes from this direction. It was called *active*, while all the other forms of knowledge, acquired through sense, were called *passive*. 'Everything that has sensation is passively affected. The good is the voluntary: the bad is the involuntary. Nothing in heaven is in bondage. Nothing on earth is free' (*Hermetica*, Exc. XI).

We find traces of the same idea of degrees of knowledge, discontinuous with one another, in the writings of the early church Fathers. Speaking of the interpretation of the Scriptures, Origen says, 'The weakness of our understanding is unable to trace out the secret and hidden meaning in each individual word.... Men make little effort to exercise their intellect, or they imagine they possess knowledge before they really learn, the consequence being that they never begin to have knowledge.... The prophetic style is allowed by all to abound in figures and enigmas. What do we find when we come to the Gospels? Is there not hidden there an inner, also a divine sense? ... The way, then, as it appears to us, in which we ought to deal with the Scriptures, and extract from them their meaning, is the following, which has been ascertained from the Scriptures themselves. By Solomon in the Proverbs we find some such rule as this enjoined respecting the divine doctrines of Scripture: "And do thou portray them in a threefold manner, in counsel and knowledge, to answer words of truth to them who propose them to thee." The individual ought, then, to portray the ideas of holy Scripture in a threefold manner upon his own soul; in order

221

that the simple man may be edified by the "flesh", as it were, of the Scripture, for so we name the obvious sense; while he who has ascended a certain way (may be edified) by the "soul", as it were. The perfect man, again, and he who resembles those spoken of by the apostle, when he says, "We speak wisdom among them that are perfect, but not the wisdom of the world, nor of the rulers of this world, who come to nought; but we speak the wisdom of God in a mystery, the hidden wisdom, which God hath ordained before the ages, unto our glory", (may receive edification) from the spiritual law, which has a shadow of good things to come. For as man consists of body, and soul, and spirit, so in the same way does Scripture' (*De Principiis*, IV.1).

.   .   .   .

In the system of Richard, the Scottish prior (twelfth century), we find the psychical activities of man divided into *six* grades, or levels. He divides these grades into pairs. The lowest pair belongs to the imagination (and sense) and of this pair the lower is not touched by reason at all, while the upper is influenced by reason, but is not reason. The second pair belongs to reason, and its lower element inclines to imagination and uses its images, while the upper is our logical reason itself which is capable of abstract thinking. Of the highest pair the lower degree is above the logical reason and not of the same order, yet it is not outside it. It is like reason, only higher; therefore necessarily more comprehensive. Finally the highest degree of all, the higher element of the third pair, whose lower is akin to reason, is outside the influence of reason, and indeed appears contrary to it. [As I said, we constantly meet with this view that there is a degree of conscious understanding contrary to our ordinary reason, or 'anti-human', as Sebastian Franck terms it.]

Now we must connect the *active* mind with the upper degrees of this psychical ladder in man and the passive mind with the lower degrees. The passive mind is influenced by all that comes in through the senses. The highest aspects of it use ideas and concepts derived from sensory experience – 'natural ideas'. The material of the active mind cannot be thought of in the same way. Its material begins with self-recognition (which is not derived from our senses). I would classify all those peculiar moments of understanding that come to us at times, in which we catch glimpses of an order of truth that cannot be demonstrated materially, as belonging to traces of the working of 'active mind'.

The realisation that one is invisible is of this order. Tennyson's experience is of this order. To realise the remarkable thing that *one is oneself* and can be no one else is of this order. It would be possible to collect a great number of such experiences, only they can scarcely be described because the meaning behind them cannot be conveyed in words – except to anyone who has had a similar experience. Actually, these moments are of more importance than anything else in life. When such experiences take an outward form – when we *see* a person or any object in a sudden and absolutely new way, it is the awakened mind that sees through the eyes.

We must remember that it is not a matter of the senses themselves. With the senses *we* see very little. When the mind sees inwardly the truth of something for the first time, this 'seeing' is of the same quality as the seeing of something outside in a new way. Such traces of active mind are one's *own* experience; they always give deeper understanding, momentarily; they are difficult, or impossible, to describe; they remain in a special part of the memory and have special associations; they are affirmative and undeniable at the moment of experience (though later we may doubt them, because the passive mind takes away their meaning); and they are connected with the 'unity of everything', although we may not notice this. I give a few examples: 'I suddenly saw the reason for everything'; 'I realised that no one knew anything'; 'I saw my hand for the first time'; 'I suddenly knew that it did not matter'; 'I saw I could only be myself'. These phrases convey very little to us. Yet they are descriptions of the experiences of different people who saw something quite unusual.

In all such moments our understanding *has power over us*. I mean that at such moments we 'see' from the authority of our own understanding, and not from what we believe to be right, not from what we think we ought to think, not from opinion, imitation, or habit. But a moment later this special kind of insight is swallowed up and we are no longer ourselves, no longer separated from the effects of things upon us which enter through our senses. The conviction of our insight passes; something quite definite has happened. What has happened? We can say that the passive has replaced the momentary activity of the active mind. Consciousness has changed its level in the psychical ladder. In terms of Fludd's triangles consciousness belonging to the upper triangle has been replaced by the form of consciousness belonging to the lower.

.   .   .   .

I have already mentioned the modern views of Hughlings Jackson about levels. Neurological teaching is aware of the existence of levels. In connection with Jackson's views – that the various manifestation of nervous disorder cannot be regarded merely from the standpoint of the nervous tissue that is destroyed or functionally out of use, but must also be considered from the side of what remains, – I wrote in 1918: 'What remains is now over-active. The fact that the schoolmaster is away will lead to uproar in the classroom' ('Conception of Regression in Psychological Medicine', *Lancet*, June 8, 1918). The uproar is the manifest side of the clinical picture; the absence of the schoolmaster is the silent side. From this idea of superior and inferior modes of function arose the general conception of psychological *regression* – that is, that under certain circumstances inferior modes of function become active apart from actual destruction of tissues. A person becomes a baby. But as I said before, the evolutionary standpoint does not give us the idea that still *higher* levels exist in us. On the psychological side Jackson spoke of two levels – the dream and the waking levels. Neurologically, a study of the cortex of the brain shows the existence of several levels of nerve-cells, more or less defined, but we do not really know what functions they subserve. I have already mentioned that there is some evidence to show that we do not use the brain as a whole.

On the psychological side the teaching of Jung has emphasised the necessity for man to reach individuation through the 'balancing of his functions'. Modern life makes him one-sided, in such a way that his unexpressed functions continually hamper him. He derives little pleasure from his work. To become 'normal', man must become balanced in such a way that thinking, feeling, sensation, and intuition play equal parts in his life. Man is sick because one or another function usurps the place of the rest. But looking back on the insight I gained through this teaching I realise that I did not understand that a man must strive towards a higher degree of consciousness to make it possible for the functions in him to reach any state of balance. I had the idea of 'normal' man only in an ordinary sense – which is insufficient because it implies, or rather implied to me, ordinary standards and viewpoints merely intensified and not absolutely new forms of understanding. That is, it implied to me continuous degrees of extension, not discrete degrees. I imagined that unity of being could be reached within the customary state of consciousness. I believed, in other words, that a radical change of being could take place *as one was*, merely through some adjustments. This is probably what most of us think, for we do not realise that in order to change anything in ourselves everything else must change, lest

225

by trying to change one thing we create wrong results in other directions. Change of being is not a patchwork process. All sorts of minor modifications are no doubt possible in people without necessarily harmful results. A person talks over his troubles with some one and feels the better for it. But for any real change that is going to be permanent, the whole standpoint has to change and for this a new understanding of the WORLD is necessary, as well as quite new sorts of effort in connection with oneself. In this respect I had no idea, save in so far as I saw that psychological regression was a movement backwards in the *life* itself, that a different understanding of time was necessary, in order to loosen deeply ingrained emotional and mental habits which otherwise cannot be loosened. It was only later that I realised the necessity of starting afresh, through a form of teaching which gave entirely new standpoints. Above all it was necessary to throw aside those evolutionary ideas that are impressed upon everyone who undergoes a scientific training, for taken by *themselves* they make it impossible to believe in an existing but unused higher structure in man, since they emphasise the view that everything that man possesses has been the result of a natural selection of serviceable variations in the past, occurring through immediate response to environment. We have, of course, always the difficulty of defining what *environment* really means. Today we have to take into account the enormous quantity of radiations with which the universe is filled and whose action on man, apart from that of light, is unknown.

.   .   .   .

From the standpoint of this volume we are living in a world of certain definite limitations as regards higher space – an abridged reality sectioned out to our weak experience. It is one of the characteristics of this abridged reality that it gives the illusion that *we can escape* from everything through passing-time. Now this is thinking according to the passive mind. It requires an act of mental creation to bring the dimension of Time itself into existence and realise that we can neither escape from anything nor lose anything. This act of creation is a form of thinking which can awaken the active mind – *which understands Time*. I must repeat that we do not and cannot understand *Time* with the passive mind; nor do we *understand* about it through any theories about dimensions. But unless we make the effort to think in that direction, and build a scaffolding of some kind, inner direct perceptions about Time will not be likely to reach us. We are supposing that it is possible to attract the action of the active mind by preparing the passive mind for it and as I said (following Fludd and Richard) we can imagine that the highest range of the passive mind takes on something of the qualities belonging to the active mind, as by descent of the higher into the lower. In dealing with this subject, indeed, Swedenborg makes the striking observation, which I do not pretend to understand, that the *natural* understanding can rise to the topmost of the three discontinuous degrees that he divides the mind into. In such a case, a man would be able to have far more than ordinary knowledge, but it would not be real because it would not influence him authoritatively, i.e. by that conviction of truth which characterises the working of the active mind; and a man will only believe in it through his self-love, when he is talking about it to others. He will not believe it when he is alone.

I said before that any proof, plainly demonstrable to sense, of higher reality would be contrary to the nature of Man. The active mind would, in that case, not be called into play. We would see with outer sense what we have to understand with inner sense. Knowing or seeing by understanding is a far more real experience than any external seeing. Since the passive mind works in connection with the senses, it is not itself the true site of this invisible *oneself*, which is capable of different degrees of understanding things that are distinct from external fact. I must beg the reader to remember that the inner perception of truth, or knowing by understanding, is something quite different from external truth, which is lodged in the outer mind and relates to the size, position, weight, etc., of objects. Such facts as the latter never really influence the spirit of a man. They never can change us. They are essential in all our external relationships to life but they do not fill those inner cisterns which, when they run dry, make life entirely barren and meaningless. The kind of knowledge which we get from such facts does not have the power over us that understanding from the active mind has, when there is a moment of insight or revelation.

Now the ordinary education which we receive in life can be thought of as developing the *passive* mind. It is gained through the senses from outside. We learn a great many 'facts' – not noticing as a rule that these so-called 'facts' are constantly changing just as everything else does in time. For we take these facts in an absolute sense, and in later life are inclined to be offended if they are exploded. I mentioned in an early chapter the inner rigidity we fall into. Now there has always existed the idea of a second education, one not given by life, and not based on shifting knowledge, but on a permanent knowledge concerning the nature of Man. If we say that the ordinary education of life is to lead forth the passive mind, we might formulate the nature of this second education as a process, involving ideas and methods of a particular kind, whose object is to lead forth the active mind.

In connection with this strange subject we find a special idea – that man only becomes *free* through his active understanding. If we recall the psychical ladder of Richard, we can perceive that the upper levels are furthest from sense-interpretation – whatever we understand by that. It was held that sense-interpretation – which I suppose we can call materialism or positivism – bound a man. This interesting idea, mentioned before, is clearly expressed in the following passage: 'The intelligible substance, if it is drawn near to God, has power over itself.... If it falls away, it chooses the corporeal world and in that way becomes subject to Necessity which rules the Kosmos' (Stobaei, *Hermetica*, VIII).

What is to be understood by the intelligible substance drawing near to God? Does it not simply mean an ascent of this ladder of degrees of consciousness within us? 'The idea of God is the idea of our own spiritual natures enlarged to infinity' (Wm. E. Channing). To put 'God' inside us is itself a reversal, for our material conception of God is as something *outside* in the sensible world. But God is closer 'than the neck-vein' because understanding is *not* outside us; and to understand differently, in a new way, is always close to us, because this ladder of consciousness is within us. Outside is the world of experience, inside are degrees of understanding; and if the intelligible substance draws near another understanding of things it draws near to 'God', i.e. to an enlargement of consciousness. It all depends upon what we make most important. As Plato said, there are three things – soul, body, and money, and all three have their place (*Rep.* IX).

It is remarkable how we put 'God' outside us – how we cannot get away from a three-dimensional view of things. 'The Kingdom of Heaven is within you, and whosoever knoweth himself shall find it.' Yet do we ever see the matter in this way? Do we comprehend that 'God' is *understanding* and that the worse our understanding the more tyrannical and 'outside' does 'God' seem to us, and the more slavery we are in?

Man gains freedom only through the use of his highest faculties. Materialism makes him more and more a slave to the forces of the phenomenal world. It is easier for us to take things as they appear – nay, even feel that we can deal with everything by means of our logic, and even 'conquer' nature. The point is, however, that such an outlook does not call into activity the unawakened higher degrees of understanding. Therefore it means that we remain handicapped, although it looks as if our attitude were extremely practical. The crux of the matter lies just in what we think about the potential nature of man. If we believe that there are no further degrees of understanding in us, that we are products of a mechanical selection, without *surplus*, then we must insist upon a purely rational or logical approach to life, since we have this degree of understanding naturally. If we believe otherwise, then we must take our reason or logic only as one partial and very necessary approach to life, but not inclusive of other forms of understanding.

The Hermetic fragment, while showing that a materialistic standpoint goes ultimately against our own interest, indicates a principle of freedom and also the source of our slavery. The more man is turned toward the corporeal world and argues from the sensible alone, the more will he fall under the power of necessity, i.e. the more enslaved he becomes by outward things. Our present-day materialism points in this direction – that is, in the direction of the enslavement of man by mechanisation and by its direct results, by state-organisations, uniformity, the sacrifice of independent intelligence, the sweeping away of individual differences, local customs, local diversity, and all the infinite branchings of humanity that enrich life. In this connection we can look further into the Hermetic point of view. Man is made free by 'truth'. The truth spoken of here is equated with *mind*. We might understand that noetic experience is meant – that at another level of consciousness we can understand infinitely better than we do at present. This more comprehensive and subtle grasp, this more delicate perception, is the beginning of 'truth' and its effect is to free us. We find in the New Testament the phrase, 'the truth shall make you free'. This kind of truth, we are told in many places, begins with self-knowledge. Truth about the corporeal world is secondary to it; some would say that any real understanding of the corporeal world is consequent upon it.

The acquisition of this kind of truth, or *Mind*, was the Hermetic goal. It was the solution of the mystery of existence, of the extraordinary, inexplicable conundrum of life. Every thing is wrong in the world, every thing in a state of confusion, because man has not this truth, and so remains *unfinished*. He lives *under its level*, and so never can understand how to act or think rightly. Viewed in the light of Hermetic philosophy, man blindly gropes his way about a dark world, using a form of understanding which can never furnish him with answers to the most important questions that vex his soul. Yet the Creator made him in the image of an eternal being and sent him down, as a mortal creature, not merely to be an ornament of the earth and become conscious of its created form, but to attain 'truth'.

For example, in a Hermetic allegory of the first century, man's situation is put in these words: 'Man has this advantage – speech and mind. Speech God imparted to all men, but *mind* he did not, not that he grudged it to any for the grudging temper comes from souls of men who are devoid of mind. (The pupil asks: "Tell me why God did not impart mind to all?") It was his will that mind should be placed in the midst as a prize that human souls may win. ("Where did he place it?") He filled a great basin with mind, and sent it down to earth; and he appointed a herald, and bade him make proclamation to the hearts of men: "Hearken, each human heart; dip yourself in this basin, if you can, recognising for what purpose you have been made, and believing that you shall ascend to Him who sent the basin down." Now those who gave heed to the proclamation, and dipped themselves in the bath of mind, these men got a share of knowledge; they received mind, and so became *complete* men' (*Hermetica*, Libellus IV, p. 151).

We must understand that this mind, spoken of here, is not our ordinary reasoning mind but something belonging to degrees above it. Is it not the second triangle? In this passage it is very clearly brought out that man is incomplete without this mind (or higher level), and that the aim of life is the reaching of it, i.e.

this is the real significance behind the life of man, to which every-thing is secondary. We know that when the rich man asked how he could gain eternal life the answer was: 'If you will be perfect follow me.' The meaning, in the Greek, is to *reach one's goal*. *Sin* meant, in the original, 'missing the mark'. The psychological idea emerges quite clearly, when we consider the real meaning of these two words. The goal is to perfect oneself, to become complete; and sin is all that that causes one to miss the goal.

This perfecting was a question of following a way, a path – *to have a path*. The rich man may not have known that in asking for eternal life he was asking for the *completion of himself*, and one that he had to bring about for himself. He is told to follow an ex-tremely difficult and scarcely understood teaching. He may even have thought that eternal life meant just what we all think, if we connect eternity with the idea of prolonged time. He is told, and told in an unmistakable way, that eternal life means, first of all, the completing of oneself *in this life*.

I think that the Hermetic allegory about the basin of Mind shows us the same thing. It did not mean to die physically. It meant beginning to struggle for something that we do not ordinarily struggle for (for we are merely *state*), something requiring great patience, something obviously very difficult to grasp. 'Let patience have her perfect work that you may be perfect and entire, wanting nothing.' And once again I venture to call the attention of the reader to the point so often mentioned before, that another understanding of time, a vision that reaches beyond time, was always held to be essential for the attainment of this higher state of man: for example: 'we look not at the things seen, but at the things not seen, for things seen are of time, but things not seen are of eternity.'

This means simply that taking everything as it appears, thinking only from the standpoint of a three-dimensional world in passing-time, we cannot get beyond the level of our natural understanding, cannot rise to another feeling of our existence – to that aeon from which we are derived.

.   .   .   .

Perhaps we scarcely notice that in every direction our natural understanding leads us to *nothing*. We come either to contradiction or to the unknown. Seeking for an explanation of the phenomenal universe with the phenomenally based mind we fail to get beyond a certain point because we have not the necessary ideas. We have remarked how the *idea* of the third dimension would explain many things to the paper-beings. For example, the entry of the third dimension into their world would be the real explanation of what appeared to them to be *growth*. The lead point of the pencil slowly entering their world would certainly appear to grow. It would surround itself gradually with a wooden covering. It would appear to them first as a small seed, a point of lead, that had the capacity for growing and secreting wood. We do not think of the growth of a seed in our world in the same way. We cannot imitate growth. Growth is from 'inside'. Higher dimensions enter our world *from inside*, from the direction of the most minute. We merely see a seed turning into a plant, or a child growing into a man, in passing-time, and think of it in an external way, as a kind of accretion of matter coming from outside. We do not see it as something coming through the seed, into our world, or through the child, from within – the entry of another dimension, which for us is passing-time. We think that the flower is potentially in the seed and that life grows from the seed, not that life enters through the seed into manifestation.

We do not conceive a generative *idea* behind the seed, and the seed as a minute receptive machine into which the generative world of form passes. In the same way we can never understand what *instinct* is because we look for its seat in material structure. But instinct is not comprehensible in such terms. The higher world enters the lower on all sides – in thought, feeling, instinct, event. Generative form which endows a thing with meaning is not to be confused with material form. It enters material form. Instinct is form, idea, in this sense. We only know serial form just as we only know events as a succession of related incidents. Higher form is gathered into a unity outside time and the relationship of material form to this higher form gives *meaning*.

The study of life is the study of the meaning and use of things, not simply analysing material structure. The circumstances under which the best expression of a thing is given is what should concern us. The study of matter does not afford this result, for it does away with *what a thing is, and is for*, by getting below its most significant level. In this way, science complicates life by continually reaching below its level and missing the idea. If we think that flower and man are potential in seed and child, in the physiological properties of their tissues, we are right in one way, only we speak from the standpoint of the three-dimensional world in passing-time, and must attribute extraordinary properties to *matter* itself. But when we think of growth as due to the entry of higher dimensions we speak from another point of view, seeing the connection between visible and invisible, between higher and lower space.

As I said, the realisation of higher space reverses the direction of our thought. Just at that point where our ordinary thought comes to an end, having gone as far as it can, so that all beyond seems *nothing*, lies the place where another kind of thinking can begin. We cannot get beyond with the form of thinking that is based on the three-dimensional world in passing-time. Another kind of thinking is necessary, one that does not belong to the passive but to the active mind, or, at least, begins to imitate the latter. The appearance of this kind of thinking, or rather the birth of active mind, has been sometimes described as revelation.

Goethe depicts Faust as having reached the place of *nothing* in his quest for truth. After investigating all branches of human knowledge, Faust finds no answers that satisfy him. He exclaims: 'And here I am at last, a very fool, with useless learning curst, no wiser than at first....' There seems to be nothing. All his learning proves to be useless. Looking round him, he sees no way out. At this point he is faced with despair. His quest becomes meaningless. Meaninglessness is the worst thing that can assail us. Like the Medusa it turns us to stone. From what direction can Faust recapture meaning – new meaning? At first he sees no direction in which to go. 'The fancy, too, has died away, the hope that I might in my day instruct and elevate mankind.' Through the best, as we usually suppose, of the human aspirations – the 'desire to help humanity' – he is nevertheless led to absolutely nothing.

In what direction does he turn? The movement of the soul is, of course, poetically treated. He opens an ancient book and catches sight of the sign of the *macrocosmos*, the great world that overshadows the visible fragment in the present moment. The hieroglyph is the seal of Solomon – the two triangles placed upside down, signifying the interpenetration of lower and higher space, the passive and active mind. A change passes over him, and he exclaims: 'Ha! what new life divine, intense, floods in a moment every sense. I feel the dawn of youth again.... Was it a god who wrote these signs?'

What moment of the soul's experience is being described? Has he not touched another degree of understanding *discontinuous* with his former level? Formerly he had tried to increase his knowledge by continuous 'degrees of extension' and it led him into *nothing*. In the light of a quite new understanding of the WORLD he exclaims: 'Oh how the spell before my sight brings nature's hidden ways to light. See! All things with each other blending, each to each its being lending, all on each in turn depending, heavenly ministers descending, and again to heaven ascending, floating, mingling, interweaving.... Can heart of man embrace Illimitable

Nature?' The visible world vanishes into illimitable nature, seen with the eye of mind freed from time and sense — from things merely as they seem.

His vision is surely similar to that seen by Jacob in the wilderness. Both can be understood as allegories, relating to the inner experience of *scale*. Jacob came 'to a certain place and the sun was set'. As in the case of Faust he is in darkness. Here a vision of a ladder appears to him, extending from earth to heaven. 'And Jacob ... lighted upon a certain place, and tarried there all night, because the sun was set; and he took of the stones of that place, and put them for his pillows, and lay down in that place to sleep. And he dreamed, and behold a ladder set upon the earth, and the top of it reached to heaven ... and behold the spirits of God *ascending* and *descending* on it' (*Genesis* 28.10-12).

Like Faust, the 'world' is transfigured for him. He perceives the scale of reality that is the true Universe and this comes just at the point when his journey had led him to darkness, as did Faust's journey in search of knowledge. Many allegorical descriptions of this experience exist in older literature in which the place of *nothing* is indicated by a dark forest, a wilderness, a desert, etc.

   .   .   .   .

Faust touches new energies. His despair turns to joy. He sees things *the other way round*. The active mind awakens. The invisible enters the visible on all sides. *Visibilia ex invisibilibus.* Faced by negation and so with petrifaction of soul, something is suddenly released in him and touches realities beyond sense. Has he not hit upon the divine science of Perseus, who escaped from being turned to stone by the Medusa (it would seem) through the art of seeing things the other way round? Perseus avoids death by looking at the Medusa in the mirror of Athena. Thereby he slays the Medusa and releases Pegasus who mounts to heaven. Is not this an allegory about man and his eternal nature?

   .   .   .   .

236

In this connection, let us reflect on the original significance of the word *faith*. Its meaning seems to have been *mental* – mental perception of the reality of the invisible. Faith is *another form of understanding*, through which force enters us. It is the *evidence* of things *not seen*. 'Now faith is ... a conviction of the reality of things which we do not see. Through faith we understand that the worlds (aeons) came into being and still exist at the command of God, so that what is seen does not owe its existence to that which is visible' (*Hebrews* II.1-3). Another definition of faith is given in the Gospels, when the Roman captain asks Christ to heal his servant. Jesus said: 'I will come and cure him.' The Captain replied: 'Sir, I am not a fit person to receive you under my roof. Merely say the word and my boy will be cured. For I myself am also under authority and have soldiers under me. To one I say "Go", and he goes. To another "Come", and he comes, and to my slave, "do this or that" and he does it.' Jesus was astonished and said, 'In no Israelite have I found such great faith' (*Matt.* 8). Here *faith* is clearly the recognition of scale, the certain knowledge that there is *that which is above* and *that which is beneath*; and that everyone stands at some point in this scale or ladder of being. [Scale = *scala*, ladder.]

Brunner defines faith as personal decision about invisible things, a question of 'I myself, not my thought, not my world-standpoint.... In faith, man becomes certain that he has himself not in himself (*Emil Brunner*). Another writer defined *new birth* as reaching an absolute mental certainty of the reality of what the senses do not show. Is not this *reversal*? We must realise the profound psychological significance of such views. In this connection let us glance at the meaning of *repentance*. As in the case of the word *faith* we probably think of some emotional attitude, even a blind one. But the Greek word translated as repentance means *change of mind* and nothing else. Is it not, then, another way of thinking about things, through which the mind is opened to a higher degree? No one can change in himself or add a cubit to his stature by taking thought just with these forms of thought which he has always used. How could he? Something new must enter him. But do we ever think of it in this way? Must he not have contact with ideas that he does not *naturally* possess? Whatever forms Christianity assumed in later times, however distorted it became, it must be remembered that its introduction was heralded by John the Baptist preaching *change of mind* as the first step towards 'eternal' life; and this change of mind was connected by him with the teaching on the Kingdom of Heaven – an idea so difficult to grasp and so contrary to all sense-thinking and external evidence that it remains a *new idea* for all time.

.   .   .   .

Long before the period of Christianity Socrates spoke of two directions in which the soul can be turned: 'The soul when using the body as an instrument of perception – that is to say, when using the sense of sight and hearing, or some other sense – for the meaning of perceiving through the body is perceiving through the senses – is dragged by the body through the region of the changeable (the temporal) and wanders about and is confused. The world spins round her. She is like a drunkard when she touches change.... But when, returning into herself she reflects, then she passes into the region of Eternity.' This movement of the soul is in the direction of that level of Mind on which it can see truth, the first aspect of which is truth about man's own invisible nature – *himself* – which he reaches through self-knowledge. It is a reversal of the natural movement of the soul. There are two sides to man's life. 'There are two ruling powers, one set over the intelligible (the invisible, mind-understood world) and the other over the visible world' (*Rep.* 509). To the visible world belongs perceptual truth. But this does not cover the whole range of truth. It does not define truth. Perceptual truth is from sensation. One who disagrees with our sensations – who says it is hot when we think it is cold – disturbs this level of truth. If we are accustomed to surrender the value of our own impressions (sensations) to the opinions of others we feel that we are not getting right impressions, and that something is wrong with us. If we believe in our sensations strongly we merely think that there is something wrong with the other person. A division of people is possible in this respect – those who are firmly fixed in their sensations, and those who are not. The latter feel that another's perceptions are more reliable than their own or are indifferent to perceptions. Of course, this has nothing to do with the interpretation of sensations, or our opinions. But the point is that 'sensation' is one level of truth only. We say: 'It is raining.' If someone looking through the window denies this we attempt to reinforce his sensations by taking him out and making him feel the rain on his skin. He then agrees with us; we cannot imagine anybody denying so perceptible a fact at the moment. But later on he may deny it, when the evidence of the senses is no longer present, and then we either think of him as having a bad memory or as deliberately lying. All this belongs mainly to the perceptual consciousness *and in the main our modern idea of truth, and what truth is, is connected with this order of truth, which is a matter of sensation or outer perception.*

.   .   .   .

All these quotations and examples show us one thing – that something must start in the mind apart from the evidence of the senses, in that journey that leads to another level of understanding. To begin with, it means that we can no longer think in the same way. We have to begin to think in a new way if we wish to enter upon that science of the soul whose aim is to effect a definite transformation of a man's nature. And it is the sense of something greater that is the starting-point. It is this and only this that can begin to effect some reversal in us which gradually frees us from the power of outer things, which completely dominates our ordinary existence, and makes us little better than machines.

It is this reversal that, in a sense, ultimately constitutes the change – not the momentary revelation of Faust, which is, after all, nothing but a prelude to all his subsequent spiritual experiences, nor the flash of another consciousness described by Tennyson, nor any emotional crisis of conversion, but a long process – a struggle between one form of understanding, on one side, and all that internally goes with it, all the features of this time and sense machinery, the succession of *I*'s, this present-momentedness of things, the distorted sense of others, consequent on our unsatisfied craving for duplication, the small orbit of meanings in which we daily revolve, the limited notions we have of existence, the narrow view of the WORLD and the narrow resultant attitudes – and on the other side, a new form of understanding that is far nearer than we imagine, that touches us, indeed, on all sides, and that we really know about only cannot hold, cannot remember, cannot make distinct and effective, save by long effort.

.   .   .   .

Is it not only through the recognition of scale (faith) in ourselves that we can escape from the negation of life? The terrible power of negation surrounds us on all sides. Some unusually bad experience, some horrible disaster, some loss, summons the spirit of negation in a moment into our thoughts. Everything turns black. We seem to be only creatures of passing-time living in a world of frustration that we can make nothing of. The world then seems only evil. Only the worst side of things draws our attention. The will becomes negative. How can we, without any new ideas of what it is that we have to do, prevent ourselves from falling into apathy, characterised by the fact that we no longer try to understand anything but 'cheerfully' or otherwise get along as best we can? Kierkegaard found the solution of saying *yea*

240

to life in willing the *repetition* of events. Barth says: 'When the excitement of "life's affirmation" has, for no doubt some quite valid reason, cooled off, men will turn to "life's negation", complaining that the world is in itself evil, that it is created in *vanity* – willingly or the plaything, maybe, of some demiurge' (Barth, *Romans*, p. 308). Then the world is seen as Ramsay saw it – as the creation of a demon. Only a special attitude can rescue us. The necessity is to create something additional in ourselves. *The whole conception of a possible higher state, psychologically verifiable, is an answer to this situation.*

Is it not only through clearly seeing that creation is subject to vanity and frustration that a man can find in himself the strength to take hold of his life and begin to separare himself from the chaos within and without? He will discover that the secret is in himself, in his willingness to become something else – to *be* something, for *Yea* lies in *I*, and *I* is to be. He will then no longer see the world merely as vanity but as a series of conditions (often of extraordinary significance to him) for the exercise of his own soul. But having no idea that there is any such exercise and never understanding that the universe is in himself, for him to change, and that its evolution for him is a series of mental transformations in himself, he will always remain concerned with what will only seem the confusion of outer life, never understanding why it does not give him what he expects, and so always *blaming* – or trying to solve problems which through the very action of passing-time are incapable of any external solution.

CHAPTER TEN

CREATION OF *NOW*

IT WAS SAID in the second chapter that because we are plunged in appearances we are not separate as regards the sense of ourselves from the external world. This is partly due to personal psychological obstacles, such as the *craving for attention*. But in part it is due to the work of the senses which put us in contact with the given world and given conditions of life which we take for granted. I will put side by side this taking of three-dimensional reality for granted and the desire for attention. They constitute one problem in my mind. The desire for attention, for the duplication of ourselves in others, the need for audience, etc., spring out of the lack of any true eternal feeling of self-existence. At the same time taking the world for granted keeps us on a level of consciousness that cannot give us any true feeling of self-existence. We need the evidence of things unseen. Only through another sense of 'reality' can another sense of our-selves arise, which in turn will modify the desire for attention.

There are, then, two classes of obstacles that prevent us seeking greater reality of being. The discovery of the particular psychological elements that especially connect us with the *outer* and keep us under its power belongs to the establishing of the personal psychology. But we are dealing rather with obstacles that are connected with our natural notions of things and with the special necessity of thinking differently about the world and our life in it. I would say that we cannot get enough strength to begin to disconnect ourselves from the continual draining-effect of outer things unless we have special standpoints. We must begin by understanding things differently, because to change oneself is to change one's understanding. For instance, the *idea* of recurrence really belongs to a new conception of the 'world'. It can bring with it an entirely new sense of responsibility towards one's own life, and arising out of this, towards the lives of other people. The tasks of life must be completed. Nothing can be avoided, for we will be brought back to the same point again and again. But such thinking is not in terms of 'visible' but 'invisible'. And it is just precisely from the latter side that we can gain the strength to do something genuinely with *oneself*. The whole notion of higher space can act on us in the form of an extremely powerful *idea* – one which gives us really another view of the 'world' we live in. Whereas, if we believe in a world in passing-time we will understand everything quite differently. We have nothing behind us. We will meet life at a point, a point of re-action.

In this connection Swedenborg observes that man is only re-action in his natural state. Mechanical philosophy could not put the case more strongly. It is not a matter of proving that man is merely re-action. There are plenty of schools today that take this view. To prove it scientifically would be useless. It is an idea that can only be realised, in flashes, individually. We are submerged in the stream of events. We are not properly conscious. Whatever we do is not our own. Swedenborg adds: 'Natural man is said to be dead however good his actions may be from the civil and moral point of view.' But this *idea* can only become effective in relationship to another *idea*. Natural man can become alive, awake, 'spiritual' – that is what mechanical philosophy will not include in its doctrine. Unless we have the second idea in mind, the first idea can have no value. It is a question which de Senancour refers to as the 'mysteries of awakening'. Man, sunk in appearances and connected like a marionette with outer things, is dead, through lack of realisation of the mystery of the world. What else but the sense of strangeness can awaken us? What else can give us new thoughts, new perceptions? We are dead because we do not try to understand, because we never face the mystery of existence with any real thoughts of our own, because we are satisfied with explanations which prevent us from beginning to think. Or, to put the matter differently, we rest content with the appearance of things – that is, we do not go beyond perceptual consciousness.

.   .   .   .

In the great discourse on re-birth and eternal life in the *Corpus Hermeticum* (XIII) the pupil is told that he must first overcome very definite obstacles and we need not be surprised to find that they are divided into two distinct classes. One class refers to obstacles belonging to the personal psychology with which we are not concerned here. But notice this: among them are mentioned especially grief, distress, *dolor*. Envy, suspicion, rashness, anger, etc., are enumerated. The second class of obstacles can be defined as referring to defects of the 'perceptual consciousness'. Can we by now understand that these defects are very great? Every thinking man must surely feel the necessity of adding something to the representation of the world given by the senses.

So the pupil in the Hermetic treatise is told he must enlarge his mind beyond the range of the senses, i.e., beyond the world of three dimensions, and the body of three dimensions which he regards as himself. The teacher refers to himself as being no longer 'an object, coloured and tangible, a thing of special dimensions (metron)'. Of course, we must understand that a long process is really meant, but it is supposed that the pupil suddenly passes into the feeling of the eternal reality of himself. How does he describe the experience? 'Now I see in *mind* I see myself to be the All.' This is his first statement. His consciousness embraces all. But it does so in two distinct ways, that refer to inner and outer. As regards the inner, in what sense is he *all*? We are not astonished to find that he is *all his life*. 'I am a babe in the womb and one that is not yet conceived, and one that has been born. I am present everywhere.' He is present everywhere in his life. This is *present*. He no longer feels himself confined to the body in space, but becomes conscious of his *body in Time*. He becomes conscious in another dimension of his life. If we had such consciousness as this, *into everything we did there would enter the feeling of all the life.* We would not re-act to the moment, but would be fully conscious, in the present. How are we to understand that *unity* of being, with which we are connecting the attainment of 'eternal life', has anything to do with what seems at first sight to be its antithesis? Unity means oneness. Why, then, this *all*, when *one* is the object? A synthesis on the path toward unity is necessary, demanding *all* as its content. Unity is attained through becoming *all*. To be one it is necessary to become *all*.

Now apart from the fact that we have no direct consciousness of the fourth dimension of our existences, our memory is partly regulated by self-esteem and self-deception, which distort the past. That kind of knowledge, therefore, that leads towards higher consciousness and unity must include this aspect of self-knowledge, which brings into ordinary consciousness sides of ourselves to which we are exceptionally blind. Or speaking of it from the standpoint of the many I's that make up our ordinary being, as Ouspensky says, it will mean that we must get to know these I's. For by knowing them do we not then cease to be any one of them? Also, will we not get rid of imaginary ideas about ourselves? The imagination makes us believe that we are something or have something when the reverse is true. But such knowledge of ourselves must be gained from direct experience, not by any indirect method.

To return to the Hermetic discourse – it is plain that a connection is made between the sense of the living existence of all the life and that fulness of consciousness called *aeonian*. Yet Tennyson felt the aeon of his individual existence only as a point of intensity which gave him the pure feeling of *I*. But we have already seen that aeon in its time-sense refers to the life throughout time and in its other sense to something beyond time. 'Aeon carries all.' And this all, which manifests itself in time, is in itself one, a whole – that is, aeon. As *one* it is beyond time. The Hermetic pupil's consciousness first expands into all the life, but that which perceives this all must be above it, and of another order. But we can imagine that the passage from this state of seeing all to the experience of a single point of intensity in which all is gathered up into one could easily happen.

The often-quoted observation of Mozart comes in here. He said, in one of his letters, that he could hear a composition in his mind, sometimes throughout its entire length, and sometimes gathered into one, altogether. I call attention to this link where *all* is felt, as a stage of heightened consciousness intermediate between ordinary consciousness and the pure sense of *one* or eternal self-existence. It is this link that concerns us in a practical way, for we must relate it to one goal of self-knowledge, and to the creation of a special memory which will have its own associations. It seems to me that this link, which is the fourth dimension, resolves an antithesis that we are inclined to make between this life and some 'other life'. Our existence is, first of all, in space of three dimensions in the present moment. It is, secondly, in *its Time*, extended in a fourth dimension. It is finally in 'eternity' where it is a new synthesis of the life. This latter is to be connected with the fullest sense of individual self-existence. And in comprehending man in these different dimensions is it not our understanding of time that is the first bridge and one that relates us both *to this life* and to *another*?

As regards *outer* the Hermetic pupil perceives himself to be all in another sense. He perceives a mystery – that he is all that he beholds through his senses: 'I am in heaven and in earth, in water and in air, I am in beasts and in plants.' He feels unity in all this diversity.

As an ancient Latin epitaph on a woman's tomb runs: '*Nec vir, nec mulier, nec androgyna, nec puella, nec juvenis, nec anus, nec casta,*

246

nec meretrix, nec pudica, sed omnia!' She is all these different sides of herself; and also *nec coelo, nec terris, nec aquis, sed ubique jacet!'*

If one could see all sides of oneself and know all these sides; if one could remember what one was yesterday and bring the feeling of it into today, this *becoming all, this universality, is to become one.* For time is *part*, division into successive little parts, each of which tries to be universal. Each little *I* becomes caliph for the moment.

.   .   .   .

The Hermetic pupil experiences a higher emotion of great cognitive value, which in its inward direction brings all his life into existence and causes him to feel and know *I am all my life*; and in an outward direction causes him to feel *I am all that I see.* This latter direction many of us may know by experience. The *receptivity* is changed, for all the higher emotions increase receptivity and entirely do away with the limited feeling of I in which we are ordinarily confined and through which the lower emotions are most easily stimulated.

But what we are paying particular attention to in this discourse is the fact that the necessity of overcoming the second class of obstacles, existing in us all equally owing to the nature of perceptual consciousness, is emphasised. Another view of the 'world' is necessary. A certain kind of effort must be made against perceptual consciousness, or things as they seem, to arouse the activity of the active mind, or the second system of Fludd.

.   .   .   .

It is only through the effect of very powerful ideas and emotions that we can come into the sense of our true existence. Recollect that whatever natural man does, whether good or bad, is *dead*. I said that he does not act from himself. It is not the *quantity* of his actions that count but the *quality*. Eckhart has a passage on this subject. There is something in everyone which, if he acts from it, gives an entirely different quality to all that he does. Whether we call this *I*, or mind, or *will* does not matter. Eckhart calls it genuine will and connects it with mind. 'Thousands die without acquiring this genuine will. Doubtless they had desires and inclinations like other animals. One man does something trifling, does it just once and sends it on the wings of praise and thankfulness up to its source. Another one does some important work which occupies him long and constantly, and yet this little thing done once is more acceptable to God than the other man's great work which cost him so much time and trouble. Why? I will tell you. Because the trivial act was carried up past time into the now of eternity, therefore it was to God's entire satisfaction. Though one should live through all the time from Adam and all the time to come before the judgment day doing good works, yet he who, energising in his highest, purest part, crosses from time to eternity, verily in the sight of God this man conceives and does far more than anyone who lives throughout all past and future time, because this *now* includes the whole of time.

One master says that in crossing over time into the *now* each power of the soul will surpass itself....' I must set beside this passage a parallel thought of Karl Barth's: 'History is the display of the supposed advantages of power and intelligence which some men possess over others, of the struggle for existence hypocritically described by ideologists as the struggle for justice and freedom, of the ebb and flow of old and new forms of human righteousness, each vying with the rest in solemnity and triviality.... Yet one drop of eternity is of greater weight than a vast ocean of finite things' (*Romans*, p. 77). One real moment, one real thought, one real feeling, one real sensation – a single moment of self-existence – is worth all the rest. There is a certain kind of action, a certain experience of oneself, that is the beginning of 'eternal' life. Without it, whatever we do, is 'natural' i.e. *reaction*. The quick and the dead are distinguished by the *quality* of their action and understanding. It is plain that Eckhart is speaking of the difference between the actions of Swedenborg's natural and spiritual man. The latter alone is active, i.e. what we have called the active mind is awake in him.

Swedenborg makes the opening of the latent spiritual degree in man to depend on the acknowledgment of God and the realisation of evil. Eckhart puts the matter rather differently as being dependent on the acknowledgment of oneself outside time. As regards the acknowledgment of God there are certain exercises whose object is to let in the sense of 'something greater' into every moment of life. God, as *idea*, is a transforming power *within* us. 'Whatever thou doest, whatever thou eatest, do all as if for me' – the words of Krishna in the Bhagavad-Gita. A similar exercise is found in the New Testament: 'Whether therefore ye eat or drink or whatsoever ye do, do all to the glory of God' (I *Cor.* 10.21). I believe that the exercise of thinking that all the life is living, and bringing the sense of the living life into every moment, is *of the same order*. We spoke earlier of the definition of God as 'beginning and end', and connected it with the idea of higher dimensions. We can now see more clearly how the idea of higher dimensions, when related to personal existence, can be effective, but when treated abstractly, in mathematical conceptions, cannot touch us. The above exercises refer to the deliberately created sense of something greater entering into every moment. The object is to emancipate ourselves from the power of the momentary I, the event of the moment.

The realisation of what passing-time is can have the same effect, i.e. we live in the world of becoming where nothing ever is. This need not only produce sadness, but, by separating us from the effect of passing-time, bring us ever closer to another level of consciousness, with its accompanying different feeling of I. This is shown in the following passage about a female pupil and her Buddhist teacher: 'There arose in her heart the insight into truth clear and stainless which perceives that whatsoever has a beginning has the inherent quality of passing away' (*The Questions of King Milinda*). Note that *insight* is said. It is not merely thinking about passing-time or thinking things are ephemeral or hopeless. It is a stage beyond that, whereby she is free from illusion and has become detached from a thousand things, seeing her relation to the visible world as from within. Nothing ever is in passing-time. That is what we do not see. The perception may bring us to *now*.

.   .   .   .

No reveries, no conversations, no tracing out of the meaning of phantasies, contain this *now*, which belongs to a higher order of consciousness. The *time-man* in us does not know *now*. He is always preparing something in the future, or busy with what happened in the past. He is always wondering what to do, what to say, what to wear, what to eat, etc. He anticipates; and we, following him, come to the expected moment, and lo, he is already elsewhere, planning further ahead. This is *becoming* – where nothing ever *is*. We must come to our senses to begin to feel *now*. We can only feel *now* by checking this time-man, who thinks of existence in his own way. *Now* enters us with a sense of something greater than passing-time. *Now* contains all time, all the life, and the aeon of the life. *Now* is the sense of higher space. It is not the decisions of the man in time that count here, for they do not spring from *now*. All decisions that belong to the life in time, to success, to business, comfort, are about 'tomorrow'. All decisions about the right thing to do, about how to act, are about tomorrow. It is only what is done in *now* that counts, and this is a decision always about *oneself* and *with* oneself, even although its effect may touch other people's lives 'tomorrow'. *Now* is spiritual. It is a state of the spirit, when it is above the stream of time-associations. Spiritual values have nothing to do with time. They are not in time, and their growth is not a matter of time. To retain the impress of their truth we must fight with time, with every notion that they belong to time, and that the passage of days will increase them. For then it will be easy for us to think it is *too late*, to make the favourite excuse of passing-time.

The feeling of *now* is the feeling of certainty. In *now* passing-time halts. And in this halting of time one's understanding has power over one. One knows, sees, feels in oneself, apart from all outer things; and above all, one is. This is the state of faith, as I believe was originally meant – the certain knowledge of something above passing-time. Faith is *now*. What the time-man understands about faith is something quite different. Faith has to do with that which is alone in oneself and unknown to anyone else. 'Every visible state, every temporal, every pragmatic approach to faith, is, in the end, the negation of faith' (Karl Barth). All insight, all revelation, all illumination, all love, all that is genuine, all that is real, lies in *now* – and in the attempt to create *now* we approach the inner precincts, the holiest part of life. For in time all things are seeking completion, but in *now* all things are complete.

So we must understand that what we call the present moment is not *now*, for the present moment is on the horizontal line of time, and *now* is vertical to this and incommensurable with it. So Barth points out that the true, living life of a man does not lie in historical time, nor is faith something that begins at a certain point in time and grows along time. He is really talking about another level of consciousness – another dimension. It is the Moment that 'qualifies and transforms time', and all else, all that is taken as faith, belongs to the 'unqualified time of sleep'. For Barth truly observes that without this Moment, this *now*, all 'men are asleep, even the Apostle, even the saint, even the lover', and in this state of sleep 'men are sold under time, its property.

They lie like pebbles in the stream of time.' Did we but awake, he says, did we but realise that we stand at every moment on the frontier of time, we should know that all we seek and all that some connect with the *future* life, has nothing to do with historical time or with visible history. The future world is not in the future of time. 'What delays its coming is not the Parousia but our awakening.'

If we could awaken, if we could ascend in the scale of reality concealed within us, we would understand the meaning of the 'future' world. *Our true future is our own growth in now, not in the tomorrow of passing-time.*

Something must be brought into every moment, the cumulative effect of which is to create *now*. *Now* is not given. While living our ordinary life we must always be doing *something else* – internally. Consider the exercise of self-knowledge in this respect. Whatever we understand by self-knowledge, one thing we certainly do not understand, that it has to do with *now*. The time-man in us does not understand this. Eckhart says: 'Mark how to know yourself. To know himself a man must ever be on the watch over himself, holding his outer faculties. This discipline must be continued until he reaches a state of consciousness....' The object is to reach a state of consciousness – a new state of oneself. It is to reach *now*, where one is present to oneself. 'What I say unto you I say unto all, *be awake.*' The translation *watch* is insufficient. Is not this idea about self-knowledge absolutely different from the moral significance we usually give it? Can we understand the New Testament at all unless we understand that it is constantly dealing with a higher level of consciousness possible to man? Is not this the treasure hidden in us, that a man can find if he seeks? 'The highest wisdom consists in this, for man to know himself, because in him God has placed his eternal word.' What is this *word* (logos)? 'In the beginning is the word.' Is it not this, the interior expression of the universe itself as potentiality, beginning with the highest meaning and existing as a scale of reality within?

.   .   .   .

If we could penetrate to the eternal reality of our own being we would find the one and only solution for every situation – in the right sense of our own existence, primarily in *itself*. The 'cause' of our existence would then be internal. This I call the *aeon* of our lives – that which is behind all manifestation of the life in time, and is summed up in the growth of the feeling of now into which all the life enters. This is the *eternal creation of man*, having no source in time whatsoever. There is nothing prior to it, in a time-sense. What is prior to it lies in the eternal order of real causes, in the scale of descent from supreme mind. Temporal and spatial existence lie at the bottom of the scale, and when taken as the scene of all existence must necessarily control us exclusively. There can be no freedom, for one is in the sea of the opposites, those robbers that steal all we have, without any possibility of walking upon that sea, having nothing above it to catch hold of. If the feeling of the life is confined to material existence we set ourselves under that ruling power that Plato refers to as controlling the sense-formed world. To overcome its dominance, it is necessary to turn the faculties inwards, to enter into *oneself*, by means of some method.

A world of *inward* perception then begins to open out, distinct from that of outer perception. Inner space appears. *The creation of the world begins in man himself.* At first all is darkness: then light appears and is separated from the darkness. By this light we understand a form of consciousness to which our ordinary consciousness is, by comparison, darkness. This light has constantly been equated with truth and freedom. Inner perception of oneself, of one's invisibility, is the beginning of light. This perception of truth is not a matter of sense-perception, but of the perception of the truth of 'ideas' – through which, certainly, the perception of our senses is greatly increased. The path of self-knowledge has this aim in view, for no one can know himself unless he turns inwards away from sense-perception, and unless he learns what to seek for. By oneself this is impossible. A man cannot get to know himself alone. His imagination stands in the way. There is no sufficient point in himself from which he can view himself aright, no sufficient knowledge. The establishing of this point is a matter of long work upon oneself with the assistance of those in whom this point is already established. This point is, as it were, the beginning of light – the light of inner perception – which begins to struggle against the surrounding darkness. This struggle marks the commencement of that inner development of man which has been written about in many different ways (yet really always in the same way) throughout all that small part of Time whose literature belongs to us, and which we think of as the entire history of the World.

CHAPTER ELEVEN

RELATIONSHIP

IF THE WORLD, experienced in its most significant aspect, be a series of mental transformations, our position in it will be determined by our *consciousness*. Viewed in this light, position in it will be according to the quality or level of consciousness. For our ordinary consciousness there are a certain number of states, fully worked out. Any state is *place*, in inner space, having its own properties; and *situation*, in outer space. The state of suspicion, for instance, is *place* which has its own properties. When we are in that state, we can study the properties of this place in inner space, if we have sufficient detachment. Externally, there will be some corresponding situation. The transition to the state of joy will mean movement to another place in inner space, having quite different properties. All ordinary human states belong to the ordinary level of consciousness, and this gives us one level of the world, the one to which we are naturally related.

Another state of consciousness opens on another level of the WORLD. We have seen that, broadly speaking, these levels are discontinuous. In other words, the psychological world is not uniform. It is not of the same order nor on the same level, just as the external, visible world is not on the same scale.

Just as that fragment of Totality, which appears as the external universe, registered by our senses, is the same for everyone, so is the unmanifested portion, apprehended by inner experience, the same. The latter I call inner space. For this reason we come to the same *place* as others do, and have the same experiences, insights, the same aberrations and insanities. Actually we continually come to the same *places* without fully recognising them – just as in outer space, in our daily movements, we cover the

255

same ground. Psychologically, we must always be *somewhere* in inner space – just as we must be in outer space.

What raises the level of consciousness and opens us to a different aspect of the WORLD is the creation of *now*. The time-man knows only state, hurrying from one into another. *Now* is vertical to this, and belongs to the scale of degrees. In now we get above state. Inner space is changed, enlarged. To feel *Time* itself is to open a corridor within. Instead of avenging demons – which must inhabit us unless we inhabit ourselves – the sense of the life comes to us. The murder of the past ceases, because the great negations that belong to the illusion of passing-time begin to leave us, and all the life begins to enter *now*. 'The righteous live unto eternity' – not for 'evermore' as the translation goes, which misses the point. To live unto eternity is to live unto *aeon*, unto unity, unto wholeness, completeness, unto *the integration of all the life*. And this is *now*. The enemy to *now* is the illusion of passing-time.

Now belongs to the second system, the second triangle of Fludd. It belongs to the realisation of time-dimensions.

When we reach *now* the world is turned the other way round. We are at the centre of things. The responsibility is ours. Had we *now* in our lives we would cease to blame. When Ramsay was in the higher state of consciousness he saw that all social relationships came out of himself. He was centred in himself. He writes: '....when one is self-centred, evidence goes the other way – i.e. Universe evolves out of one's own mind. *The whole thing* turns on this point – all social relations – all develop out of the recurring stage ... far more than you can imagine.' He saw that all 'quarrels and reconciliations, woes and fears, are no longer the chief thing of the Universe'. He saw also that they develop out of the recurring stage – in himself. One can go round and round in the same circle of woes – not seeing it as *inner* state but as *outer* situation – as other people's fault. Yet, seen from the strength of a new consciousness, he perceives that it all comes from himself. And we have already seen that he had perceived that it was possible to get beyond recurring stages, beyond ever-repeating states, *because the* WORLD *is a series of possible mental transformations.* He saw, for example, that the feeling that the world was the creation of a demon always recurred at a certain point in mental evolution, and by realising – by *remembering* – that it always recurred it was possible to get beyond it.

Is not this the only solution of the life and its problems? Is not this the key? Otherwise, must not our lives be always re-action? The solution is in the creation of *I* and the creation of now, which are one and the same – in the sense that *I* dwells in *now*, and not in passing-time. Then, in the reversal of everything and the transvaluation of everything, there springs up a new understanding of the meaning of life – *of what we have to do*. Our lives can no longer be left to reaction – from the lower triangle.

.   .   .   .

It is our relationship to the second triangle that must change our lives in recurrence. I will give in brief my personal views.

I believe that in the recurrence of one's life there are phases when the *momentum* wanes and then it is possible to change the life. The Egyptian diagram, given on the title page, is one that I believe refers to the recurrence of the lives in the mystic ocean of existence. Origen says the Egyptians taught the idea of recurrence. The diagram represents a snake, sometimes called *Apophis*. The snake is often representative of *time*. The snake swallowing its own tail was supposed to represent 'eternity', i.e., the circular movement of time, or the circle of the life. Apophis is the *destroyer* that has to be overcome. We find many Egyptian diagrams of this serpent being pinned down or transfixed by knives. Time, from one standpoint, is the destroyer. As mere passive creatures of passing-time, we are continually destroyed by time. We are eaten by Apophis. The four sets of coils depicted in the diagram on the

257

title page suggest to me that there may have been some teaching about four forms of recurrence, i.e., four kinds of life that we have to undergo in recurrent form, perhaps having to do with the four castes. I think Plato mentions only three successive choices of the life.

The Egyptian diagram might be interpreted as meaning that we pass into some particular form of life that recurs and recurs until the momentum of this spiral 'rocket' wanes and we reach a point of possible transition, when another form of life might be entered upon. Of course this is purely speculative. But it would mean that when fully in one form of life, we would be under a certain momentum. We must certainly admit that we see people whose lives seem obviously wound up, and go strongly under their own momentum. We also see people whose lives are not so obviously wound up and who seem to be in some stage of transition. Or to change the metaphor – some people easily find ready-made shoes and walk without difficulty; others find that they have to make shoes for themselves.

It is just those people who do not find that life easily opens out to them who may be in a position to change something in themselves and turn in new directions.

In this connection I make the following tentative reflections. It must be remembered that the emphasis falls upon *this life* when it is seen in the light of recurrence – this life of ours here to which we must learn to say *yea* and towards which we must find a new and *individual* responsibility. The most important things are other people, and significant experiences. Of the latter we have spoken. There are significant people in our lives. Or there are people who become significant as soon as we feel the strong necessity to deal with ourselves. They are not necessarily those whom we, or others, suppose to be significant at first sight. We touch one another differently, affect one another in quite different ways. Two people may be useful to one another – or quite useless

– or quite useless in this recurrence. It is not a matter of propinquity, but of position in psychological space.

From the standpoint of the re-entry of the life our relationships to certain people begin to have a new and quite peculiar value, one that cannot ever be given by the notion of passing-time. We meet again. Thus, our relationships always lie *ahead* of us. This is the chief change of standpoint that it is necessary to make, for otherwise significant elements in our lives will not be understood. If we are blind to significant elements and do not value or understand them, they remain *inactive* in the life. But if we see them in a special light they become active. We will give inner attention to them, inner feeling, inner thought, in a way impossible when we are gripped by the illusion of passing-time. *Conscience will begin – or consciousness in Time.*

Now these active points lying in the life are to be thought of as capable of spreading their influences in either direction in the recurrences of the life, i.e. backwards and forwards, obliterating useless parts of the life by growing into them. By useless parts I mean accidental circumstances, contacts and phases in the life which have no real significance or only a harmful one. We must form the picture of the life as a growth, *transverse to time*, and capable of growing not merely in one part but in many parts, i.e. we must get rid of the idea that the life only grows from the present. This gives a wrong relation to the moment. The life may grow in all parts of itself and we may be affected by these growing directions (in other parts of our personal Time) even in the 'present'. But a certain point of view is necessary to let in these growing influences, namely, a new sense of what the life means, and with it a new realisation of what is significant, based on the constantly created feeling of *all the life*. In the recurrence of the life we cannot then suppose that we will meet everything in just exactly the same way.

Passing-time brings us to each moment of our lives, as if to review it in detail. Were our consciousness different, each moment would be registered. We would see *into* each moment and thus leave a *trace of ourselves*. But this would be to dwell in *now*, wherein alone anything can be done. The potential of consciousness would be raised. But the time-man lowers this potential, so that our energy is never gathered into *now*, but distributed in a hundred directions of the imagination. So we are always 'thinking', as we call it, not realising that these thoughts lead us always in circles and never give us any real starting-point. Only through some specially-guarded understanding can we increase the sense of the life as a whole, and so leave a *trace*. The 'unrighteous' man's life is compared in the Wisdom of Solomon to 'a ship that leaves no trace in the sea, or a bird that leaves no track in the air'. This is the time-man. 'So soon as we are born we begin to draw to the end and leave no trace.' The righteous, living 'unto eternity', leave a trace, i.e. they leave a trace, over and above reaction. Kierkegaard remarked that as soon as he fell out of his 'religious understanding' he felt like an insect. He found in the idea of repetition – of willing the repetition of things – a special way of meeting life – of leaving a trace. One must not always try to get out of things. We begin to leave a trace when we bring new attitudes to bear on life, if we continually re-create them by a certain kind of effort. Life is a labyrinth in which we get lost and are unable to find the way out. The Minotaur consumes us – because we leave no trace, because we lose sight of ourselves at every moment and forget to unwind the thread that Ariadne has given us.

If we leave a trace perhaps we may, in recurrence, meet people earlier or later than before; or even the order of things may be changed. Parts of our lives from which we have got all that is possible, or parts that have no significance, may be looped up, so to speak, so that the life is joined together in a new way, some parts being shortened, others prolonged. I believe that people who are really very significant to us are met with just *when it is possible* to

260

meet with them – that is, when we are ready. If the life as a whole grows we may meet them earlier *if this is possible* – or *as soon as it is possible*. We must remember that there are different 'times', or periods, on different scales, finally involving cosmic processes; and all this turning machinery of wheels within wheels must sometimes render things possible and sometimes impossible.

If someone is significant to us, that person may or may not be influenced by this fact. But if there is a special understanding in common the influence *must* be mutual, and then the growth of one will be connected with the growth of the other. The inter-relation of these two people will not then be haphazard and accidental as is the relation of people in general. And in this significant inter-relation all the different aspects and possibilities of human relations must be thought of.

We cannot think of development as solitary, because the inter-connection of humanity in higher dimensions must be extraordinarily complex. We might suppose that any significant relation will always contain very emotional elements, which without some special understanding, shared in common, may take a negative form and lead to violent disruption. If this happens, we can imagine that the growth of this complex inter-connection called humanity is impeded at that point; whereas if the relation is established, it will be advanced. Without special understanding, this form of growth of humanity is probably – I would say undoubtedly – impossible. Every organism grows from its separate cells. All real relationship, I believe, in this sense, remains impossible without special understanding shared in common.

We can imagine that if this growth takes place at one point in humanity it may affect the entire human organism to a very slight degree. Many of us, as a result of our reflections on life, must have come to the conclusion that something quite definite holds humanity back, not connected with commercial agreements or political questions. It cannot get beyond the stage in which it

261

is, and keeps on turning in a circle. Civilisation fails to get beyond a certain point. Some further growth of it is demanded which it seems incapable of undertaking, and from which it turns back. We might suppose that the questions of special understanding and significant relationship come in here; moreover that a certain number of people most likely have a particular duty in this respect and a special opportunity at certain points in the general recurrence of all things. As I said, the Egyptian diagram suggests to me that four points are indicated in all the cycles of the life. Above all it is necessary to reflect on what is meant by *special understanding* – for which special ideas are necessary – ideas which can become new causal elements in the life.

This life on earth is only one bit of *Totality* – perhaps the most difficult bit of all.

.   .   .   .

The whole question is about this *higher level of consciousness and what will awaken it.* In other words, what will awaken the active mind, or second triangle. Nothing gained from books can possibly do this. It always remains a question of the *inner perception of ideas.* As I said at the beginning, this book is about one or two *ideas* – that is all. The attempt to present ideas of this kind is probably a legitimate undertaking, though I am not quite convinced of this myself, because if taken literally, they can be nothing but poison, i.e. if they fall on the passive mind. If the presentation of *ideas* is legitimate up to a certain point, there must be a particular form of literature which constitutes the medium for the expression of these ideas. *Ideas* cannot be presented in a logical form or a scientific form. To present an idea one must aim at producing a certain kind of effect. In this volume I use the method of analogy, quotation, and illustration – really always talking about exactly the same thing, namely the idea of *higher space*, which Ouspensky has especially made his own. This *idea* can be very useful, but if taken just in that way, pragmatically, it will be entirely useless.

Ouspensky compares *ideas* to very powerful machines. If one attempts to go up in an aeroplane without knowing anything about its mechanism, perhaps not even understanding what it is for, the result cannot be *useful*. All *ideas* require preparation for their full meaning to engage the soul. This volume is therefore nothing but an *advertisement* of ideas (which have an immense background). There is no question whether they are true or not. One *buys* for oneself. There is no *absolute* truth. All truth is relative – relative to one's needs, relative to one's position in psychological space, relative to one's *pocket*. No one need burden himself with the dilemma as to whether what we have spoken about is truth or not. To take the ideas we have discussed in this way is just as wrong as asking whether a picture is 'true' or not. The question is merely what the soul engages with – what can touch the understanding.

.   .   .   .

The universe is intelligent in so far as we are intelligent. It becomes what we think and feel about it – what we make our own. The universe is *infinite response*. Mentally understood, it is *all possibilities*. Every point of view is possible, and because it 'exists' it is *right*. But it will give us what we make of it. One last word must be said about this response. The response is *more* than what we furnish to produce this response. To everything that is genuine and real in us, to everything that we really think from ourselves, the universe gives more than we give – 'full measure and running over'. It is not simply response by reaction in a mechanical sense. The mechanical law of action and reaction does not apply where the mind and heart are concerned. Because response is *more*, negation is dangerous. This is why, when we give up trying to understand anything, we do not merely halt but begin to *die*. And this is why, in the other direction, if we struggle to create a special understanding of life, something begins to assist us. The universe undergoes a significant transformation for *oneself. The universe is a series of possible mental transformations, one way or another.* It is useless to try to settle, at the outset, whether the universe is good or bad. It is useless to start from any point outside oneself. All the standpoints that all human people reflect form a minute part of the WORLD. The universe is *universality*, and therefore is *All* and *One*. So it is indifferent, neutral – that is, perfectly balanced. Only when one begins to change oneself does the universe change. That is the secret.

．　　　　　．　　　　　．　　　　　．

We have the main idea of higher space. Associated with this we have the idea of *higher levels of consciousness* connected with *higher space*. We have the idea of the existence of things *in Time itself* – of all the life; and of the existence of a sense of *I* not comparable to any that we know while under the illusion of passing-time. We have the idea of seeing things the other way round, as in the Mirror of Athene, and with this the idea of awakening another psychological system in man related to the cognition of higher space. We have the idea that when a thing ceases to exist for us (in lower space) that its disappearance is comparable to the disappearance of the pencil from the range of vision of the paper-world of beings. We have the idea that nothing perishes and that the illusion of perishing arises owing to our limited perception of dimensions. We have the idea of faith being a form of *mental* effort to awaken the second system in man. We have the idea of the *passive* and the *active* mind. We have the idea of natural and spiritual interpretations of life and of different *orders* of truth and reality. We have the idea that man is 'natural' and incomplete, because the second system is unawakened in him, because he has no true sense of self-existence, no real sense of *I* which belongs to a higher level – i.e. to the second system. Finally we have the

264

general idea that unless one sees the world differently, unless new *ideas* touch our consciousness we cannot rise to any apprehension of the second system. To all that we know naturally we must *add* something, and in this volume this addition is taken in terms of adding first the dimension of Time *to our own lives* and considering what this means *for oneself*.

CHAPTER TWELVE

THE INTEGRATION OF THE LIFE

THE ATTITUDE WE come into possession of when the World in Time is seen brings a new sense of environment. This corresponds to something innate in the soul. Our life surrounds us. It does not lie merely in tomorrow; it does not pass away. We need no longer put this sense of environment into some future *hereafter* to satisfy the soul. We labour in the *permanent* field of our own lives.

And we labour also in the common and immense field of living Time of which we inhabit a small portion. It is only our senses that turn all this into passing-time and death and destruction.

From other parts of living Time we receive a few signals – in literature, architecture, art. What we read, coming from those parts that surround us, belongs to the *living* World. Can we think, then, that we have surpassed the ideas that reach us from what we regard as the dead past? No – because all history is a living *Today*. All thought is in the Today of humanity. Throughout all its extension in Time humanity is thinking. Placed somewhere at a point in this immense circle of humanity, that is *ever-present* to the eye of eternity, we so-called moderns are now witnessing one angle of totality, one section of the WORLD, one radius of truth. This little today of ours, which we take as the summit of progress, is a fraction of Today itself. But unless passing-time falls away from us, we can never understand. The time-sense must change. We must think beyond time, out of time, and unless we question our temporal existence, unless we begin to think differently about everything and give quite a new interpretation to our lives, we cannot change our standpoint, which is the standpoint of *illusion*. To think *Time* itself brings us near the sense and meaning of Eternity. The rushing movement of passing-time ceases.

There comes, from an indefinable direction, and intermittently, the sense of *now*. The feeling of the life changes. The direction of effort changes. The valuation of all our experiences changes. We perceive what it is that we must escape from – the meaningless circle of our reactions. And perceiving that the purely temporal outlook gives us nothing, or takes away as soon as it gives, we realise the unspeakable boon of transcending the major illusion of the senses. Then new affirmative emotions reach us, that cannot reach us otherwise. A new action of the mind begins – a rethinking of everything in terms of *all the life* and *now*.

Above space appears Time, and above the enduring World in Time the enduring World of all possibilities, which is the World of Eternity.

This new sense of environment makes for the *integration* of the life. The mere sense of passing-time goes against it. For, in relation to passing-time 'each one of us is made up of ten thousand different and successive states, a scrap-heap of units, a mob of individuals' (Plutarch). Under the illusion of passing-time we can have no unity. To *be* is to have the permanent sense of *something else*. And as Plutarch says there is no *now* in passing-time, for '*now* is squeezed into the future, or into the past as though we should try to see a point which of necessity passes away to right or left'. Without the sense of the invisible there can be no unity, no integration – nothing but successive states, the ever-turning kaleidoscope of *I*'s. For integration, ideas that halt time are necessary, and these ideas must feed us continually. And it is only through that peculiar kind of effort, whereby we realise our own invisibility, that such ideas can reach and feed us. Without this effort we fall every moment, prone and lifeless, into the overwhelming stream of time and event, and the circle of our re-actions. For at every moment we can sink down into our habitual state of consciousness – where no integration is possible – where, indeed, we are, and can only be, divided up into innumerable little contradictory parts, which continually steal us from ourselves. Then we lie asleep in appearances, lost to ourselves, for then the sense of ourselves is derived only from the ever-changing response to the flicker of appearances. Then every event carries us away. Every event fastens its mouth upon our energy and consumes it. Life carries us away, now up, then down. And the illusion of passing-time, and the thinking only in terms of time, cause us to fix our eyes always on tomorrow *which never comes* – for it is always tomorrow. So we live ahead of ourselves, strained out in time, and are never here, never in the place where we really are, the only place in which anything real can happen – in *now*.

Were two people to meet in this place they would indeed meet. They would know one another. But in passing-time we cannot know one another. Our bodies jostle one another, but we have no *time* to know one another, nor do we have *time* to know ourselves – for we can only meet ourselves in *now*. All else is theory and phantasy.

The mystery of time is in ourselves. We can struggle to awaken to a new sense of time and to a new sense of ourselves and so get beyond what we think we are already and what we think we know already. But in every struggle of this nature we will inevitably realise more and more that it is *oneself* that is the mystery – that the whole thing is in oneself – *in what one takes as oneself.* One will be *forced* more and more on to what is oneself. The mystic ocean of existence is not to be crossed as something outside ourselves. It is in oneself. A man must surely realise that it is invisibly in him. And when he really touches *now*, he will know that all his lives, lived and unlived, meet here, beyond all conditions of passing-time, and that he has in himself all that is necessary for the overcoming of his most difficult problems – in this *now*, which, if he fails to discover, will be always replaced by the stream of passing-time. Realising what it would mean to hold now, he will catch a glimpse of the meaning of that strange phrase

in the *Wisdom of Solomon*: 'He, perfected in a short time, fulfilled
a long time.'

.   .   .   .

A double-thought is necessary in all problems connected
with higher space. In the spiral of our lives we may turn ceaselessly in one circle, in absolute recurrence. All that is possible,
potential, will remain unrealised. It exists but does not exist – for
us. There is the *already-thereness* of everything in higher space and
the lack of individual realisation of it in oneself. The road is there
but we do not necessarily go along it, but may walk round and
round the same point unable to escape from the circle of our associations and habitual reactions. Every further stage of ourselves
is within us, above us. Below us lies what we are already, what we
have done before. Below us, behind us, is the passive surrender to
things, the inertia of the past, the habits of years, and the passive,
sensual mind – the mind of the senses – with its sole belief in appearances and passing-time.

At any point in our lives we are thus between two opposing
forces – the force of the realised and the force of the unrealised,
what we are and have been, and what we may be. And what we
may be is *already there*, as unhappy feeling, as incompleteness.
It lies along an untrodden road which the *active* mind can only
find. Thus there is always hidden in the centre of man's heart a
problem, capable of so many different inadequate renderings and
formulations. Seen from one angle, in order to go forward, a man
must overcome the sensual interpretation of life which feeds the
passive mind, and weights the past too much. He can only relate
himself to new forces, coming from that which he has not realised, through seeing things differently, through touching ideas
that have transforming power and that can only be proved by his
own experience of them and never evidentially, by an appeal to
the outer world of the senses.

269

From this standpoint the world that we really live in is not the phenomenal world but the psychological world, in which there is a *psychological* past and a *psychological* future. Here time passes into psychology. There is that which lies behind or below us and that which lies in front of or above us, *psychologically*. That which lies above us is not in the future of passing-time. Mere length of days will not bring us to it, for we can remain, *psychologically*, in the same part of the psychological world for all our remaining years, if we continue always to think in the same way and act with the same self-satisfaction. Time will then pass, but psychologically we will remain *stationary*, ever turning round the same circle in inner space, with weakening pleasure.

Our real future is our own growth, and the latter can only be into what is already there – but as far as each of us is concerned only potentially there – just as the North Pole is already there and forms a part of some people's experience but for me still remains a possible experience in the already-thereness of known space. But if I think that I only live in the world registered by my senses and confuse growth with the passage of time, I will never be able to understand the direction in which my possible growth lies. I will always see it as outside me, in external activities and in the direction of tomorrow. And the idea that I am not only always and necessarily somewhere in visible space, but also always and necessarily somewhere in invisible space will remain incomprehensible.

But are we not always in *two* places – one in known three dimensional space, the other in inner space – one in the 'material' world, the other in the 'spiritual' world? I am *here* in this street, in this house, at this moment; and I am also *here* (in the psychological world) in this state, in this mood, in this re-action, in this feeling – and at *this point* in the spiral of lives, in the ocean of existence. Could I realise this fully then would I know fully that what I do *now* is the only important thing. For to realise these two *heres* together is already to realise something of *now*, in which time halts. And if I can once begin to reach *now* I will realise that every experience of it penetrates and recalls every other experience of it, in a manner that has nothing to do with sequence or date in passing-time. For all moments of understanding lie close together.

Realising *now*, I perceive something that does not change, something that is both spectator of myself and really myself, in relationship to which all my temporal troubles and problems become small. Only then can I say those words that are so difficult to say in the right way, and are constantly used exactly in the wrong way – *'nothing matters'*. For then it means that nothing matters save this feeling of *now*. And this is because in the presence of greater meaning all lesser meanings, that fill our ordinary mind full to the brim, shrink to their true proportions and cease to steal from us. For in the presence of greater meaning we are redeemed from everything small and trivial and absurd – and unless there were greater meaning men would have nothing to do, no goal, no aim, no direction save that given by the outward senses.

.   .   .   .

A part of the total WORLD is outside us, the remainder inside us. Where the visible world leaves off, man invisible begins. Where the manifested world, *common to us all* as immediate sensory experience, leaves off, the unmanifested WORLD begins – *individually* for each of us. And at the meeting-point in every man of these two aspects of the total world the phenomenon of passing-time enters. The higher invisible degrees of the WORLD are in us; and outside us, in experiences that we share with others, are its lower visible degrees. Outside us is outer truth; within us, inner truth, and both make up All – the WORLD. And as inner truth – supposing that I experience some degree of it – it is seen and demonstrated *within* me, individually. I cannot show it or prove it to others – whatever I may discern of it in my spirit – for it is

271

within, as is heaven or hell. I can only find evidence, in literature and elsewhere, that others have discerned similar things. But in the realm of outer truth the case is different. Whatever I discover about the visible part of the WORLD – which we think of as the entire world – can be demonstrated to others and become accepted as part of the collective, or outer, scientific truth belonging to the period. This outer truth will lie in that part of my mind turned outwards towards the senses, towards that part of the total world that is manifest – that is, it will lie in the passive mind. It will not and cannot change me in myself, for change is through the inner active side of the mind. It will not make me a different kind of man. It may give me fame, but it cannot do anything else, because it does not belong to me as inner experience and does not enter me from within.

Nor will mere flashes of inner truth, entering from within, necessarily change me. To perceive that the universe is in oneself or to perceive the fact of recurrence, as did Ramsay, is merely fleeting inner experience. It is like catching a glimpse of a framework that is quite devoid of content. For a moment the soul is turned in a new direction and tastes another order of things. Drugs, anaesthetics, etc., sometimes can briefly turn the soul in this direction. But in itself this is nothing save that it shows that there is a further range of experience of the WORLD. It shows a new order of knowledge. But experienced in this way, one has no connection with this knowledge, and turns back to life as did Ramsay. It is necessary to find some kind of *way*, some form of work upon oneself, that will connect one legitimately with knowledge of this order, through a gradual transformation of oneself. And the starting-point of work of this kind is, as Karl Barth says, to realise the *ambiguousness* of temporal life. There must be the feeling and conviction of something else. And it is not only necessary to feel that there is some other interpretation of things but to *desire to hear and know it*. A clear attitude, a distinct thought, must exist, similar to what was in William Law's mind when he wrote that once a man understands that he is down here in time and space *in order to awaken to another state of himself*, everything that happens to him, whether good or bad, comes to have a new meaning.

In the light of such a standpoint the ambiguousness of life vanishes. A continual state of doubting and vacillation is replaced by the beginning of a new kind of knowledge. One no longer stares at life, trying to decide whether it means something or means nothing. One perceives that with the ordinary knowledge that one gains from life, one can never solve any of those conundrums which preoccupy us secretly and which we never know how to think about distinctly. Incapable of reaching ourselves, we remain wandering about in a growing indistinctness, and drowned in the illusion of tomorrow, we see no reason why we should make any efforts to struggle with ourselves now. We cling to all the negations that belong to the illusion of passing-time, and perhaps, as life seems to pass swiftly and for ever away, comfort ourselves with the deadly dream that we have tried to do our best.

To begin to awaken it is necessary to begin to think what all this literature, philosophical, religious, mystical and otherwise, is about – this literature of ideas which always reads so strangely. What is it about? In its true essence it is always about the same thing – about knowledge without which we can never begin to understand the meaning of our existence. If we can ever find the right approach to it, we will find that it begins to answer just those questions that we are secretly preoccupied with, that have existed in us since childhood, and that belong to that part of ourselves that we have had to go on living without, as it were – we have had to leave behind.

. . . .

I mentioned that the Egyptian diagram on the title-page might have to do with the four castes, i.e., man must experience

273

in recurrent form four samples of lives beginning with the most menial. In other words, in crossing the ocean of existence he crosses humanity itself in its main aspects. This diagram, if it has any connection with the repetition of the life, refers to four episodes, each one re-traversed seven times, i.e., the same kind of life recurs seven times, and I would take it as meaning recurrence in the same part of time for any one episode, or sample of life. Once worked out, once the spiral is accomplished, a new sample of life is begun, and I suppose that this would be in a different part of time. This is entirely speculative, but it gives a point of view that explains some of the inconsistencies of life. At this moment every separate person in the visible world is at a certain point in this invisible system of four spirals that bridges the ocean of existence.

If the two figures on either side of the Egyptian diagram are of different sex, this may mean that a change of sign takes place in the passage across the mystic ocean of existence. The termination of the life in full consciousness necessarily means the full awakening of the *active* mind and this I understand as the *head* in the diagram which is next what I will take as the figure of Osiris. The life begins from the *passive* end – taken as Isis.

Man, as a spiral of lives, lies between opposites – man as time, man as four-dimensional, five-dimensional, six-dimensional. If this interpretation has any truth in it the diagram indicates an increasing consciousness in man who is developing, as we might expect. Starting from a passive state in which he is only reaction to his senses, he can undergo a growth in consciousness and pass from a passive to an active state. I mean only that this is a possibility, because it is understandable that he may turn ceaselessly at one point in the spiral of lives, in absolute recurrence, and not advance through the pathway possible to him. A double-thought is necessary here, as in all problems connected with higher space, namely the *already-thereness* of everything and the individual realisation of it. The road is there but we do not necessarily go along it but may walk round and round the same point unable to escape from the circle of our habits.

Isis as 'mother' and Osiris as 'father', thought of as passive and active, can be connected with the two triangles of Fludd, 'material' and 'spiritual'. The overcoming of the mother will then mean the overcoming of the sensual man, i.e. the material interpretation of life. This will mean that there is always hidden in man's heart a problem, which obviously can be interpreted in all sorts of different and inadequate ways. Everyone has always something to overcome in himself or herself – this 'mother', this passive mind, this passive surrender to things, this inertia, this past, this belief in appearances and passing-time. At any point in our lives we are between two opposing forces. At every moment a man is between 'Isis' and 'Osiris', as a possible form of Horus.

BIBLIOGRAPHY

KARL BARTH. *Commentary on Romans*, Oxford. *The Message of Karl Barth.* by W. G. Hanson. Religious Tract Society. 1931.

WM. STURGIS BIGELOW. *Buddhism and Immortality.* Ingersoll Lecture. 1908.

WILLIAM BLAKE. *Jerusalem. Milton.*

JOHN BURNETT. *Greek Philosophy.* Macmillan. 1928.

E.A.BURTT. *The Metaphysical Foundations of Modern Physical Science.* Kegan Paul, Trench, Trubner and Co. 1928.

EMIL BRUNNER. *The Word and the World.* S.C.M. 1931.

W.K.CLIFFORD. *Lectures and Essays.* Vol. I. Macmillan. 1886.

HERMANN DIELS. *Die Fragmente der Vorsokrutikar.*

JOANNES SCOTUS ERIGENA by Henry Bett. Cambridge University Press. 1925.

GUSTAV FECHNER. *Dr. Mise's Kleine Schriften.* 1846.

ROBERT FLUDD. *Utriusque Cosmi.* 1617.

SIR WM. HAMILTON. *Lectures in Metaphysics and Logic.* (6th edition. 1872.) Blackwood and Sons.

FREDERIC HALL. *An Ether Vision.* Open Court Magazine. Dec. 1909.

HERMETICA. Edited and translated by Walter Scott. Clarendon Press. 1924.

HUGHLINGS JACKSON. *Selected Writings.* Hodder & Stoughton. 1932.

WILLIAM JAMES. *Collected Essays and Reviews.* Longmans, Green & Co. 1920.

THE WORKS OF WILLIAM LAW. 1749. Privately reprinted, 1893.

TAYLER LEWIS. *Six Days of Creation.* Chapman. 1855. *Plato against the Atheists.* Harper & Bros. 1875.

MINKOWSKY. *The Principle of Relativity.* Methuen. 1923.

D. MCKENZIE. *Aromatics.* Heinemann. 1927.

M. NICOLL. *Conception of Regression in Psychological Medicine.* Lancet. June 8. 1918.

P.D. OUSPENSKY. *Tertium Organum. A New Model of the Universe.* Routledge, Kegan Paul Ltd.

ORIGEN. *Contra Celsum. De Principiis.*

DU PREL. *Philosophy of Mysticism.* Redway, Paul. 1889.

PLATO. *The Laws. Phaedo. The Republic. Timaeus.* (Jowett's translation.)

SELECTED ESSAYS OF PLUTARCH by A.O. Prickard. Oxford. 1918.

E.H. PLUMTRE, D.D. *The Spirits in Prison.* Wm. Isbister. 1885.

PROCLUS. *Commentary on Timaeus.*

PROPOSITION 199 OF PROCLUS by E. R. Dodds. Oxford. 1933.

DE QUINCEY. *The Wider Hope.* Fisher Unwin. 1890.

SIR WILLIAM RAMSAY. *Partial Anaesthesia.* Proceedings of the Society for Psychical Research. Vol. IX. 1894.

LEON ROBIN. *Greek Thought and the Origin of the Scientific Spirit.* Kegan Paul, Trench, Trubner & Co. 1928.

SWEDENBORG. *Arcana Coelestia.* Swedenborg Society.

SYNESIUS. *The Essays and Hymns of Synesius of Cyrene*. Oxford. 1930.

TERTULLIAN. *Concerning the Resurrection of the Flesh*. (Souter.) S.P.C.K. 1922.

A.E. TAYLOR. *Commentary on Plato's Timaeus*. Oxford. 1928.

ALFRED, LORD TENNYSON. *A Memoir by his Son*. 1897. Macmillan. Rep. 1924. *The Questions of King Milinda* ('Milindapañha').

AVAILABLE FROM THE PUBLISHER:

P.D.Ouspensky *A Record of Meetings*
P.D.Ouspensky *A Further Record*
Bob Hunter *P.D. Ouspensky: Pioneer of the Fourth Way*
Bob Hunter *The True Myth*: Beryl Pogson's teaching on
Gurdjieff's *All and Everything*
Bob Hunter/Beryl Pogson *Brighton Work Talks*
Bob Hunter *A Pupil's Postscript*
MauriceNicoll *Psychological Commentaries on the Teaching of
Gurdjieff & Ouspensky* 6 Vols
Maurice Nicoll *The New Man*
Maurice Nicoll *The Mark*
Maurice Nicoll *Living Time*
Maurice Nicoll *Selections from Meetings in 1953*
Maurice Nicoll *Simple Explanation of Work Ideas*
Maurice Nicoll *Notes taken at Meetings in 1934*
A Few Recollections of Dr Nicoll and Amwell 1949-1953
Beryl Pogson *Royalty of Nature*
Beryl Pogson *In the East My Pleasure Lies*
Beryl Pogson *Maurice Nicoll: A Portrait*
Beryl Pogson *Commentary on the Fourth Gospel*
Beryl Pogson/Bob Hunter *Mind and Energy*
Beryl Pogson/Bob Hunter *Meetings with Beryl Pogson* 3 Vols.
Bob Hunter *Catherine Nicoll - A Wakeful Wife*
Beryl Pogson & Others *Unforgotten Fragments*
Beryl Pogson & Others *Centenary Fragments*
Beryl Pogson *Work Talks at The Dicker–More Work Talks–Work Talks
in Brighton*

Samuel Copley *Portrait of a Vertical Man*
Anon. *Words on the Work*
Anon. *A Recapitulation of the Lord's Prayer*
Anon. *A Point in the Work* (Two Volumes)
Irmis Popoff *Gurdjieff-HisWork-OnMyself-WithOthers-FortheWork*
Solange Claustres *Becoming Conscious with G.I.Gurdjieff*
Annabeth McCorkle *The Gurdjieff Years 1929-1949:
Recollections of Louise March*
Paul Beekman Taylor *The Philosophy of G.I.Gurdjieff*
Paul Beekman Taylor *Gurdjieff's Invention of America*
Paul Beekman Taylor *G.I.Gurdjieff: A New Life*
Paul Beekman Taylor *Gurdjieff in the Public Eye*
Paul Beekman Taylor *Real Worlds of G.I.Gurdjieff*
Paul Beekman Taylor *Gurdjieff's Worlds of Words*

E-book and printed by Amazon

May 2020

© **Eureka Editions**
ISBN 978 90 72395 18 4

Herenstraat 4-A
3512 KC Utrecht
The Netherlands

www.eurekaeditions.com
info@eurekaeditions.com

Made in the USA
Coppell, TX
31 August 2021